Beckett's Critical Complicity

Winner of the 1987
Midwest Modern Language Association
Book Award

Beckett's Critical Complicity

CARNIVAL, CONTESTATION, AND TRADITION

Sylvie Debevec Henning

THE UNIVERSITY PRESS OF KENTUCKY

*PR
6003
.E282
Z674
1988
147679
Nov.1989*

Library of Congress Cataloging-in-Publication Data

Henning, Sylvie Debevec.
    Beckett's critical complicity : carnival, contestation, and
tradition / Sylvie Debevec Henning.

    p.   cm.
    Bibliography: p.
    Includes index.
    ISBN 0-8131-1664-3
    1. Beckett, Samuel, 1906-   —Criticism and interpretation.
I. Title.
PR6003. E282Z674   1988
848'.91409—dc19   88-15569

Contents

Acknowledgments

Many people have contributed to the writing of this book. I am, however, especially grateful to my colleagues at the State University of New York at Plattsburgh for creating an environment in which scholarship can be pursued.

Most of this material is published here for the first time. Parts of it have appeared elsewhere and are reprinted by permission: "The Guffaw of the Abderite: *Murphy* and the Democritean Universe," *The Journal of Beckett Studies* 8 (1985): 5-20, © 1985 by John Calder, Publishers, London; "Samuel Beckett's *Fin de Partie*: Variations on the Hermeneutic Theme," *Boundary 2*, 8, 2-3 (Winter/Spring 1985): 371-92, © 1985 by *Boundary 2*, SUNY-Binghamton, Binghamton, N.Y.; "Narrative and Textual Doubles in the Works of Samuel Beckett," *Sub-Stance* 29 (1981): 97-104, © 1982 by the Board of Regents of the University of Wisconsin; "*Film*: A Dialogue between Beckett and Berkeley, *Journal of Beckett Studies* 7 (Spring 1982): 89-100, © 1982 by John Calder, Publishers, London; "Samuel Beckett's *Film* and *La Dernière Bande*: Intratextual and Intertexual Doubles," *Symposium* 35, 2 (Summer 1981): 131-54, reprinted with permission of the Helen Dwight Reid Educational Foundation, published by Heldref Publications, 4000 Albemarle St., N.W., Washington, D.C. 20016, copyright © 1981.

Abbreviations

The following abbreviations, rendered in parentheses with appropriate page numbers, are used throughout the text and notes.

Samuel Beckett

D   *Disjecta: Miscellaneous Writings and a Dramatic Fragment,* ed. Ruby Cohn (New York: Grove Press, 1984).

E   *Endgame* (New York: Grove Press, 1958).

F   *Film* (New York: Grove Press, Evergreen Books, 1969).

FP   *Fin de Partie* (Paris: Les Editions de Minuit, 1957).

KLT   *Krapp's Last Tape* in *Krapp's Last Tape and Other Dramatic Pieces* (New York: Grove Press, Evergreen Books, 1958).

LD   *Le Dépeupleur* (Paris: Les Editions de Minuit, 1970).

LO   *The Lost Ones* (New York: Grove Press, 1972).

M   *Murphy* (New York: Grove Press, 1979).

P   *Proust* (New York: Grove Press, 1957).

George Berkeley

PC   *Philosophical Commentaries* in *Berkeley's Philosophical Writings,* ed. David M. Armstrong (New York: Collier Macmillan Publishers, Collier Books, 1965).

PHK   *A Treatise Concerning the Principles of Human Knowledge* in *Principles, Dialogues and Philosophical Correspondence,* ed. Colin Murray Turbayne (Indianapolis, Ind.: Bobbs-Merrill, Library of Liberal Arts, 1965).

TD   *Three Dialogues between Hylas and Philonous* in *Principles, Dialogues and Philosophical Correspondence.*

Marcel Proust

RTP   *A la recherche du temps perdu* (Paris: Bibliothèque de la Pléiade, 1954).

The Accompliced Critic

Samuel Beckett's work is commonly regarded as symptomatic of Western anxiety and self-doubt in the twentieth century. Often it has been considered representative of modern existentialist or absurdist movements. This view tends, I believe, to obscure Beckett's more critical relation to our cultural context, a relation in which certain fundamental philosophical issues are frequently addressed in satirical, or even carnivalizing, fashion. In jesting confrontation with major representatives of our cultural heritage, his work offers serious challenge to many of their basic assumptions, for example, the desire for final resolution, including every form of integral totality, closed system, the comprehensive dialectic. By embodying, moreover, the enduring tension between our impulse to order, structure, and identity, and a counterimpulse to question or even oppose such phenomena, carnivalized dialogization also provides a more affirmative and dynamic manner of staging "messy" relations in the face of anxiety that is never entirely sublimated.[1]

When the desire for unification is predominant (as, for example, in the epigraph to Beckett's essay "The Two Needs"), there arises a totalizing point of view that is intolerant of significant differences. Beckett shares Mikhail Bakhtin's criticism of the repressive monologism that is so characteristic of Western thought with its penchant for abstract integrality. *Murphy*, for example, can be read as a Menippean satire on totalitarian thinking in general. In many of Beckett's "threshold dialogues," such as *Malone Dies*, objective unity is recognized as an illusion, yet the protagonists continue struggling to establish authoritarian control over one another or over their own unruly selves. The desire for subjective oneness remains strong, although not unchallenged.

Bakhtin's generally hostile view of modern fiction suggests that he would have placed Beckett among those who perpetuate the "Romantic" deformation of the folk carnival.[2] Romantic aspects do exist in Beckett and constitute a definite tendency perceptible in both his critical essays and his literary work. His subjects, whether fictional characters or fellow artists, often retreat into solitary chambers to savor solipsistic pleasures and sorrows. Another tendency exists, however, and counters the first with parody and irony that is frequently self-directed.[3] Moreover, the private chamber generally becomes the scene of a confrontation, both intra- and intertextual, between characters and their provocative doubles. These garrets, padded cells, hospital or boardinghouse rooms function as stages for carnivalized encounters analogous to those that occur in Dostoyevsky's parlors. When, as in *Endgame*, these rooms can be described as "cranial boxes" (*D* 126), the mind itself has been transformed into a carnival agora.

The dialogic quality of parody and irony resides in the fact that they imply an inner debate between a mocked and a mocking "voice" each actively eliciting the other, while vying for control.[4] The two may test and contest one another, as well as all related aspects of society and culture. Those that stand the test may well be reinforced. In other cases the process helps prepare the way for transformations.

Carnivalized dialogization places everything in irreverent quotation marks.[5] Official philosophical, scientific, or artistic positions are set against the background of a problematic reality they cannot accommodate within their narrow boundaries. By creating parodic images, Beckett reveals the limitations and deficiences of such canonical or "serious" views, without, however, discrediting them completely. Instead, they are brought back into the play of hermeneutical comprehension.

Laughter is a chief weapon in the struggle against the monologic tendency of official forms. Carnivalizing laughter is internally dialogized, simultaneously affirming and denying not only the parodied phenomenon but also the parodying, which is itself kept open thereby to further review and revision. The mockery is thus not simply that of a satirist or ironist who assumes a position of authority vis-à-vis his object—all participants are subject to it, including the author himself.[6]

In Beckett's work, as in Dostoyevsky's, laughter is most often muted, or reduced. As such it has no direct expression. It does not, so to speak, ring out. Nevertheless, its traces remain and can be discerned, particularly on the level of style and structure.[7] Buster Keaton (the star of Beckett's *Film*) personifies this approach in which the mind may smile but the face remains grave (*D* 89).

The stylistic reflection of the carnival is a pluridimensional mode of language that Bakhtin terms dialogized heteroglossia.[8] From the standpoint of monologic criticism such pluridimensionality is typically regarded as either jibberish or silence, which may amount to the same thing. Yet, it is not simply "a conglomeration of alien materials and incompatible principles of design."[9] Such a style also makes possible agonistic encounters among phenomena embodying different historically situated ideologies, the "poles of becoming," or the metamorphoses of the self.[10] Through dialogized heteroglossia language discloses itself as a "space" in which disseminating and consolidating forces may actively engage one another.

Any textual or discursive level can be invested with different and differing points of view, or "voices." The privileged tendencies of a text or aspects of an idea may then be confronted by latent or repressed ones. The impulse to stage this confrontation entails what might be called the deconstructive strategy of dialogization that exploits the "loopholes" through which a subversive "voice" may insinuate itself into the discourse of the dominant perspective.[11] There, as in the pluridimensional soliloquies of the Unnameable, this strategy may take advantage of unthematized reservations, hesitations, and contradictions to create ironic interferences that undermine the impression of self-identity or harmonious integrity.

The different discordant perspectives may be past, contemporary, or potential avatars of either the dominant or the latent "voice." Thus in *Film*, the explicit Berkeleyian theme is brought into contact with its Sartrean "doubles." And the different voices may engage in an intertextual dialogue, as *Krapp's Last Tape* does with both *Remembrance of Things Past* and Beckett's own *Proust*.

In much the same manner, competing philosophical, cultural, and religious systems that coexist within the Western heritage may be permitted to contend with one another, as in *Le Dépeupleur* [*The Lost Ones*], where their dialogic inter-involvement reveals their differences and, more importantly for Beckett, their similarities. Related systems are then in turn implicated in a larger dialogue with the submerged carnivalesque tradition. Heteroglossia may suggest alternative formulations, evaluations, and developments that, in a dialogized context, could be accommodated or even privileged, yet without the elements of repression and exclusion that characterize the established order.

An acceptance of internal diversity and the attendant possibilities of genuine conflict and genuinely self-critical reflection, are aspects of the pluridimensional situation that help to account for its transformative, as well as its more obvious regenerative, potential. The numerous and often highly complex cultural references that appear in Beckett's fictional work suggest an awareness of the extent to which creative art may depend (like all truly revolutionary activity) upon an ability to engage other "voices" from both the present and the past in authentically contestatory dialogues.

Though often denied or restricted, the disturbing dialogic quality inherent in all discourse makes linguistic nonreferentiality an impossible dream. Beckett displays a strong drive toward an aestheticist solipsism of this sort. He recognizes, however, that the multiple aspects of language are as productive as they are painful or frustrating, and that they could not be eliminated without deadening consequences. The blank wall of hyperformalism is accordingly both proffered as the solution and scrutinized as a part of the problem. Works such as *Endgame* reveal, moreover, an awareness of the fact that the ideal of nonreferentiality is itself historically situated and that to espouse it is already to enter implicitly into dialogue with its entire genealogy.

The dialogic quality of a text or discourse may engender a variety of interpretations, depending upon how the multiple "voices" are accentuated. A single text may both agree with and criticize the same ideas. Among them may be some which the author himself will elsewhere appear to espouse in more one-dimensional fashion. Even in his more straighforward critical essays, however, Beckett's position is often ambivalent. His own ideas are not sacrosanct. They may be among those subject to carnivalized investigation. The danger in interpreting a pluridimensional work, however, is that one voice will be so privileged that the sedimented quality of the text becomes obscured. Beckett's fiction has often suffered this fate. Its serio-comic quality has been inadequately treated, so that complexly dialogic texts have commonly been regarded simply as expressions of existentialist anguish or nihilistic despair.

The somber quality of Beckett's work reflects the pain experienced in confrontation with a paradoxically both indeterminate and overdetermined world that cannot easily be assimilated and often encourages an attitude of stoic resignation or life-denying withdrawal. The carnivalesque dimension counters this tendency, commenting ironically upon our culture's repeated attempts to do away with the problematic aspect of existence and even mocking our desire to do so. Beckett's uneasy interweaving of somber and carnivalesque perspectives suggests a confirmation of the view that suffering and anguish are fundamental to life and are, at the same time, an affirmation, however subdued, of their relation to cultural vigor and creativity.

Thus, it may be possible to argue that parody and satire are never simply demoralizing, and that even extensive recourse to them need not be interpreted as evidence of cynicism or cultural despair.[12] In Beckett, indeed, these and similarly "comic" devices may even be directed against just such reactions. I shall consequently endeavor to establish that his severe critique of the Western intellectual tradition does not presume or necessarily entail the loss of all positive values and beliefs.

His use of carnivalesque and dialogized modes in particular suggests, on the contrary, a transformative dimension, heretofore unappreciated.

Beckett should not, therefore, be considered an embittered simply negative opponent of the Western tradition. In his novels and plays, the tradition's strongest elements are brought forward the better to confront its most lively antagonists in an encounter that is often both profound and disturbingly comic. The result is positive insofar as it promises to revitalize tradition by resituating it within a richer, if less settled, cultural context.

The works I shall examine are neither exemplary nor necessarily representative of Beckett's literary production. They are, however, important parts thereof. Moreover, they permit the testing of my hermeneutical hypotheses in a wide range of genres. I have chosen his first novel, *Murphy*, because it sets the scene, as Beckett has said, for all the subsequent novels.[13] His most sustained piece of literary criticism, *Proust*, will be considered together with the play to which it is most closely related, *Krapp's Last Tape*. A major play, *Endgame*; Beckett's only cinematographic venture, *Film*; and an example of his later short fiction, *Le Dépeupleur*, will bring the itinerary to a close. Beckett's *Trilogy* and his last novel to date, *How It Is*, I have reserved for a second study, now nearing completion.

Beckett is an intellectually challenging writer because he works through complex problems. To deal honestly with his writing, my book had necessarily to reflect that difficulty. It is an attempt to remain faithful to the high level of Beckett's own thought without completely sacrificing the paradoxical spirit of his seriocomic playfulness. Consequently, I have varied my own critical style somewhat from chapter to chapter as Beckett's texts seemed to require.

Beckett's multilingual puns (he is fluent in at least four languages) and cross-disciplinary allusions create complex networks of interpretive possibilities. In trying to suggest this cultural richness, I too have found it necessary to employ foreign words and expressions from time to time. Translations have been provided whenever possible. When Beckett translates his own works he often modifies the wordplay. He may retain or emphasize only certain aspects of the original, or even add different connotations. I have therefore ventured to provide my own translations of the French whenever Beckett's English versions differ from them in significant ways.

Beckett's highly allusive style can also be a source of difficulty. His references to people, places, objects, and dates are neither gratuitous nor affected. Rather, they tend to signal major philosophical issues, situating them simultaneously in a particular sociohistorical moment and within the entire Western cultural tradition. From *Murphy* to the later short fiction, however, these allusions become less frequent or, at least, less explicit. Overt clues increasingly give way to scenarios that stage or play out the problems addressed by major thinkers, often exploiting the carnivalesque potential of their own metaphors and imagery.

I have sought to work through Beckett's text, following the meanders, detours, multiple leads, backtracking, false starts, and circuitous paths, until more or less distinct patterns emerge. Although it is clearly possible to discover in this way any number of coherent and meaningful patterns, it seems impossible to integrate them all into a single, comprehensive thesis, schema, system, or perspective. The elaboration of one pattern requires that certain aspects or pieces of the text be highlighted, casting others into shadow. Sometimes the latter may be incorporated into the momentarily privileged pattern through generalization or analogy. They may, however, lead in directions that cannot even be related dialectically, although they may form aspects of other distinct patterns.

Some groupings of elements may suggest structures that remain incomplete, and whose very incompleteness is not without significance. Still, other elements may remain outside the authority of any structuring principle whatever. In addition, elements selected for inclusion within a particular pattern may themselves suggest a range or plurality of meanings, and these may accordingly be comprehensible in terms of the same pattern, several different patterns simultaneously, or none at all.

I have chosen to enter into this play of multiaccented images and discourses to which Beckett's texts invite us. Without simply mimicking, I have allowed the thinking embodied in my interpretative analyses to be guided by his style—one, that is, which stages and actively engages problems that cannot be adequately encountered by means of conventional generic, logical, or even linguistic forms.

CHAPTER 1

The Poet Membered

Beckett's art and literary criticism provide one important means of approaching his fiction and drama. Unfortunately, these essays have until recently been all but inaccessible.[1] Most appeared in obscure periodicals and exhibition catalogs; some remained in manuscript form. Only two long pieces were readily available. Yet *Proust* and "Three Dialogues" do not by themselves allow the reader to perceive the manner in which Beckett's nonfictional work developed over time.

Its bearing upon his fiction and drama, is not easily described. The latter are never simply illustrations of the former. Rather, Beckett's literary works engage his criticism dialogically, accepting certain of its premises, challenging others, and treating still others with ambivalence. His novels and plays create "concrete" situations in which recurring themes of the criticism can be tested, especially those whose inherently problematic nature the criticism itself has neglected. Indeed, conflicting tendencies that remain implicit in the essays are highlighted and explored in the literary works. This does not mean that Beckett's fiction and drama can be said to supercede his discursive writing. On the contrary, what ultimately emerges is that the author's deep dissatisfaction with prevailing modes of thought and action must contend against his own uneasiness over the apparent alternatives.

Beckett's first published essay, "Dante . . . Bruno. Vico . . Joyce" (1929), relates *Finnegans Wake* to the works of three significant antecedents. In doing so, however, it raises an issue that is repeatedly addressed in various ways throughout all his fictional and nonfictional work: the relation between abstraction and concrete particularity on the epistemological level, or between spirit and matter on the ontological. The fundamental problem here (as for Plato and Aristotle) is the nature of the "between" that both separates and joins the two elements of each pair. Philosophy is the traditional go-between. But for Beckett all philosophy is ultimately idealist, and he therefore doubts that it can be an adequate mediator. Philosophy relies too heavily upon processes of abstraction in which the temporal and sensual are most often simply eliminated as dross (D 19). The order established is thus merely formal or ideational.

Taking his cue from the Renaissance humanists, Beckett would replace philosophy with philology (or literature), which discovers order in existence without completely subsuming the individual and the particular. The latter is preserved as an "empirical illustration" that successfully rerelates material diversity to the formal rationality of the system. Beckett does not yet consider the problem whether this formal rationality is situated in the perceiving subject or in the perceived object. In his later writings, the question is usually decided in favor of the former. The object remains unavailable, impregnable, unknowable.

The obvious problem with "Dante" is that Beckett seems often to be replicating the dichotomizing gesture he has rejected. Philosophy and philology are starkly opposed: the domain of pure metaphysical abstraction vs. that of concrete empiricism, with nothing significant in common. The poet would thus be justified in banishing philosophy entirely. Along with it, however, goes the possibility of genuine mediation.

On several occasions Beckett has insisted that his literary production is not philosophically informed. The drama especially is to be apprehended through the senses and not by the intellect at all. At times Beckett has instead emphasized the importance of an emotional reception of his work.[2] The affective domain, the "heart," has traditionally occupied the intermediate position between mind and body, reason and senses. And the heart has always been a problem for dichotomous logic, as it later is in *Murphy*. In it are harbored apparently incompatible elements.

Beckett has often "related" these elements in his nonfictional statements by simply downplaying or rejecting outright the intellectual component. It is also apparent that Beckett's neat categorical distinctions are themselves without an adequate empirical foundation. Even at its most rarefied, intellection remains a "sensuous untidy art" (*D* 27). When, in a letter to Axel Kaun (*D* 170-73), Beckett recognizes the metaphysical constitution of the *philo-logos*, he rejects the Word entirely, as if absolute silence were not itself an established metaphysical analogue.

In "Dante" we are advised that *Work in Progress (Finnegans Wake)* is not to be read as an "explicit illustration" of any philosophical system (*D* 20). The peculiar manner in which it plays with philosophy indicates, rather, how any such system necessarily distorts the reality it would explain. In particular, the dual nature of Joycean *logoi* concretizes language through "direct expression" (*D* 26). Unlike the classical-Scholastic tradition, which regarded the sensible as (at best) the means to a nonsensible, and therefore higher, reality, Joyce resists this desire to leave the material dimension behind. He remains instead in "an extremely comfortable position between two stools" (*D* 29).

Beckett goes on to suggest that a more general tension between processes of incorporation and elimination is the precondition for all dynamic activity, whether in life or in art. Nevertheless, he does not himself seem comfortable in that position. In this essay, as in many of his later texts, opposed elements either converge into an identity (for example form = content) or alternate within a closed system. The ongoing relational interaction that Beckett defends in Joyce is accordingly threatened in his own work by monism or dualism in turn.

Beckett's monograph *Proust* (1931) focuses upon time, the problem that all attempts to comprehend existence within a formal structure must confront. Traditional means of dealing with temporality can be subsumed under the ascetic principle, "ablation of desire," that underlies the operation of habit, as well as of voluntary memory (*P* 7). Habit creates security, but only by generating a degree of what Beckett will later call "rigor vitae" (*D* 95), as one learns to avoid (or simply to ignore) potentially disturbing differences. Habit, like abstraction, is a matter of consistent or common qualities. The "discordant" element that distinguishes one thing from another, its "essential" particularity, is cast off (*P* 53). With it go the enchantment, cruelty, and deliciousness of life, whose very impermanence only increases our attraction. Thus, although differences frustrate the quest for security, they are also appealing (as passional relations demonstrate) and ultimately life-enhancing.

Proustian time is a "dualism in multiplicity" in which the diverse temporal perspectives converge into a double-faced one, like "the spear of Telephus that both kills and cures" (*P* 1). Beckett, however, would keep the faces apart. Moments of habit, "the boredom of living," are separated by painful yet fertile periods of transition, the "suffering of being." The passage from one to the other remains mysterious, since "by no expedient of macabre transubstantiation can the grave sheets serve as swaddling clothes" (*P* 8). The suffering is in fact caused by the apparent impossibility of this transitional movement through which and in which "being" is simultaneously deformed and formed anew.

Involuntary memory, "the Proustian solution" to the problem of time enables us to capture, as phenomenal Idea, the "essential" difference (*P* 56). The resultant art form, like Joyce's direct expression, would be both ideal and real, formally stable yet existentially dynamic. Its implicit final goal, however, is to negate both time and death. In the end, then, it merges not only with asceticism but also with the habit that has been here so explicitly criticized, ablating all pain and creativity, in quasi-Schopenhauerian negation of the will (*P* 69-70).

In "Concentrism" (1930), Beckett provides an openly carnivalesque perspective upon many of the same problems and solutions that receive a "serious" treatment in *Proust* and other of his more monovocal essays. With insistent parodic reference to an entire philosophical heritage, this lecture describes the Buddhistic Cartesianism of "Jean du Chas," whose *Discourse*

on the Way-Out [Discours de la Sortie] advocates retreat into
self-contemplation as the way to truth. The way out is through
the way in—provided one can negotiate the (inverted) needle's
"I" [chas] of anal-ytic asceticism.

Beckett's deadpan discussion of the Chasian aesthetic implicates, however, the concentrist tendency with which he
sympathizes in Proust, just as the irony of his autoparodic (and
seemingly un-Cartesian) style implicates the romanticism of
the intuitive approach that "du Chas" shares with Marcel.
"Concentrism" generates an art that is "perfectly intelligible
and perfectly inexplicable" (D 42). Though Beckett has elsewhere espoused a similar position, it is difficult to view this
conclusion simply as the serious punch line of an elaborate
joke. Self-directed irony is too much a part of Beckett's work.
The double-voiced quality of his carnivalizing humor commonly expresses both sympathy for, and a critical distance
from, his protagonists' worldview. His "comic" writings accordingly play out the tension between conflicting tendencies
more often than they decide the issue in favor of one or the
other.

Dream of Fair to Middling Women (1932), Beckett's unfin-
ished and unpublished first "novel," returns to the mode of
"Concentrism." Published excerpts[3] rehearse the ways in
which Beckett had tried to make the "between" position more
comfortable in "Dante." Beckett, "Belacqua," and the narrator
are not equatable, nor do their statements add up to a consistent
doctrine. Their voices are related dialogically. Each comments
ironically upon the other's statements, often revealing the traditional presuppositions of apparently revolutionary formulations.

The narrator continues Proust's discussion of subjective
instability, but links it more directly to the formal opposition
between order and disorder within the novel itself. Inasmuch
as the traditional novel depends upon the construction of
monadic characters held in artificial or "chloroformed" stasis,
its traditional "Pythagorean" structure is grounded in the principle of identity (D 43, 47). In the narrator's "new" novel, characters never completely coalesce into melodic units or single

sounds. In principle, however, they exist as a simultaneity of notes that form a symphonic unit. This musical analogy signals the affinity between the narrator and those Romantics who, like Wordsworth, conceived of a multeity-in-unity to replace the monolithic ideal they found repressive. The unconventionality of this aesthetic is further complicated by the fact that its principal representative is "Nemo." *Simultaneity* is thus associated with a negative identity, a "no one." Perhaps this is why the characters' "ipse-mos-ity" is so "precarious" (*D* 45).

Although, like the narrator, Belacqua insists that "the reality of the individual . . . is an incoherent reality," he too will not accept a real "simultaneity of incoherence," particularly in the affective domain. *Simultaneity* must be rationalized so as not to contravene the law of noncontradiction (*D* 48). An individual may be a conglomerate of atomistic character traits and emotions among which he/she alternates, but no irreducible indeterminacy is conceivable. Similarly, Belacqua interprets the fluid continuum of reality as a series of audible statements punctuating "insane areas of silence," thus approximating what Martin Heidegger calls the everyday notion of time. Ultimately, Belacqua hopes that this alternation will be resolved into complete silence. "Hölderlin's *alles hineingeht Schlangen gleich* [all things are intertwined]," is thus transformed into a wish for dissolution and death, the "Pauline *cupio dissolvi* [I desire to be dissolved]" (*D* 49).

"Belacqua" and his ironic narrator-double reject the ideal of totality because it represses the fertile pathos of existence. Each, however, still seeks to eliminate life's painful "chaos" by transforming it into a negative totality ("Nothing"). Thus, they reiterate the nihilistic implications of the abstracting gesture that Beckett had earlier criticized.

The Belacquan novel itself, however, does not appear to aim at the negative absolutism of its central figure. Dehiscing, it manages to sustain an interplay of forces without attempting to resolve them in nothingness (*D* 49).[4] The "ecstasy of décollage"[5] implied by the characters' monstrous ipseity threatens, it is true, to whirl the novelistic structure apart. Yet there are moments of "centripetal backwash" that prevent this (D 46). The result is neither absolute order nor total chaos, but a fluctuating combination of relative order and disorder. In this respect the fictional work may actually be more persistently unsettling than either characters or narrator realize.

Beckett's book reviews of 1935-1936 return to the mediatory process, attempting to articulate the relation between structuring and destructuring forces within a coherent artistic form. All efforts to create order out of disorder are now regarded as deadening falsifications (D 64). Instead, reversing the process, the artist should strive to discern "the principle of disintegration in even the most complacent solidities," a task for which knockabout comedy is particularly well suited (D 82). This reversal reveals the ultimate incommensurability of world and mind, object and subject. It should not be confused with the absurdist maneuver that repeats the "crass antithesis" that Beckett abhors (D 66). The two terms are related, but their relation is irrational. Between them is a "space" whose nature remains undetermined: "no-man's land, Hellespont or vacuum, according as [the artist] happens to feel resentful, nostalgic or merely depressed" (D 70). Through this "space" the artist-subject continues to strive toward the unattainable, but real, object.

The will to attainment, the process, is what matters, not the result. Yet, Beckett criticizes those who would erect a merely "fidgeting" artistic consciousness into a new subjective center, or I-God [Ichgott]. His admiration is reserved for those who manage to maintain the tensions in their creative work. Jack Yeats, for example, does not clearly distinguish between structuring and destructuring within a process that Beckett called "analytic imagination" (D 89). Although Beckett's oxymoron may imply that opposites still coexist within a whole, his description of the process, both in "An Imaginative Work!" and in "Proust in Pieces," suggests that interjacent movement does not take place within a space external to the elements, but rather through some kind of internal spacing.

Proust had opposed the "suffering of being" and the "boredom of living." In a review of Denis Devlin's poems (1938),

Beckett links them both to fundamental human needs, but only
to separate them further: on the one hand, a need for pragmatic,
utilitarian solutions; on the other, an indeterminate eternally
unfulfilled "need that is the absolute predicament of the human identity" (*D* 91). Each now characterizes an entirely different type of art. The utilitarian either denies the paradoxical
aspects of life or treats them as mere puzzles to be solved in
time. Beckett counters with an art that would ask, rather than
answer, questions and produce something nearer to consternation than to clarity. *Identity*, for example, it regards as a
conjunction of "cathexes not only multivalent but interchange-
able" (*D* 92).

Alongside the more radical remarks that call into question
the concept of monovocal "truth," there is again a strong Romantic current that carries Beckett back toward a negative idealism. The distinction between artistic and pragmatic concerns
leads to a separation of the solitary artist from (bourgeois) society. The appreciation of, or even desire for, disorder and the
nonrational is placed on the side of the former, where they
oppose the rational order of church and state. Beckett then
transforms this disorder into the negative order of a pure antithesis in which autotelic "Need" takes the place of God (*D* 91-
92).

The 1937 letter to Axel Kaun openly expressed the nihilism
parodied in "Concentrism" but implicit in Beckett's earlier
essays. Attacking the "apotheosis of the word" (*D* 172) which
occurs not only in the imperturbability of classical grammar
and prose but also in Joyce's direct expression (praised in
"Dante"), he swings to the opposite extreme and advocates a
"literature of the Unword" (*D* 173). Joyce lacked the irony of
a nominalist. He believed in the reality of his word constructs.
His verbal formulations aimed at comprehending all aspects of
existence, but excluded all absence. To make space in Joyce's
completed word, Beckett puts language in the place that philosophy had occupied in "Dante" and its tedious analogues,
habit and voluntary memory, in *Proust*. Beckett now opposes
it with silence, and replaces the pathos of being with a form

of unbeing. His painful but fertile interjacency has become a purgatorial hollow out of which one climbs into the Void.

"The Two Needs [*Les Deux Besoins*]" (1938) attempts to thematize the problem of the rival strains that have contributed to the stresses in Beckett's thought since his earliest essays. Conflicting tendencies are no longer viewed as separable opposites, but as partners locked in a tense embrace that shapes the psyche itself. The fact that this important essay remained unpublished until 1984 is not unrelated, I think, to the pathos of this fundamental tension. The struggle between a utilitarian need for order and an exorbitant desire that disrupts all order, the artistic "need to need," is emphasized in the opening words, an epigraph from Flaubert's *Sentimental Education*, in which the "revolutionary" forces of order strive to repress the joyous unruliness of a carnivalesque scenario. Ostensible opponents, in politics or art, may indeed come to resemble one another in the world.

"The Two Needs" makes explicit the ontological quest at the heart of artistic endeavor. The true artist turns around this focal point, the nature of being, trying in vain to express it. Most people (including many writers) wallow in the boring life "of thinking, and even right-thinking, cabbages [*de choux pensant et même bien pensant*]" (D 55). When the quest and its object are recast in terms of two divergent needs, the inaccessible center becomes the "need that is needed" and the artistic drive a "need to need" (D 55). The two needs can be related as goal to process, as in the Devlin essay, but not without modifying in significant ways the conventional meaning of *telos*.

That the movement of process depends upon want in the double sense of desire and lack had already been asserted in *Proust's* discussion of passional relations. Ultimately, it derives from Aristotle's understanding of change. But here the "goal" is not only what is desired but also what is lacking and must always remain lacking. This does not mean simply that no end is possible. It expresses serious doubts about the very idea of final resolution or satisfaction of desire.

Beckett represents the two needs in the form of a six-pointed star, while allowing that no such concrete image can be fully adequate. Even falsifications can have value, however, and in this case the schema brings out some of the metaphysical presuppositons that repeatedly emerge and counter Beckett's attempt to break with traditional modes of thought. The two needs are objectified as opposite but equal Pythagorean equilateral triangles. Motion toward the apex of the need-goal triangle brings awareness of the need-desire, with the result that at the apex, where the goal should be attained, one finds instead the "chaos" of simultaneously seeing and wanting sight. As one moves downward toward the apex of the need-desire triangle, one becomes aware of the need-goal or rather, of the needed-goal.

This corrective is crucial, for the need-desire triangle does not lead to a completely indeterminate state as expected, but to "the Nothingness of having seen" (D 56). Instead of "chaos," we have at this end a negative plenitude. The need to have need is interpreted, not in the more complex Aristotelian sense of that exigency required for all change or motion, but reductively, as a desire for simple privation. It is thus related to both the ascetic tendency in *Proust* and the nihilism of Beckett's letter to Axel Kaun. The central area created by the intersection of the two triangles is the domain of art. It could have been the battlefield of opposing forces. Instead, it becomes "the creative autology" in which an awareness of the need to need is resolved, inexplicably, however, into an awareness that the need was needed (D 56).

Beckett contradicts his own explanation of the diagram by calling the latter a regular dodecahedron. The significance of this gesture lies in the fact that the regular dodecahedron is the form whose existence embarrasses Plato's Demiurge in the *Timaeus* by exceeding the limits of its harmonious fourfold schema. Moreover, as Beckett observes, it is not a purely rational figure, depending as it does upon "the incommensurability of the square's diagonal with the side, subject without number and without person [*l'incommensurabilité de la diagonale de carré avec le côté, sujet sans nombre et sans personne*]" (D 56).

Beckett's own two needs are similarly incongruous: the need for order or structure, and the need that contests the possibility, or even the desirability, of that order. Man is here regarded as the being who needs. His "being" is "need," in the double sense of desire and lack. He seeks a center, inasmuch as his own essence is a noncenter, a striving. From this "hell of unreason [enfer d'irraison]" there arises "the silent cry, the series of pure questions, the work [le cri à blanc, la série de questions pures, l'oeuvre] (D 56). The "logic" of art, its "effective principle," is neither that of mathematical science nor of theology, both of which rely upon "the holy sorites" in order to bring their dialectical debates to an end in monovocal Truth. Art, by contrast, ever-questioning and self-questioning, is necessarily inconclusive.

Most of Beckett's subsequent essays (1938-1967) deal with painters, as if the distrust of language apparent in his letter to Axel Kaun had led him to test out his aesthetic in an apparently nonlogocentric context. His studies of the van Velde brothers describe the tension-ridden "occasion" of their artistic activity: a distance or spacing that makes possible the interaction of artist-subject and object to be represented. Ultimately, however, that object is "unavailable" to the subject, and there can "be" no real relation between them. For the object exists in a corporeal realm about whose radical otherness the mind can have no certain knowledge. Such skepticism, which develops out of the extreme dualism of the Cartesian Occasionalists, leads on the one hand either to the intuitionist position of Proust or to the implicit nihilism of Beckett's subjective idealist assertions. Alternatively, it points toward the more perspectivist tendency in Beckett's thought, in which the object does not exist independently of the relation that simultaneously joins it to, while separating it from, the subject. What Beckett does not do at this point is investigate the "objectivity" of the subject and the extent to which the same could be said of it as well.

"The Painting of the Van Veldes or The World and the Trousers" (1945) describes how the brothers deal with the inaccessible and enigmatic "thing." Their two ways are viewed in a

manner that repeats the overly neat distinction between philosophical abstraction and empirical reality from "Dante." The
Heraclitean flux of Geer van Velde's painting is opposed to
Bram's phenomenological enterprise. Inverting his earlier hierarchy, however, Beckett now favors the latter's putative capture and suspension of the indeterminate "thing" by means of
an epochal perception that dispenses with time and motion in
a manner reminiscent of *Proust's* involuntary memory. Here
again Beckett leans toward the fixating, limiting, ultimately
repressive philosophical order he criticizes elsewhere—an inclination that is situated in a critical and perhaps self-mocking
framework by the epigraph to "The Two Needs."[6]

In his second van Velde essay, "The Painters of Impediment"
(1948), Beckett continues his investigation of "the object's be-
reavement" (D 135), now focusing upon the problem of mimesis. Attempting to reproduce its quiddity, modern art has
discovered not simply that the essence of the thing resists representation but that this essence *is* resistance to representation
(D 135). Art can only "represent" the conditions of this elusion
[*dérobade,* D 137]: the instability of the subject and the indeterminacy of the object. Beckett accordingly underscores the
subjectivism of the phenomenological perspective and then
undercuts the possibility of a true *epoche* by problematizing
the observing ego. These conditions are regarded, however,
both as obstacles to the older representational ideal and as the
appropriate subject/object of a new one.

Beckett's shift here from problematic subject/object as the
condition of essential evasion to subject/object as hindrance to
essential representation and hindrance itself as the thing to be
represented in the future replays the reduction of complex
needs in "The Two Needs." (*Impediment* and *hindrance* imply
a thwarted desire for representation; they do not carry with
them the possibility that the thwarting is itself both fundamental and desired.) Moreover, these hindrances put the artist
into that same "state of privation" that had there finally decided the question of "want" in the direction of lack (D 137).

Ontological elusion is initially described in terms reminiscent of the early Heidegger: a combination of unveiling and

veiling that proceeds toward a core that can never be fully unveiled (*D* 136-37). The attempt to represent this unrepresentableness leads to an infinite series of approximations: not because all earthly representations are inadequate, but because the essence is itself "a place of impenetrable proximities" (*D* 136). The essence is not a quid in any traditional sense. When Beckett interprets it as pure absence, however, the object is in danger of simply vanishing and the artist of being imprisoned within his own subjectivist cell.

Beckett has long meditated upon the "nothing." Indeed, in a letter in Sighle Kennedy (June 14, 1967), he wrote that one of his points of departure is the dictum "Naught is more real than nothing" (*D* 113). Playing upon the two negatives of ancient Greek, Democritus, from whom it is borrowed, had proposed a distinction between *no thing*, which signified the gap or spacing between (and perhaps even within) entities, and *nothing*, which signified a more total negation. The latter had no real existence; it was simply an illusion. Beckett repeatedly struggles with these two "nothings," unable to deny either one completely. This gives rise to the muted carnivalization of his Socratic parody, "Three Dialogues," in which the overt confrontation between "B" and "D" masks the more intense conflict within "B" himself.

The crucial problem in "Three Dialogues" is how to stage indeterminate relations among object, medium, and artistic subject. The difficulty is compounded because each component is itself already internally constituted by similarly irrational relations; each is therefore a no thing, that is, not really a *thing* at all. It is no longer possible to disregard their fundamental incongruities. The artist must attempt to express the inexpressible, make the unmakable, know the unknowable. A new art "form" is needed, one that would exceed the conventional boundaries of knowing and making without aspiring to the old ideal of total knowledge and perfect structure.

This new art is consequently always a failure, both as objective representation and as subjective expression, and its indigence insuperable.[7] Although "B" has experimented with this failure, he believes that Bram van Velde is the "first whose hands have not been tied by the certitude that expression is an impossible act" (D 143). Yet, it would be a mistake to say that his friend's painting is "expressive of the impossibility to express" (D 143). All attempts to represent or express the impossibility of representation or expression, "B" understands, remain within the limits of traditional mimetic art ("the bosom of St. Luke") with its dubious ontotheological basis (D 143), as Beckett himself had in his second van Velde essay. The occasion of van Velde's art is not the predicament of an art that considers itself inadequate to either world or self: "the pathetic antithesis possession-poverty" (D 144). "All that should concern us is the acute and increasing anxiety of the relation itself, as though shadowed more and more darkly by a sense of invalidity, of inadequacy, of existence at the expense of all that it excludes, all that it blinds to" (D 145). Van Velde has neither world nor self in the traditional sense. Indeed, such an awareness may keep artistic failure from becoming a simply negative concept.

My case, since I am in the dock, is that van Velde is . . . the first to admit that to be an artist is to fail, as no other dare fail, that failure is his world and the shrink from it desertion, art and craft, good housekeeping, living. No, no, allow me to expire. I know that all that is required now, in order to bring even this horrible matter to an acceptable conclusion, is to make of this submission, this admission, this fidelity to failure, a new occasion, a new term of relation, and of the act which, unable to act, obliged to act, he makes, an expressive act, even if only of itself, of its impossibility, of its obligation. I know that my inability to do so places myself, and perhaps an innocent, in what I think is still called an unenviable situation, familiar to psychiatrists. [D 145]

In "Dante," straddling two stools was said to be "extremely comfortable." In "Three Dialogues," "B" seems more alive to the anxiety involved in trying to maintain that position.

For "B" the Void, as negative plenitude, is unacceptable, for by promising to eliminate the unattainable object, it merely offers another possibility of transcendental relief. This implies a criticism of all forms of asceticism related to Beckett's other point of departure mentioned in the Kennedy letter: the Geu-lincxian "where one is worth nothing [there one should want nothing]." "B"'s dissatisfaction with will-less Nothingness thus marks a change from Beckett's explicit approval in *Proust*.

Nevertheless, "B" falls back into aestheticism when, in a kind of tropism toward darkness, he expands the exclusiveness of representer and represented until no interaction remains. The undecidability of the relation between unstable object (no thing) and indeterminate subject (no one) is reduced to an absence of relations.[8] The "irrational" becomes after all the Void. Like the tradition he criticizes, "B" at times reveals a kind of "Pythagorean terror" before "the irrationality of pi" (*D* 145). The result is an analogous tendency to silence all unruliness like that of the early Pythagorean Hippasus, who revealed incommensurability to the uninitiated. The Babbler was drowned but the problem he represents did not go away.

"Homage to Jack B. Yeats" (1954) continues Beckett's consideration of this anxious problem, the modulations between the French and English versions replacing the "voices" of "Three Dialogues." Although his own English translation is terse to the point of obscurity, it actually resolves the ambiguities of the original French in a traditional direction by giving the artistic object a subjective source. The French signals a double movement by which "a hiddenmost of spirit" (*D* 149) simultaneously spawns and questions [*soulève*] the idea of artistic self-referentiality (*D* 148). Similarly, the artistic medium or technique [*facture*] is both inspired and stolen away by [*soufflée par*] "the thing to be made [*la chose à faire*]"[9] (*D* 148-49). This is not simply the awesomeness of the *telos* shaking the technical confidence of the artist by scattering images beyond the limits of his human vision, as in the English version. Here the violence of need both releases images and upsets them by leading beyond their established limits. In the English version, full mastery is impossible because the true nature of the subject/object simply exceeds the grasp of artistic comprehension. The artist submits to it in fear and trembling, looking for a quasi-mystical union through intuitive processes. The French version suggests that the essence is not just indeterminable but indeterminate, and so renders questionable the very desire for mastery.

"The Painters of Impediment" had understood the indeterminacy of subject and object in terms of hindrance. In a 1952 essay on Henri Hayden, it is described as "this double effacement" (D 146). Although Beckett apparently means disappearance, his text also suggests a more dynamic interplay of presence and absence that is closer to the veiling/unveiling of "Painters" and announces the "trace" of his Arikha essay: "Scant [à peine] presence of the one who makes, scant presence of what is made" (D 146). The work of art results from the interaction of these shadowy "entities."

In attempting to represent this situation, Hayden has discovered the "strange order of things" founded upon a twofold suffering: order suffering the need of things, things suffering the need of order (D 147). What both fascinates and repels is "the little order [le peu d'ordre]" that seems to promise and yet to deny the artist that greater degree of order he "wants." To satisfy this double need and escape their aporetic position, most artists flee into either versions of totalitarianism or nihilism. If they abstract a complete order from "the little," they begin to produce not art but analytic intellection and systematic science. If they deny "the little" and see only chaos, they fall into despair. Both, however, are attempts to avoid the inherent dis-ease of art. Hayden has chosen to live this disease and to produce artworks from it. His is not an asceticism that rejects, but a kind of nonrationalist stoicism that accepts the unsettling (dis-)order of things.

In 1961 a brief, but very important, comment on Bram van Velde attempts to relate this anxious interplay of order and disorder to a more encompassing struggle between death and life. Death belongs to the essential matrix, or underlying "text," of existence. In earlier critical pieces (for example, the Kaun letter and Dream) the essence was viewed simply as a core of silence, or Void, at the heart of all words. In his comments to Lawrence Harvey[10] and in fictional works (such as Endgame) that develop a similar imagery, it is regarded more in terms of disintegration.

In the 1961 comment that death which belongs to the essence is countered by the unruly vitality of existence, the essential "orthographic mistake [faute]" that continually disturbs an otherwise entropic system (D 151). The embalmed stasis of abstract reflection, so often the butt of Beckett's criticism, is characteristic of those who are too fainthearted to confront, accept, and even welcome the consequent "suffering of being," except as a means of atonement. To such "lovers of natron" Beckett adds implicitly those whose stoic resignation is rooted in a heartfelt regret of the faultiness of existence. Beckett's earlier commentaries, which distinguish Bram's work from traditional art, still seemed to lack this unrepentant quality.

Now, he insists that all existential resentment should be swept away. Van Velde's paintings neither create a formal order that perfects a "fallen" natural world nor represent the ground of existence as absurd chaos. Rather, they flow like lava from fissures whose eruptions profoundly disturb both the system of death and the traditional aesthetic of perfect order that corresponds to it. In a manner reminiscent of Heidegger, the new art is said to supplement the text of death by explicitly staging the essential strife of existence: an endless, double contest that pits ordering against disordering processes, both of which are present on each side of a similar struggle between the forces that build up and those that break down.

Beckett's last critical statement, "For Avigdor Arikha" (1966-1967), correlates many of the important strands running through his art criticism. A dialectic between subject and object is initially postulated. Within the "I," however, the same opposition reappears as eidetic eye and manufacturing hand modify one another reciprocally (D 152) in an avatar of the mind/body relation already found in "Homage to Jack B. Yeats." In the French, their interaction constitutes an eye-hand that resituates on an epistemological level the hybrid ideal-real that Beckett no longer finds acceptable. The interinvolvement of mind and body, knowing and seeming, generates a being-self, which then confronts the nonself without being ontologically implicated in it. The corporeal dimension of the I/eye is apparently spiritualized. Nevertheless, both the French and the English versions also raise doubts about this rather conventional opposition.

From the conception, found in earlier essays and repeated here, of an ultimately unattainable object existing in a domain of absolute alterity, we move to an object constantly involved in the processes of seeing and making. The "shuttle" back and forth between eye and hand and within the eye as it attempts to negotiate the space between the unseeable object-in-itself and its unmakable artistic image leaves "traces" that replace the autotelic Subject as the true origin of art. The interplay of presence and absence that constitutes a trace makes it possible to stage the unrepresentability of subject, object, and their nonlogical relation without a reduction to either utter chaos or absolute Nothing.

Beckett's nonfictional writings are supplemented by "Beckett" 's published interviews.[11] In the first, granted to Israel Shenker in 1956, Beckett returns to the novelistic problem of *Dream*, now recast as the relation of form to anguish or consternation. "Classical" writers, including modern figures such as Kafka, would employ the one to neutralize the other. Relying once again upon a radical separation both of words from silence and of subject from object, Beckett advocates a form constantly threatened from outside itself. Words, subject, and form are aligned in opposition to silence, object, and anguish. The first series represents Beckett's subjective, and even subjective idealist, tendency, which is not unrelated to the nominalism suggested in the letter to Axel Kaun. The second suggests both the disturbing indeterminacies of the temporal world and the attempt to sublate them into silent nothingness.

Beckett seems to go over to philosophy, but with a painful awareness of the all-strange-away gesture this constantly requires. The artist is incapable of creating a form that can withstand the onslaught of these threatening "outside" forces. He has neither the capacity nor the knowledge for coming to terms with the anguish of an existence in the world. His art, similarly impotent and ignorant, is consequently a failure. Beckett associates knowing and making with the Apollonian but refrains from linking his own position with the Dionysian. Explicit statements made elsewhere (e.g., in *Proust* and the letter to Axel Kaun) suggest that Beckett has inclined to interpret Nietzsche's early formulation in a Schopenhauerian light: an ecstatic unruliness finally dissolving into a nihilating oneness.

Tom F. Driver's 1961 discussion with Beckett reformulates the issue in terms of the traditional opposition between eidetic form and irrational "mess." While classical art closed off its borders to the latter, Gothic art accommodated it.[12] Beckett is critical of all classicism for attempting to deal with the problem of existence by means of a fully rational, neatly ordered schema of values. The classical aesthetic is objectionable precisely because it tries to clean up a *significant* "mess." Instead, Beckett advocates an art that would suspend all conclusions with a *perhaps* that repeatedly questions the very answers it proffers.

What Beckett does not do here is acknowledge the divergent tendencies within the Gothic itself. Though anticlassical in many respects, its Christian theological framework was still firmly grounded in the classical metaphysics of Plato and Aristotle. All the imperfections of this most imperfect world were ultimately to be transcended in reunion with a God who was perfectly rational. A more unsettling "pagan" strain, which has come to be known as the carnivalesque, was oriented more toward maintaining the tense interrelatedness of "form" and "mess."[13]

Beckett's literary work does not simply illustrate or represent any aesthetic theory that these critical writings may be said to express. Beckett, indeed, is unsympathetic to conventional conceptions of art as an act of representation. I should like nonetheless to argue that, in the dialogic and often carnivalesque dimension that figures so prominently in his fiction, the revolutionary art form advocated and at times adumbrated in the criticism is in fact played out. Scenes of this nature serve as a double-voiced response to the abstracting and systematizing tendency in Western thinking, but also to his own closely related idealist or even nihilistic inclinations, which often approximate that tendency in more or less inverted ways. A struggle between established and more contestatory strains is, after all, fundamental to the carnivalesque mode, allowing its playfully relativized structure to accommodate both the centripetal and the centrifugal forces described in *Dream.*

The spirit of investigation and inquiry that is fundamental to carnivalesque dialogization aims simultaneously to destroy and to renew. Bakhtin describes its destructuring aspect in terms of dismemberment and analysis (which are also implied in Northrop Frye's use of the term *anatomy* for Menippean satire).[14] In Beckett's critical writings the analytical spirit is associated both with the desire for a perfect, closed system and with the disintegrative force of death. Like *Proust's* conception of time, it is thus a dual-faced phenomenon that is then further implicated dialogically in the equally indeterminate processes of artistic re-petitioning and re-memberment.

Past orders are repeatedly recollected and then broken down in order to be creatively surpassed. The title Beckett selected for the collection of his analytic essays invokes the Dionysian/ Orphic tradition, in which a similar process is celebrated.[15] Carnivalization enacts this eternal struggle between ordering and disordering tendencies. The carnivalized heteroglossia of antagonistic forces eschews the sort of final resolution to which the predominant tradition has always aspired. Instead, its *membra disjecta* are bound up together in a tense pluridimensional dialogue that continues to be painfully creative because it does not fear to remain fertilely destructive.

CHAPTER 2

Murphy's *Caelum*

Murphy has often been interpreted as an illustration of philosophical principles, usually, since Samuel Mintz's study, those of Arnold Geulincx, the Occasionalist disciple of Descartes.[1] The novel, however, does not so much embody a specific philosophy as satirize what is perhaps the dominant strain of the Western tradition: a general faith in the reality, or possibility, of ultimate identity or totality.

Whether it manifests itself in a monist, dualist, or pluralist philosophy, this desire, like the Demiurge of the *Timaeus*, reduces or suppresses "the reluctant and unsociable nature of the different into the same." This unruly difference, which thwarts complete integration, contributes to what Beckett calls the "mess" "invad[ing] our experience at every moment."[2]

Beckett goes on to say that the task of the artist is "to find a form that accommodates the mess." The Menippean, or carnivalizing, satire offers a possible solution. It makes room within its very structure for a dynamic interplay of elements and voices. Like other carnivalesque works—Sterne's *Tristram Shandy*, Carlyle's *Sartor Resartus*, Flaubert's *Bouvard et Pécuchet*—*Murphy* engages the reader in the worldly adventures of an "idea."[3] The various episodes are not meant as positive illustrations. Rather, they constitute scenarios in which the "idea" can be provoked and tested. Actively investigating the problems inherent in the way an idea manifests itself in the works of particular thinkers, they bring it back into contact with all that its abstracting power has eliminated—the excrescences and deficiencies of existence, including laughter.[4]

Carnivalization generates an ambivalent interaction between the terms of the basic oppositions of our traditional logic—for example, life/death, body/mind, object/subject, effect/cause. Barriers are also broken down betweeen styles and genres usually considered incompatible. Disrespectful of hierarchies, carnivalization blends the high and sacred with the low and profane. Beckett's comparison in "Dante" of philosophy and philology to "two nigger minstrels out of the Teatro del Piccoli," for example, mixes serious and popular culture. It also reveals that the similarities between *sophia* and *logia* are more than blackface deep. The mingling of supposedly self-enclosed systems is carried further in *Murphy* where Pythagoreans and Newtonians, Spinozans and Hegelians meet and are reflected in each other. Instead of being strictly separated, the opposed elements are shown to be mutually implicated.[5]

Often these scenarios are suggested by philosophers themselves. "I am interested," says Beckett, "in the shape of ideas, even if I do not believe in them. . . . It is the shape that matters."[6] Beckett accumulates the striking images and metaphors of philosophy and, exploiting its repressed carnivalesque dimension, turns them against the ideas they would illustrate. In *Molloy*, for example, he takes Descartes's image of wandering through a forest in search of a methodological way to truth and transforms it into Moran lost in the woods. In later works, identifiable images borrowed from specific philosophers are rarer, though they have not been eliminated. Instead, Beckett builds his own images to illustrate the general "shape" of an idea found in an entire genealogy of thinkers, for example, the cylindrical world of *Le Dépeupleur* or *Imagination Dead Imagine*.

The Menippean situation challenges the "truth" of a philosophical principle by embodying it in a seeker who uses it to order his or her life. Murphy himself, the "seedy solipsist," is of course the principle seeker in this particular Menippea. Yet he is not alone. All the characters resemble, in fact, *morphai*—the various forms in Western culture's recurrent dream of unity and ultimate reconciliation. Although they illustrate the stages in the history of human consciousness, they do not replace one another in a linear progression. Nor do they move dialectically toward a total system of knowledge. On the contrary, they remain in perpetual carnivalized and carnivalizing dialogue.

From the onset *Murphy* addresses parodically the classic ontological problem of being and becoming. A realm of true being, ideal and timeless, where "the light that never changes cast[s] its rays . . . over the mind," has often been opposed to the temporal and spatial realm of "the quid pro quo . . . cried as wares and the light [that] never wane[s] the same way twice" (*M* 6-7).[7] Or phenomena have been perceived as exhibiting only a perpetually self-repeating series of "mews" that at best reassure with their orderliness and regularity, and at worst induce a feeling of *ennui*: "the poor old sun in the Virgin again for the billionth time" (*M* 1-2). Genuine change is thus either irrelevant or illusory. Really there is "nothing new." In either case what is eliminated are those elements of disorderliness and discontinuity that thwart the desire, common to both philosophy and science, for total integration and complete identity.

Into the phenomenal world Murphy had fallen and is now "detained" in a bodily "cage." This is the "big world" to which he does not belong or so "he fondly hope[s]" (*M* 2).Alienating himself from what "never truly is" in order to attain true being, Murphy sits "out of it," clothed only in his thoughts, his senses bound and his eyes wide open. There, in his own chair guaranteed by the maker not to change, he experiences something akin to that spiritual pleasure some have called freedom.

To remind the reader that a measure of change is, however, undeniable, the narrator returns to a time when Murphy was part of Neary's circle. Then he was in contact with those who, despite their apparent diversity, all sought harmony among opposites. Neary sometimes espoused Pythagorean apmonia [*sic*], at other times Alcmaeon's isonomy, and even the attunement of Simmeas (*M* 4); nevertheless, all are similar concepts for the coexistence of differing "notes" within a coherent structure.[8] Must these elements be held in equilibrium, or is there room for unresolvable dissonance? *Murphy* repeatedly investigates this question already posed in *Dream*.

Apmonia, for example, is the Latinized but actually non-transliterated form of the Greek word for harmony. At the same time it approaches the Greek phrase *apo monoas* ("away from the unit") or the verb *apomonoein* ("to be excluded from a thing," "to leave quite alone"). Taken together they signal an ontological ambiguity, the former emphasizing the consensus that binds the group together, the latter the setting-apart of the individual. By rendering the Greek *rho* as *p*, moreover, Beckett has brought the word closer to the Latin *admoneo*. (*Ap* is an assimilated form of the Latin *ad*—*OED*.) The various meanings of admonish point to an ethical ambivalence. It is not clear what Murphy is being exhorted to do or what he is being warned against. This rather undecidable quality of *apmonia* thus repeats the conflict between centripetal and centrifugal forces earlier discernible in Beckett's art and literary criticism and his own problematic attitude toward it.

Neary comprehends life as an organized form, a "tetrakyt" or Gestalt, outside of which there is nothing but dross, or what William James called "the big, blooming, budding confusion" (*M* 4).[9] Its unity can only be achieved through love that, creating a short circuit, fuses the opposites (e.g., Miss Dwyer's closed figure and Neary's penetrating desire). Nevertheless, it depends upon mastering whatever threatens to be excessive, in particular the immoderate "heart." Neary usually manages to stop his, at least momentarily.

By contrast, Murphy, who cannot forgive himself any compromise with corporeal existence, perceives life in more idealist terms as simply a "passing through," the wanderings of the lost one back toward his originary spiritual abode. He scornfully rejects Nearyean love as an instinctual return to the level of Teneriffe apes.[10] Murphy's extreme dualism makes all intercourse of mind and body impossible. In the process his own pineal gland has "shrunk to nothing" (*M* 6). Nevertheless, if Neary's sensuous love is Greek to Murphy, it may be because he would forget that his own more idealized conception derives from the ascetic tendency of that same Pythagoreanism.

In Chapter 2, the dualism that would reduce Murphy to mere mind unencumbered by body would, at the same time, reduce the body, one's own or that of another such as Celia, to mere empirical data (*M* 10). What attracted Murphy to her, he claims, however, was not her figure but her form, a form so enticing that it caused him to abandon *caelum* gazing for Celia gazing (*M* 15). As he tried (futilely) to demonstrate with syllogistic logic—"in Barbara, Baccardi and Baroko, though never in Bramantip"(*M* 16)[11]—his love was not a result of physical desire but rather of pure beholding. It was love at first sight. This is not to imply that Murphy's perception of Celia was simply spiritual or intellectual. *Eros* and *nous* need not work at cross-purposes. The former will be sublimated, if the seer is wise, into a passionate but spiritual commitment to the Absolute. Sensuous beauty may lead the lover upward to ideal Beauty known only through the intellect.[12] So that there might be no uncertainty about the precise nature of his relation with Celia, however, Murphy would like it brought into harmony with the "heavenly" order. (It never was.)

After reading the where, how, and when of Celia's first meeting with Murphy, although in an unsatisfyingly eliptical and expurgated account (*M* 12-17), the reader, like Mr. Kelly, would like to know, who is this Murphy? Celia's answer is that "Murphy [is] Murphy" (*M* 17). Upon closer inspection, the reader will find that this classical formulation has obscured something important. It appears from the equation M = M that M is not, in fact, self-identical. And Murphy, therefore, not one with himself. The *copula*, indeed, marks an internal difference. Beckett had already suggested something similar in his analysis of *Remembrance of Things Past*: "The most ideal tautology presupposes a relation and the affirmation of equality involves only an approximate identification, and by asserting unity denies unity."[13] This difference will undercut the attempt of any *morphe* to see itself as a whole. Murphy, however, is as yet unaware of this fundamental issue.[14]

Consider Murphy's Thema Coeli (*M* 32). The genethliac horoscope reveals one's entire existence as foreordained by the position of the stars. A microcosm in harmony with the macrocosm, an individual life is only eternal being projected onto time and space. Murphy's nativity, however, resists comprehension. Its predictions, like those of all horoscopes, are contradictory, both among themselves and internally. It is difficult to decide precisely what certain elements mean. Murphy's patron, Mercury (*M* 31), for example, is simultaneously a trickster, thief, and Antichrist, on the one hand, and a divine messenger, on the other. Through Mercury, or Hermes, Murphy is associated with Hermetism, which, although tied to the Neoplatonic tradition by certain of its aspects (particularly the quest for ultimate reunification of the microcosm with God as macrocosm), also includes many nontraditional and indeed subversive elements (e.g., a belief in the creative potential of chaos).

Moreover, Murphy was born under the sign of Capricorn, which in Bruno's *Expulsion of the Triumphant Beast* is the animal allowed to represent the divine in things. This is not surprising since as (scape)goat, Capricorn is the animal of the God-man Christ. Yet, the goat as satyr or devil is also associated with evil and lust. Capricorn is in addition the sign at the winter solstice—Christmas or Saturnalia. (Murphy's birthday is December 25, when "four degrees of the Goat was rising"— *M* 32.) And Saturn himself is an ambivalent figure, simultaneously destroyer and procreator, patron of abstract contemplation and carnival revels, god of egalitarian harmony and chaos. And also disseminator of seeds and meanings. The reason for this excessiveness may be, as Swami Suk (incongruous name for an ascetic) reveals, that "few Minds are better concocted with this Native's" (*M* 32). A not always well-digested mixture of rather messy ingredients (e.g., "intense love nature . . . with inclination to purity"), it may provoke an upset, such as Murphy's "heart attack" (*M* 30) or his final fiery disaster.

What then does Murphy mean? He himself offers little help. "Sometimes Murphy would begin to make a point, sometimes he may have even finished making one, it was hard to say" (*M* 22). His discursive points, unlike Descartes's geometrical points or Leibniz's metaphysical monads, are far from clear and discrete. It was hard to decide either their beginning or end. Their effect on Celia was to make her feel "spattered with words that went dead as soon as they sounded; each word obliterated, before it had time to make sense, by the word that came next" (*M* 40).

Murphy's indeterminate words, like his undecidable points, make quite an interpretative "mess." Celia can at present only understand them as obliterating each other, producing meaningless static. Or at least, "in the end she did not know what had been said." Nevertheless, she still recognized that Murphy had said something. His chaotic utterances could not be equated with empty silence. "It was like difficult music heard for the first time." Less traditional interpretive strategies may be needed.

In the third chapter, Celia pauses on her way to see Murphy to consider a crucial question: "What difference . . . would it make now, whether she went on up the stairs to Murphy or back down them into the mew? The difference between her way of destroying them both, according to him, and his way, according to her" (*M* 27): the dissolution of spirit in the "mercantile gehenna" (*M* 41) of the big world or the extinction of the body in the little world of darkness and silence. Does it really come to the same thing in the end?

Murphy finds disgusting "the charVenus and her sausage and mash sex" (*M* 37). Not only is it, like Nearyean "love," a natural appetite that drags man into the wallows of the material world, it is also inferior desire belonging to the flux of the phenomenal world. "You can want what does not exist, you can't love it" (*M* 36). Love, by contrast, is pure and static. "What do you love? . . . Me as I am" (*M* 36).[15]

Underlying their dispute is a fundamental ontological conflict. For the more pragmatic Celia, being is doing. She would have Murphy demonstrate his true meaning and worth by working in the world. Murphy, on the other hand, is already Murphy. For him, being precedes and is independent of doing. Indeed, only a fraction of one's being is ever actualized. He perceives action with a "cash value" as prostitution: "walk[ing] the streets for work." Thus, the only possible "course" before him is "inaction" (*M* 38). Murphy "does nothing that [Celia] could discern" (*M* 17). He lives instead by messing with the rent accounts sent to Mr. Quigley, just as he subsists by defrauding restaurants. Murphy's livelihood depends on what exceeds, like his irrational heart, the bounds of a supposedly static system. Yet, since he is really not concerned with earthly subsistence, he adheres to the Archeus of ethical dynamics—doing "no more than he would be done by" (*M* 21)—and expects Celia to do the same. Thus, "apperceiving himself into a glorious grave and checking the starry concave," he would withdraw from ever-recurring earthly torments and allow Providence to provide. (Unfortunately, it never did, at least not enough to make ends meet.)

Although "to die fighting was the perfect antithesis of his whole practice, faith and intention" (*M* 38), Murphy willingly chooses, not only to defend his "course of inaction" but also to contest Celia's "course of action" (*M* 36). What would have caused this "grisly relic" from the depraved days of "nuts, balls and sparrows," when he, like Augustine,[16] was a student of materialism, to upset his habitual state of ideal passivity (*M* 38)? Murphy explains that "he has been carried away by his passion for Celia"(*M* 38).

Murphy's heart attacks have an analogous effect. But only when Celia is absent. When Murphy is able to sublimate Celia's provocative rhythm (she could not disguise her walk) into the sequence of "serenade, nocturne, aubade," he has neither need for his rocking chair nor heart attacks (*M* 30). The rhythm of passion, contained within the formal patterns of Platonic *mousike*, restores the emotions to their proper balanced order.[17] Without this musical harmony, Murphy's passion, heartfelt and irrational, literally bowls him over, turning his ascetism into a carnivalized crucifixion (*M* 28).

Mr. Kelly, Celia's grandfather, as if recognizing the nihilism inherent in Murphy's undertaking, had advised Celia to "terminate an intercourse that must prove fatal . . . while there [was] yet time" (*M* 25). Celia's passion could not, however, be foregone. Before going in to see Murphy, she had drawn a distinction of her own: "It was not she, but Love, that was the bailiff. She was but the bum[-]bailiff" (*M* 27). Celia apparently sees herself as love incarnate.

In order to cope with such an indeterminable creature, Murphy must transform the mind/body dichotomy into the Platonic trichotomy, an essentially "monstrous proposition": "You, my body and my mind" (*M* 40). Celia, in the place of soul, should occupy an intermediate position between mind and body. (Murphy, however, as if refusing to recognize her spiritual qualities, places her entirely on the side of the body.) Like the heart, the soul has often been perceived as problematic: immaterial and immortal, yet somehow animating the body in which it dwells.[18] In Neoplatonism, for example, the soul is said to reflect the ideas in the divine intellect, transmitting them in turn to material forms. This arouses in the latter an erotic desire to be reunited with the former. Matter, aware of its insufficiency, thirsts for sufficiency. Celia's love may represent a desire for comprehension. Nevertheless, "its inception and its continuance," as Beckett wrote in *Proust*, "imply the consciousness that something is lacking." Celia, it appears, unlike Murphy, understands intuitively that "one only loves that which one does not possess entirely" (*P* 39). Celia's passionate love, then, like the cool, bright *caelum* that reminded her of Ireland, is full of both the movement of desire and the light of love.

Neary's confrontation with the bumbailiff passion assumes the form of a direct frontal attack on the "Red Branch Bum" (*M* 42) in chapter 4. When Miss Dwyer allowed him into her closed figure, she became, to his dismay and against all Gestaltist principles, indistinguishable from the ground. Any mixture of opposites, no matter how harmonious, became simply chaotic. What Neary seeks is not Pythagorean harmony but a union in which neither he nor the other abandons his/her alterity.[19] Neary wants it both ways.

This burning need then drove him to Miss Counihan[20] from whom, however, he was separated by a distancce no less great than that between Dives and Lazarus (*M* 48). She had unfortunately already found her savior in Murphy. Despite the fervently argued tractate, *The Doctrine of the Limit*, he had borrowed from his master's disciple Philolaus, Neary failed to convince her to abandon Murphy and allow him to insert his principle of limit into her unlimited womanliness.[21] ("All centre and no circumference," says Wylie, bringing Cusanus down to earth.) Miss Counihan, however, might reconsider if Murphy were found lacking. Unable to locate his query despite Cooper's fervent efforts and frustrated by his *âme damnée's* (*M* 54) conflicting telegrams, Neary turned in desperation from Miss Counihan's "hot buttered buttocks" to the "deathless rump" of Cuchulain, the Yeatsian symbol of Neary's "love" problems.[22]

Neary understands that because its end is full union, love requires that "nothing" remain covered (*M* 47). On the other hand, its secrets (like the existence of the fifth regular geometric solid in the *Timaeus*—"the construction of the regular dodeca-hic-dodecahedron"—or "the incommensurability of side and diagonal") must not be made public. They exceed, as do Neary's hiccups, the limits of propriety (*M* 47-48). And the secret of love is desire, the "morsel of chaos" that his system cannot accommodate.

Desire is a want in the double sense of a craving and a lack. It is an overflowing movement toward what both creates and marks a space (a no thing). Like the Schopenhauerian will, desire is insatiable, thrusting itself blindly toward ever-changing objects: Miss Dwyer, Miss Counihan, Murphy, Celia, and so on.

While waiting to see if Cooper's mission succeeds, Neary would contain his desire for Miss Counihan within a system of "counters," another Pythagorean variant of Murphy's "music": "There [in Mooney's] he sat all day, moving slowly from one stool to another until he had completed the circuit of counters, when he would start all over again in the reverse direction. He did not speak to the curates, he did not drink the endless half-pints of porter that he had to buy, he did nothing but move slowly round the ring of counters, first in one direction, then in the other, thinking of Miss Counihan" (*M* 56). Neary's attempt here (as in the case of Miss Dwyer) to contain the e-motion of desire within a permanent form might be described as his passion.

Passion derives from pathos that generally refers to the suffering that results from tense conflict. It can be interpreted in several ways, each of which is related to a tradition in Western thought. When associated with Christ, passion describes an agony whose goal is atonement for sin and reunion with God. Christian pathos thus serves the dominant ethos that affirms as a fundamental principle the overcoming of all division and dissension in a loving unity. Love may therefore be described as sublimated passion.[23] Perpetually frustrated, however, the quest for unity and wholeness leads to the metaphysical pathos characterizing Western culture. Associated with Dionysus, on the other hand, passion involves intense emotion, disorder, and excessiveness that transgresses all limits and contests all established structures. Rather than reconciliation and harmony, we find here participation in a world that can never be completely mastered.

When the indelible residue of motley passion takes the carnivalized form of being down-faced by a deathless rump, the only way out (or in) is to dash one's head against it.[24] The parodic attempt at "harmonizing" mind and body is really an attempted suicide. Neary's primal unit, it appears, is merely an inversion of Murphy's solipsism.

Wylie, however, was there to stop his former mentor from making a complete mess of himself and to show him another way. The diffusion of life that so upset Neary's harmony cannot, and need not, be concealed. It can instead be incorporated into a closed, mechanistic system based upon the law of conservation of wantum. Of course, in this process all indeterminacy must be suppressed. Consider the case of Newton. He sought relief from this world of paradoxical hypotheses in the insulating laws of simplicity and uniqueness. As a result he perceived motion as adiabatic, that is, occurring without gain or loss. "Humanity is a well with two buckets . . . one going down to be filled, the other coming up to be emptied" (*M* 58). In this system, nothing is left over; "there is no rump" (*M* 57).

If the quantum never varied, as Wylie's first law of thermodynamics affirms, then the system of desire would be closed: "Of such was Neary's love for Miss Dwyer, who loved a Flight-Lieutenant Elliman, who loved a Miss Farren of Ringsakiddy, who loved a Father Fitt of Ballinchashet, who in all sincerity was bound to acknowledge a certain vocation for a Mrs. West of Passage, who loved Neary" (*M* 5). Or at the moment: Neary who loves Miss Counihan who loves Murphy who loves. . . . Since, however, according to the Clausian premise, heat always shows a tendency to pass from hotter to colder bodies, Neary must convince Miss Counihan that he has reduced his temperature before the direction of the flow of wantum can be reversed. Neary would then be able to receive the heat Miss Counihan could no longer dissipate in Murphy's direction (*M* 60-61).

Murphy, however, still remains a problem. What could women possibly see in "that long hank of Apollonian asthenia . . . that schizoidal spasmophile" (*M* 49)? Perhaps it is his languidness prone to sensual fits, or the inconstancy of his willessness. Perhaps it is his amorous style, flacid but easily excited. Women, it seems, are attracted to the peculiar temper of his reserve. Wylie, however, can only perceive the "surgical" quality that he and his master share with Murphy and his historical doubles.[25] Whether in philosophy or in bed, what matters to the analytic mind is an ability to undo the strands and loosen the ties without too quickly losing its head. Nevertheless, something is abstracted from Murphy's nature in the process, for, as the narrrator points out, surgical quality is "not quite the right word" (*M* 62).[26]

In chapter 5, this analytic side of Murphy's nature is both graphically manifested and problematized by the pleasure he derived from the "linoleum of exquisite design, a dim geometry of blue, grey and brown" in the Brewery Lane room he shares with Celia (*M* 63). Although it reminded him of Braque's analytic cubism, it is later referred to as the "dream of Descartes." Latent in this abstract design, however, as in Murphy himself, is a certain irrational dimension. Baillet recounts in his biography how the young Descartes, passionately seeking truth, "fell into a kind of enthusiasm that disposed in such a manner his already dejected spirit that it put him in a state to receive the impressions of dreams and visions." On November 10, 1619, he went to sleep "full of his enthusiasm and completely occupied with the thought of having that day discovered the basis of an admirable science." During the night he had three consecutive dreams that Frances Yates has compared to Hermetic trances.

These dreams reveal an openness to "enthusiasm" that exceeds the usual opposition between reason and unreason, and undermines the priority of the former: "the divinity of Enthusiasm and . . . the force of imagination that make the seeds of wisdom (that are found in the spirit of all men like sparks of fire in rocks) sprout with much greater facility and even much greater brilliance, than can the Reason of Philosophers." But this excessiveness is then excluded by a gesture that realizes Descartes's more conscious dream of unlocking the secrets of nature by establishing mathematics, and particularly analytic geometry, as the sole key.[27]

Thus, like a piece of linoleum, Cartesian "analytic geometry" might be described as a fabric of interwoven contrasting strands into which a mixture of rhapsodic Linus's flax and wise Minerva's olive oil has been rigidified, forming an artificial ground.[28]

Murphy repeats Descartes's "surgical" gesture when he tries to classify jokes analytically (*M* 65). Only someone with "an imperfect sense of humor" would have tried to fit into clear and distinct categories something as fundamentally double and paradoxical as the pun. Furthermore, to assert, as does the narrator, that "in the beginning was the pun" is to undercut any attempt at categorization. If there is no *Logos* in which thought can become present, there is no immediate and natural relation in which word and thought are one. Instead, there is only an approximate equivalence between word and thought, giving rise to a number of more or less synonymous words, for example, *apmonia, isonomy, attunement*. And words can provide a number of differing meanings. The "right word" (*le mot propre*), however, does not and can never quite present itself.

This disseminating quality of language should not be confused with a polyvalence in which the multiple meanings coalesce into a unified whole as they do in medieval biblical exegesis (or in Frye's *Anatomy of Criticism*) and in the Romantic understanding of multeity-in-unity. Neither, however, should it be seen as leading to a totally subjective use of language. Although there appears to be no natural connection between signified and signifier, the connection is not simply arbitrary. Neary cannot in fact call *apmonia* "what he liked," for its different variants are at least historically determined. Nor finally does it mean that language is hopelessly inadequate to describe reality that is excessive (a position to which Beckett at times seems to adhere).

Rather, it suggests that both difference and absence are required for there to be anything like signification. The possibility of signification presupposes both some difference between signifier and signified and the absence of the latter. Hence, the origin of meaning can never be a unique, singular reality, but must be constituted within the play of difference.[29]

The problem of difference again becomes apparent when Celia attempts to comprehend Murphy. She interprets "everything that happen[s]" as "yet another reason for Murphy's finding work": "From such antagonistic occasions as a new arrival at Pentonville and a fence sold out in the Market, she drew the same text" (*M* 64). Celia's attitude suggests that the "antinomies of unmarried love," if understood as converging in work, would lead Murphy out of the daily routine of the "nothing new" into a progressive perfecting of his being. To Celia, this means making a man out of Murphy, an act of incarnation that would at the same time redeem her, as it had Mary Magdelena, from her fallen state of prostitution. Only Murphy, it appears, perceives the implications of this attitude. If the quest for work were ever to attain its goal, Celia's visible universe would be annihilated, for without the willing and nilling, there would be nothing left. Celia, however, might even accept this, for she believes that "then there will be nothing to distract [her] from [Murphy]" (*M* 65).

With the visible world gone, with will and desire satisfied,

Celia would be free to contemplate directly the true source of meaning for her: Murphy. ("Everything led to Murphy"). Yet, only if Murphy were engaged in work elsewhere, or in other words, absent. It seems that the "nothing" that would make it possible for Celia to be one with Murphy would at the same time be the "no thing" that would keep them apart, to adapt the old Joe Miller from Democritus that Murphy finds such a bad joke. And well he might, for it will return to upset his own quest for monadistic unity.

As Murphy sets out in search of a job, the inhumanly regular cycles of Ecclesiastes to which he adheres come into contact with the teleological conception of time found not only in the mercantile world, but also in the Book of Job, specifically in Blake's vision of *Job*.[30] "Members of the Blake League" might think "that the Master's conception of Bildad the Shuhite had come to life and was stalking about London in a green suit, seeking whom he might comfort"(*M* 70).[31] "But what is Bildad but a fragment of Job, as Zophar and the others are fragments of Job." Job's would-be comforters, as Joseph Wicksteed has commented, are only concrete manifestations of his own egotistical (and therefore for Blake "corporeal") creed. Job's friends had accused him of wrong actions, but they should have rebuked him, like Elihu, for the importance he attached to his struggles to perfect his own isolated individuality or "great Selfhood."

Job's materialism and his individualism are analogous in that they ascribe ultimate value to the individual as a physical entity rather than to a spiritualized "natural" community. Thus, Blake's Job finally discovers that it is useless and even destructive "striving to Create a Heaven in which all shall be pure and holy in their Own Selfhoods."[32] Murphy on the jobpath, then, is Murphy on the Jobpath, since "the only thing Murphy was seeking was . . . the best of himself" (*M* 71). Indeed, his quest might even be described as a carnivalized history of growth and development.

In the act of having been born, Murphy fell out of tune with the heavenly spheres. His vagitus "had not been the proper A of international concert pitch, with 435 double vibrations per

second, but the double flat of this" (*M* 71).[33] His loss of spirit
occurred at the latest in "the moment of his being strangled
into a state of respiration" (*M* 71). Later, as a theological student, he meditated on how man, fragmented by his fall into
terrestrial life, might be redeemed by the "it is consummated"
of a conjugal love, celestial or otherwise. Nevertheless, during
"those sanguine days" of hard abstract reflection, he came to
prefer the egotistical love of Selfhood to that unitive love of
the whole. This preference is concretely manifested by the suit
he then acquired that "admitted no air from the outer world;
it allowed none of Murphy's own vapours to escape" (*M* 72).
Yet, Murphy had not forgotten his origin, for he refused to wear
any coif, so much did it remind him of his painful partition (*M*
73).

Consequently, he perceives his new life with Celia as an
asylum on his pilgrim's regress toward the home from which
he had been originally exiled. The "serenade, nocturne and albada" (*M* 74) of the Celian spheres, although too rhythmic to
be totally satisfying, can at least be temporarily soothing. Thus,
in the meantime, Murphy shows a marked preference for an
antepurgatorial state, between the heavenly mere of Milton
House and the mire of the infernal concourse: "This was his
Belacquan fantasy" (*M* 78). (This might be tripe, as the narrator
suggests, but at least it did not seem offensive to others; "it
did not smell.")

Murphy's growing dissatisfaction with astrology, like Augustine's, can also be interpreted as necessary to his quest, that
is, as a casting off of yet another tie with the material world.
Furthermore, such astral determinism must be overcome if he
is to continue on his way toward freedom. All astrological prediction is based upon a determinism which claims that the
inner life is dependent not only upon bodily changes but,
through the body, upon celestial configurations. Murphy now
denies that the stars occupy a privileged position as if they,
and they alone, were powerful enough to condition the vicis-
situdes of human life (*M* 75-76). Like Pico, Murphy insists on
the disorder that results from astrology's application of the laws
of physical causality to the realm of human consciousness:

"There seems to be a certain disharmony between the only two canons in which Murphy can feel the least confidence. So much the worse for him, no doubt" (*M* 76). There seems, in other words, to be a conflict between determinism and free will.

The progressive working out of Murphy's system first takes him to a chandlery, where among base and earthly men he would work as a smart boy, heating animal matter so that it might be abstracted into candles for the spirit. Unfortunately, he is refused the job. His nature is too irrational to be incorporated into the chandlers' system of classification: " 'E ain't smart . . . No 'e ain't a boy . . . 'E don't look rightly human to me . . . not rightly" (*M* 77).

Exhausted by the ordeal, Murphy longs for the negative theological way "out of all knowledge," but unfortunately he is too far from his own chair (*M* 79). He has instead to settle for an anti-Pavlovian lunch ordered following the analytic Kulpe method, contemplated with the theophanist reverence of a William of Champeaux, but indigested according to an absurd procedure of his own. Although Murphy is only an "off and on" adherent of these (and other) positions, his syncretism remains as problematic as that of Leibniz who tried to connect "Plato with Democritus, Aristotle with Descartes, the Scholastics with the Moderns, theology and morals with reason."[34] Its messy problems should not, however, be skimmed off in order to make it conform to any one system, philosophic or hermeneutic. Rather, it attests to the existence of differing, if not openly conflicting, tendencies within his "system." These tendencies, however, do not appear ever to be sublated into a higher philosophy. Thus, Murphy himself remains the scene of numerous contests and his solipsism truly "seedy" (*M* 82).

Similarly, Murphy's "successful attempt to defraud a vested interest" disrupts his "perfected balanced meal"(*M* 80) "to the honourable extent of paying for one cup of tea and consuming 1.83 approximately [or more precisely 1.83333333 . . .]" (*M* 84). Moreover, the excess that thus appears is not quite balanced by the profit the company makes (*M* 83). Too much is given or taken, on one side or another; the system is not perfectly closed.

Murphy then sets out to continue in his imagination toward his next cockpit. He has regressed mentally into the proto-classical Archaic Room of the British Museum in order there to recruit his strength from the dark mysteries of the Harpies' Tomb, when he is aroused by Austin Ticklepenny. An Irish Renaissance man, Ticklepenny exhibits the sterility of his ped-erastic pedantry by merely inverting classical adages and Ar-istotelian poetics, having been advised to turn from emptying pints into "gaelic prosodoturfy" (*M* 89) to washing them for the profit of the Magdelena Mental Mercyseat (M.M.M.). Ticklepenny thus seems the descendant of those carnivalized humanist pedants found in Rabelais's *Gargantua* or Bruno's *Chandler* and the contemporary of the autodidact in Sartre's *Nausea*. Moreover, he "knew nothing" (*M* 90). Not only was he incapable of intuition (*Anschauung*), he sneered at it as be-yond rational comprehension. (Nevertheless, Murphy may be more like Ticklepenny than he would admit. Ticklepenny, af-ter all, is attracted to him as an apparent kindred soul.) Tickle-penny had sought to flee from the Mercyseat for fear of losing his mind.[35]

Murphy has no such fear; on the contrary. Although he does merit the narrator's scorn, Ticklepenny unwittingly reveals to Murphy, as Faustus did to Augustine, the direction his journey should take—into the M.M.M. This sudden oxymoronic "sy-zygy in Suk's delineations" of lunatic and custodian radically changes Murphy's perception of his nativity. Having apparently revealed its systematic quality, it becomes "the poem that he alone of the living could write" (*M* 93). As he unriddles its secret chit, he may find, like Schelling playing Romantic varia-tions on Plotinus, that it narrates "the Odyssey of the spirit which, wonderfully deluded, in seeking itself, flees itself," only to return in the end "completely to itself."[36]

Finally settled in the Hyde Park Cockpit, Murphy prepares to consume his solid nourishment, from the primary ginger (a rather unstable origin) to the ultimate Anonym. His prefer-ences, however, astringe the natural variety within the closed system of the five, thus violating the very "essence of assort-ment" (*M* 96). During an ecstatic vision of the multeity-in-unity that would result, he believes, from the lack of willful differentiation (Schelling might call it indifference), Murphy wrestles with the "demon of gingerbread." He appears particularly susceptible to those things that are destined to disturb his closed system. He finds it impossible to deny his "small but implacable appetite" (*M* 81), as well as "his deplorable susceptibility to Celia, ginger, and so on" (*M* 179). (Celia and ginger—both are stimulants and both are, oddly enough, connected with the chaos of gas: ginger as a carminative and Celia as a celestial whore.) Such willful movements seem fundamental to Murphy's nature.

Murphy is awakened from his sleep of biscuit plenitude, not by the sublime revelation of a rosy-fingered dawn as was Wordsworth's Pedlar, but by the grotesque Rosie Dew. A duck like Ticklepenny, but of a different albeit analogous breed, her earthbound body afflicted with Panpygoptosis (a carnivalized version of panpsychism) is mismatched to the spirit of a medium.

Rosie Dew has come to the garden, her dog, Nelly, in heat and her protector, Lord Gall of Wormwood, "in tail male special" (*M* 99) on a Romantic argonautic in search of the golden love so dear to Shelley. As if following the Aristippean dictum, "*non me rebus, sed mihi res* [not myself to things, but things to myself]" (*M* 98),[37] Shelley reinterpreted the Neoplatonic concept of spiritual circuit in a more sensuous direction. "[I]n his poetry," comments M.H. Abrams, "all types of human and extrahuman attraction—all forces that hold the physical, mental, moral and social universe together—are typically represented, both in myth and in metaphor, by categories which are patently derived from erotic attraction and sexual union."[38]

Lord Gall of Wormwood's "painful position" is to be a broken link in this great chain of union and procreation. "Spado of long standing in tail male special he seeks testamentary pentimenti from the *au-delà*" (*M* 99). Lord Gall needs an heir; he is the unfortunate victim of a predestined order of succession that now leads up to an issue that does not and cannot exist. Because he is incapable of an apocalyptic climax, there can not ever be a first, not to mention a second, coming. Thus, he would like an earlier and presumably less rigid version of the family will to emerge so that he might inherit (*M* 104). Rosie Dew's function as medium is to unite heaven and earth, past and present, in order that the lord's will might be redone.

Rosie Dew's Manichaean control, however, can only offer her the hope that with the millenium will come salvation. Until the time is right, both she and her employer will have to endure the passion of a grotesque nature that thirsts for union with the sublime. Until then, her aphrodisiacal offering of lettuce will not complement the sheep's hunger, nor will the depravity of Nelly's appetite match Murphy's desire to indulge in a "rutting cur's rejectamenta" (*M* 102). Love, it seems, at least in its natural form, is incapable of fulfilling what is incomplete and reintegrating what has been divided, whether in the individual psyche or in the social order.

Consequently, when *Murphy* turns to examine the relation between nature and man, particularly in the Rosie Dew episode, it finds no evidence of that harmony with the natural world that brought solace to the Romantics. This only confirms Murphy's decision to exclude all that was natural from both his big and little worlds. Unfortunately for him, he could not do it entirely. Man and nature, mind and body—they can be neither completely harmonized nor completely separated. For Murphy, it appears they combine oxymoronically to form that stimulating chaos he perceives as a "murk of irritation" (*M* 104). Murphy is unable to reason even a spark of light out of this muddy mess.[39]

Since union with nature is undesirable, at least as far as he is concerned, and mastery impossible, Murphy chooses another course.

He therefore went to the other extreme, disconnected his mind from the gross importunities of sensation and reflection and composed himself on the hollow of his back for the torpor he had been craving to enter for the past five hours. He had been avoidably detained, by Ticklepenny, by Miss Dew, by his efforts to rekindle the light that Nelly has quenched. But now there seemed nothing to stop him. Nothing can stop me now, was his last thought before he lapsed into consciousness, and nothing will stop me. In effect, nothing did turn up to stop him and he slipped away . . . to where there were no pensums and no prizes but only Murphy himself, improved out of all knowledge. [*M* 105]

Murphy is apparently striving to out Hegel Hegel. His spirit refuses to arrest its development with the absolute knowledge that derives from its contemplation of itself. Instead, it continues one step beyond to the negation of that self-consciousness. Following the negative way, Murphy puts himself, as it were, under a cloud of unknowing. There, stirred by a love of a different sort, he reaches out toward that which is beyond all rational knowledge: the unnameable, unknown *Deus Absconditus*; the No Name or Nothing. The two extreme possibilities proposed by Murphy—renunciation of the will and withdrawal from the sensory world—thus may be seen as analogous, or mutually interrelated, forms of nihilism.

Murphy calls consciousness this negative state in which the self comes to know itself as participating in a "unity that transcends oneness," in the "No Name Above All Names."[40] There the mind acquires immediate and intuitive knowledge of itself, *sub specie aeternitatis*, to use Spinoza's expression. Reinterpreted by Murphy this divine self-consciousness becomes solipsism: "*amor intellectualis quo Murphy se ipsum amat* [the intellectual love with which Murphy loves himself]" (*M* 107).[41] Consequently, instead of the union of man with nature in the Divine Mind postulated by Spinoza, or in Absolute Spirit described by Hegel, or in the artistic imagination proposed by Wordsworth, there is instead only Murphy's mind.

In Chapter 6, "Murphy's mind picture[s] itself" as a monadic contraction of Plato's Primal One or Spinoza's *Deus sive Natura* into the self. A true microcosmos, it sees within its "hollow sphere" the entire world—virtuality and actuality; past, present, and future—including, therefore, unlike classical Being, becoming, movement, and space. It does not think itself tarred with idealism, for it accepts both the mental and the physical fact. Nevertheless, it does distinguish between what

Schopenhauer terms, *abstrakte Vorstellungen* ("forms with parallel in another mode"—*M* 108) and *intuitive Vorstellungen* ("forms without parallel") as between the kick and the caress.[42] In the description of Murphy's mind, light, traditionally symbolizing reason, is associated with abstract representation, while darkness designates knowledge of a more mystical sort. Intuitive knowledge, then, is "light fading into darkness" (*M* 108).

Regarding the relation between mind and body, Murphy's mind sides with the Occasionalist Geulincx against both Leibniz and Schopenhauer. It has to admit some sort of intercourse between the two but is "content to accept this partial congruence . . . as due to some process of supernatural determination" (*M* 109). Mental activity, however, is determined by the mind alone, the only domain where man can presumably be free.

Finally, Murphy's mind, adapting the Spinozan way to salvation, distinguishes within itself three zones. The first represents an empirical abstraction from the "dog's life" of physical existence. The second, rational intuition, is associated with Belacquan contemplation. This speculative stance, however, still requires too great an element of intellectual effort and willful choice to be entirely satisfactory (*M* 113). The third zone is beyond dualism. It is a zone of darkness and will-lessness: "nothing but commotion and the pure forms of commotion."[43] This "non-Newtonian" "matrix of surds" with "neither elements nor states, nothing but forms becoming and crumbling into the fragments of a new becoming" (*M* 112) suggests neither (Schopenhauerian) Nothing nor (Aristotelian) Substance, but rather chaos. Regardless of whatever this is or is not, Murphy's mind can no more be one with it than the Leibnizian monad can subsume its passive component of "prime matter" into its principle of activity or substantial form: "Here he was not free, but a mote in the dark of absolute freedom" (*M* 112).

Murphy's mind does not appear aware of this fundamental problem. Leibniz was, but he attributed it to the imperfection of created substances. There is, however, another problem that plagues all integralists in their attempts to comprehend the identity of mind. The mind is necessarily the "gravaman of these informations" (*M* 107). By reflecting upon itself, that is, by picturing itself to be, from the internal distance of apperception, it inadvertently reveals that it is not one with itself. The self cannot be totally present to itself. When it thinks and is aware of itself thinking, when it perceives itself and is aware of itself perceiving, it is both subject and object. (And each aspect, both subject and object.) If the object and the subject of consciousness were ever to be united, they would no longer be able to describe themselves or think (about) themselves. They would no longer exist. It is in these very acts of thinking and apperceiving that it constitutes "itself": *cogito ergo sum*. Paradoxically, the "self," in other words, only "is" insofar as it "is" not.[44] Thus, after having considered the inharmonious relation between man and the big world, Murphy turns to what its protagonist following Aristotle calls the "little world" of the self, there too it finds only nonidentity.

Moreover, the self can never be made totally present to itself. Every attempt to reveal what is behind the veil, reveals yet another veil. And as one veil is pushed aside, part of what had previously been unveiled is also obscured. Instead of self-identity, there appears to be only this perpetual interplay of concealing and unconcealing, of seeing and not seeing, of being seen and not being seen.[45]

Furthermore, the alterity that the self perceives when it thinks (about) itself is irreducible. No matter how much time the protagonist of *First Love*, for example, devotes to "supineness in the mind, the dulling . . . of that execrable frippery known as the non-self," he can never do away with it.[46] This "not-I" is the whole realm of matter, space, and time. It is the external world, all that is not mind or consciousness. Man and world are intricately bound up with one another, not in Fichte's sense that *das Nicht-Ich* is but a derivation of mind, the raw material of spirit, but rather, as Heidegger explains, that each contributes to the constitution of the other.

Man does not exist apart from the world in which he finds himself. Neither, however, can the environing world exist as such until it is so fashioned by man's dwelling within it. At the same time, the "not-I" does not merely represent those demands and expectations of society that have been accepted by the self, that is, the internalized Other that Sartre condemns as obliging us to live not in freedom but for others. The "Other" is already there within, before any subsequent internalization of this or that external norm. The inmates of the M.M.M. are not alone in having to confront their schizoid voices, for one is always to some degree an "other" to oneself.

Murphy, in chapter 7, may be satisfied for the present, presumably at one with himself by having repressed all elements of alterity. The remaining characters, however, all seek to be at one with an "Other." Fittingly, these attempts at (re)possession take place on October 7, 1935: Yom Kippur. This is, moreover, "the first day of [Time's] restitution to the bewitching Miss Greenwich" (*M* 114), the end of daylight saving time and the return of an extra hour of sunlight to standard, or mean, time. Yet this restitution can only be partial, for mean time is already an artificial construct. The "mean sun" can never recapture the "real sun." The distance that forever separates them, like the textual distances that keep the characters apart, serves as an ironic comment upon the quest for total redemption.[47]

A lonely derelict grandfather, Mr. Kelly, who has trouble keeping his own body and soul from fragmenting, wonders if he will ever be reunited with his Celia: "Celia, s'il y a" (*M* 114). His granddaughter lost to Murphy, he has turned to the heavens (*caelum*), like a parodic double of his rival. In the hope of rejoining earth to heaven, he bides his time repairing his six-pointed creation, his crimson kite. Unlike Neary's tetrakyt, Kelly's kite draws him skyward, its material existence in time and space indispensable to its ascent toward perfection: " 'I shall fly her out of sight to-morrow' . . . 'God willing,' said Mr. Kelly, 'right out of sight' " (*M* 25).

Abandoned and alone, Neary reflects upon his need for Murphy. It appears that his worldly desire for harmony has been transformed by Orientalism into a desire for friendship. Like Schopenhauer, he now apparently scorns sensuality, considering disinterested friendship based upon compassion and self-sacrifice as true love. Neary's quest for friendship, however, is destined to fail because it is still too willful, too self-seeking.

At the same time, Wylie and Miss Counihan enjoy a carnivalized at-onement as "oyster kisses passed between them." Wylie's objective approach, monoglot and positivistic, seems to require this "slow-motion osmosis of love's spittle" (*M* 118). As a result, the rhythmic "serenade, nocturne, albada" of Murphy and Celia, is here graphically scored as "a breve tied, in a slow amorous phrase, over bars' times its equivalent in demi-semi-quavers" (*M* 117), that is, the quivering of desire restrained by calm "four-square" notes. Nevertheless, because Wylie refuses to remove by strict analysis "the clapper from the bell of passion," the depraved innuendoes of polyglossia cannot be stopped from vibrating.

The Menippean satire in general and particularly in Murphy tests and contests integralist abstractions by bringing them back into contact with the concrete world from which either they are said to derive (*"mihi res"*—*M* 98) in the Aristotelian sense or which they are said to control (*"me rebus"*—*M* 98) in the Platonic. *Murphy* does not, of course, confront these *morphai* with "real life" situations, but rather with somewhat fantastic ones. Although part of the stock of comedy, these scenes nonetheless do raise some serious points. First, by standing the traditional dichotomies on their feet, they revalue the corporeal. Then, not content to remain at the stage of reversal, they attempt to problematize these oppositions in more radical ways by pointing out what the abstracting process has attempted to distort or master (*"quod erat extorquendum"*—*M* 184), but what, in fact, escapes at least partially its circumscription.

This concretization can also be observed on the level of language. A telling series of examples derives from Beckett's use of sports terminology. Sports are obvious forms of *agon*, or conflict, between individuals or groups of individuals. Because they involve continuous physical motion, they cannot be static in either space or time. Nevertheless, this motion is not random, but follows (more or less strictly) the rules of the game. Yet, it is always threatening to exceed these rules, despite the surveillance of guardians and the inflictions of penalties. Indeed, it might be said that in sports, "ruly" and "unruly" activity, oppositional tension and momentary harmony, work or rather play together. Total mastery or destruction of the opponent is not the goal of such a contest. Although a winner is declared at a moment designated the "end" of the game, the winner is in no way an absolute victor. He or she enjoys only "relative dominance."[48] The spirit of competition dictates that the antagonists should meet again and again.

Furthermore, "scoring" is the object of the game. Sportive strife, in other words, involves an attempt to disrupt the stillness and silence of the blank scoreboard by leaving marks upon it. The "naught" score, such as "love" in tennis or "duck" in cricket, is a sign that a player is not engaged in a lively way. In fact, the repeated failure to score is described in cricket terminology as an unhealthy situation of disease: a plague of ducks. Nevertheless, even a zero score is better than not playing at all.

The "love game" of Wylie and Miss Counihan (M 118) is interrupted by Cooper, as problematic an element as ever disrupted a union. Akathisiac and triorchous, his diabetic walk, bloodshot glass eye, and baggy moleskins further attest to his eccentric nature. Nevertheless, this "ruthless tout," (M 54) whose profiles do not even match (M 123), is assigned a significant role in a grotesque tripartite merger of mind, body, and soul proposed by Wylie as the beginning of their own parodic replay of the *vita nuova*.

Like his namesake, A.A. Cooper, Lord Shaftsbury, Cooper sees his private good as consisting in the attunement of his appetites and desires. This Cooper can attain only by strict self-control. But because he is part of a social system, his appetites cannot truly be balanced unless they are in harmony with others. Cooper, however, is not forced to choose between self-love and altruism. His regard for his own private good may be consistent with the public good and even contribute to it. This, at least, is what he may infer from Wylie's interrogation (M 123-24). Cooper, it seems, like Neary, would accord his self-regarding and his altruistic impulses.

Miss Counihan, that "sentimental lech" (*M* 126) seems equally problematic as "heart and soul." In her the material component predominates, as the obscene connotations of her name suggests: "Her instinct was a menstruum, resolving every move [a man] made, immediately and without effort, into its final implications for her vanity and interest" (*M* 127). She might therefore embody that "corporeal sensibility" that the *philosophes* considered "the sole mover of man." This sensibility manifests itself in self-love, directed toward the acquisition of pleasure which many considered the basis of human conduct. Miss Counihan, as a carnivalized version of Murphy, would be a material monad. Yet, at the same time, the pleasure she seeks requires the presence of the Other. Thus, "the only points at which [she is] vulnerable [are] her erogenous zones and her need for Murphy" (*M* 127).

Like her rival and celestial double, Celia, she is faced with a thorny problem: "Is it its back the moon can never turn to the earth, or its face? Which was worse, never to serve him whom she loved or perpetually those, one after the other, whom she scarcely disliked" (*M* 131). From this confusion Miss Counihan is rescued, not by her passion for Murphy, but rather by Wylie's attraction. Like the Enlightenment disciples of Newton, Wylie sees no reason why, for the purposes of scientific philosophy, such problems should be solved. His business is to correlate phenomena in a systematic way rather than to deal with questions for which there are no observable answers.

As a voyeur, Wylie cannot go beyond the range of empirically verifiable phenomena unless he wishes to enter a realm where no sure knowledge is attainable. In the societal sphere, this leads to the assertion of an intimate connection between self-interest and the performance of social duty. Thus, Wylie's task is to "draw [Miss Counihan] back to a more social vertigo" (*M* 131), to make clear to her that she, like Cooper, should employ her powers for the common welfare and happiness.

Chapter 8 reveals these various quests encountering certain problematic elements that, by resisting complete assimilation, thwart the desire for plenitude and perfect self-perception. Miss Carridge, for example, a hapless wayfarer as badly born as Murphy, struggles, unlike her double, Miss Counihan, against the continuous outpourings of her bodily vapors. In order to regain her "pristine" state (without of course exceeding her strict economy), she tries to eliminate, or at least mask, this corporeal excess through a ritual of purification, anointing herself with "free samples of various sorts, shaving soap, scent, toilet soap, foot salts, bath cubes, dentifrice, deodorants and even depilatories" (M 132), much as Murphy tries to contain his within a "holeproof" suit (cf. M 74). Miss Carridge's instinctual insight (or as Condillac might call it, "insmell") into this tragic problem that plagues all philosophical systems, inspires her, in other words, to sacrifice her caper (M 134).

While Miss Carridge is disturbed by an excess, Celia's "Aegean" distress (M 134) results from a lack: the deathly stasis of the Old Boy upstairs. It is Friday afternoon, "day of execution, love and fast" (M 142), and he, like God the Son, has scapegoated himself. As skeptical as Pilate, Miss Carridge refuses to believe in his felo-de-se, finding it irrational. His death must have been an accident, a chance occurrence resulting from one of the fits he was prone to have (usually on days of absurdity, e.g., Shrove Tuesday and Derby Day). As scandalous as it might seem, however, God's self-sacrifice is considered by Christianity as the crucial stage in man's pilgrimage of atonement.

Or perhaps this death of that "old boy of a God"[49] the deity dismantled by analytic thinking, whether rationalist or empirical. In the debate between reason and faith, those who emphasize the latter insist that God exceeds rational comprehension. Rationalists, such as Bishop Butler, Descartes, Newton, and Berkeley, on the other hand, insist that reason can by itself prove the existence of God. Indeed, they assume his existence as the first premise of their systems. It is not surprising, therefore, that the Old Boy in dying should dilapidate the dream of Descartes.

Moreover, such rationalist proofs were often based on disadvantageous foundations. As the workings of the universe were explained by scientific laws, God became progressively less necessary, often being relegated to First Cause. Finally, by applying the philosophical razor, He was excised altogether as superfluous (as Berkeley had feared).[50]

Yet this does not explain why He should commit suicide. Hegelian determinism, however, does make room for both the self-immolation of the Crucifixion and the self-sacrifice of God to Enlightenment protopositivism. They are seen as necessary stages in the historical journey of Spirit toward its ultimate self-realization in the Absolute.

Murphy is "at a loss" (*M* 139) to understand why the death of this former butler should have undermined Celia's world. After all, Murphy, not the Old Boy, should occupy the center of her attention. Nevertheless, his own responses to her distress—a discourse of suicide and a joke on the creation of the world—offer two possible answers. The first suggests that the Old Boy's disappearance reduces her world to nothingness, as it would, for example, in the Berkeleyian system where God keeps all things in existence by divine perception. (Celia's visible universe, however, has not been annihilated; she is still aware of Murphy's presence, although only in "fits and starts.") Murphy, who has already shown an interest in negative theology, finds the benefits of such an action "inutterable" (*M* 135).

The second suggests that without God the universe would return to primordial chaos! Murphy's "Milky Way joke" parodies all rationalist attempts—philosophical, scientific, religious—to explain the creation of the universe by casting it in the form of a pun: "In the beginning was the pun. And so on" (*M* 65). The pun, like the Gilmigrin wine of the Lilliputians, produces an excess (e.g., of laughter or meanings) out of which arises a clonic state that can disrupt the rational processes. In *Murphy*, the result is a hysterical replay of the Old Boy's suicide that could also be said to ruin Descartes's dream with its hyperbolic enthusiasm.

Although it resembles Murphy's heart attack, it does not lead to a passionate union with Celia. Times have changed. Murphy now feels himself in excess. Concerned with the absence upstairs, Celia had paid him little mind. Nevertheless, this is supposed to be his lucky day, a day to raise himself up again and set out on a new venture. Like Adam's "fortunate fall," Murphy's expulsion from the Celian paradise will lead to a fiery apocalypse in the M.M.M. And indeed, long after his departure, Celia will remember him in the attitude of a pilgrim, "leaning on a staff"(M 142) irresolutely continuing his journey toward the Mercyseat. She will, moreover, continue to see him multiplied in the burlesque imitations of the other questors.

Murphy's way, however, is only half of a double journey. Celia's quest for comprehension had led her to take up Murphy's rocking chair during his absences. "In spite of herself she began to understand as soon as he gave up trying to explain" (M 67). Although what she experienced resembled Murphy's trance it was not quite identical. She preferred the interplay of light and dark, of sound and quiet to Murphy's silent darkness. Moreover, the "peristalsis of light worming its way into the dark" (M 66), aroused in her a *voluptas* distinct from Murphy's intellectual pleasure. The impulse "as for an exquisite depravity to be naked and bound" remained, after all, "the trembling of her body to be made fast" (M 67).

As Murphy sets out for the M.M.M., Celia continues on her own way, moving up, like Beatrice, into the light of the Old Boy's room. (But she is alone, having lost both her Dante and her God.) There in the rocking chair she now savors "the silence not of vacuum but of plenum, not of breath taken but of quiet air. The sky" (M 148). After recollecting the strands from the weave of her history, she can, like Penelope, untwist and scatter "the days and places and things and people" "hackle" them into primordial "tow" and then lie down in "paradisiac innocence" (M 149).

Time, unfortunately for Celia, continues to flow on. The Round Pond must now serve as a substitute Eden, complete with that snake-in-the-grass Cooper. Above the soothing waters she observes the kites replaying the Fall and Redemption under the skillful eye of the Child. This youthful double of Mr. Kelly, however, ignores her call, forewarning that there may be no salvation for her. Furthermore, the Father is missing;

Mr. Kelly is nowhere to be seen. At home, Celia finds that "there [is] nothing to go back to" (*M* 153), for Murphy has definitely abandoned her, or so it seems. Celia must now go up alone into the darkness caused by the Other's absence. It is a darkness that no "candle of vision" can dispel—neither Miss Carridge's virginal "insmell" nor the subjectivist revelation of A.E.'s Eastern mysticism. The light of those candles is an inner light. It cannot fill the space between self and other; it can only highlight it. Perhaps this is the price one must pay for solipsistic integrality.

In chapter 9, this problem of the relation between the solipsist and the other is signaled by the quotation from *The Human Condition* that announces Murphy's entrance into the purgatorial M.M.M. "Ideally situated on its own grounds on the boundary of two counties," the Magdelena M.M. appears to Murphy as a halfway station between the gehenna of rational society and the paradise of the mad (*M* 161).

There he can retreat into his own private mental mercyseat, his Leibnizian garret illuminated by "an immense candle," his own individual light.[51] He no longer needs to curtain off the sun; a frosted skylight veils it by day and opens onto "the galactic coal sack" by night (*M* 188). Murphy, however, does not mind the starless sky. His rejection of astrology has progressed to the point where he sees himself as the prior system and his nativity as "the poem that he alone of all the born could have written"(*M* 183). Soon this "vitagraph" will appear a "superfluous cartoon" of his own system. He seems to be ascending the gnoseological ladder toward the godlike state of absolute self-awareness. The narrator warns him, however, that there is no coming back down again (*M* 188).

His "indoor bower of bliss" abstracted from the animation of phenomenal existence is consequently unheated. Yet, he knows that "he cannot live without fire" (*M* 163). Because there does not appear to be any preestablished harmony between his cell upstairs and the supply of fuel below, someone will have to help him make the extremes meet. Ticklepenny provides the occasion by hooking up a derelict radiator to a source of natural gas in the WC, following Descartes's plumbing blue-prints.[52] The only issue open to debate is "who starts the flow" of gaseous animal spirits. Murphy, we know, does not much care about the answer. It is only important that they be per-fectly sublimated, preferably by Murphy's own candle of vision.

Integrality, as perhaps the consummate abstract idea, rep-resents in an encapsuled form what is deadly and deadening in the process of abstraction. All that is dynamic and changing, all that is vital and warm in sensory experience is eliminated. Man is thus left to dwell, writes Nietzsche, "in the empty husks of the most indefinite terms, as though in a house of cobwebs." Nietzsche's attack upon abstraction was explicitly directed against "the rigor mortis of the coldest, emptiest con-cept of all, the concept of being." Heidegger has shown this fundamental concept to be bound up with the ideas of identity and presence, which have appeared throughout the history of philosophy in varied shapes, for example, the Christian *Logos*, the Platonic *Nous*, the Kantian Pure Ego, even the Neoplatonic conception of pure love as the *virtus unitiva*.

Abstract integrality is not, however, limited to forms of ide-alism, as *Murphy* itself illustrates. Leibniz's dream of a deduc-tive scientific metaphysic, of which logic and mathematics would be essential parts, is not unrelated to Plato's ontological schema. Nor are Newton's notions of absolute time and space free from association with traditional conceptions of the divine or with what Kant would later term "transcendental ideal-ism."[53] The list could be extended to include even the example of Locke's paradoxical abstract matter with which Berkeley took issue.

Following the logic of abstraction, the ideal mind would be pure ego, that is, autistic like the Aristotelian divinity. *Murphy* thus describes the insane as microcosmopolitans. Each con-tains his own world. No two are exactly alike, for then they would be one. Yet, a few do share some repeatable qualities, like impenetrability or "absolute impassiveness."

Mr. Endon, for example, exists in an imperturbable state of languor (though "never so profound as to inhibit all move-ment"—*M* 186). His life, such as it is, he holds "within" (*en-*

don) him, or rather he attempts to, as does Murphy by wearing his holeproof suit that does not allow his bodily *pneuma* to escape. This is, in fact, Endon's preferred suicide method: *apnoea*. Were it possible, not allowing one's "vapor" into the world, it seems, would eventually lead to death. (Killiecrankie, however believes *apnoea* to be physically impossible. The conscious, rational mind may will to withhold breath from the body. Nevertheless, when loss of breath brings loss of consciousness, the "involuntary" nervous system takes over and the body begins to breath again, reaffirming the irrationality, as Schopenhauer calls it, of its will-to-will.)

Paradoxically, it is the impermeability they would share if they were truly monads that, according to Leibniz, would allow them to coexist, without ever truly interacting, in peaceful groups. Carnivalized, this preestablished harmony becomes the "kinship" of Murphy and Endon "engaged" in a chess game in which each moves in the absence of the other, and no piece is ever lost or checked (*M* 187-88).

Nevertheless, it should not be forgotten that many of the M.M.M.'s insane are schizophrenic. They are therefore anything but at one with themselves. The split within their selves has reached an irremediable level of psychosis. And autism itself is a form of schizophrenia, for it posits both a self (much like Murphy's own) cut off from the sensory world and a self cut off from the sensory elements within itself.

At the same time, Murphy's *Bodenkammer* resembles a *caelum* of sorts, both the "hollow sphere" of the mental firmament and a cave. On its walls Murphy beholds what is ironically termed "the beatific idols" (*M* 181). These he believes reveal the truth that lies, not in the light of reason as Plato asserted, but rather in the darkness of unreason, or perhaps in the darkness beyond reason.

In Murphy's turn toward insanity, certain tendencies already visible in his earlier forms acquire prominence while others are muted. His rejection of sane society is still an attempt to withdraw from technology and mercantilism. Now, however, the big world is identified as the world of rational operations, from Aristotelian bookkeeping to Skinnerian voyeurism. Evidently, he no longer sets great store by his "surgical quality" or his syllogistic logic. His quest has brought him to the understanding, which he dimly had all along, that reason cannot penetrate to the underlying reality: "It was not to obtain an obscene view of the surface that in days gone by the Great Auk dived under the ice, the Great Auk now no longer seen above it" (*M* 193). Murphy's *Bildungsreise*, in other words, continues to lead him toward "a repudiation of the known."

Moreover, he now rejects the "reasonably balanced way of life" (*M* 177) in which everything is done in moderation and the extremes are harmonized. Explicitly directed against the adaptationism of certain post-Freudians, Murphy's position also takes issue with the atomist view of the social structure. On another level, it implies a dissatisfaction with the conception of "well-being" as rational equilibrium. The swaying of Murphy's rocking chair thus proves definitely inadequate. In fact, it has always been inadequate. Murphy's state of freedom, of at-oneness with self, could only occur, it might be recalled, when his rocking chair stopped rocking: "Most things under the moon got slower and slower and then stopped, a rock got faster and faster and then stopped. Soon his body would be quiet, soon he would be free" (*M* 9). Murphy has now come to realize that "nothing less than a slap-up psychosis could consummate his life's strike" (*M* 184). Perhaps, then, in order to be truly unbalanced, Murphy must be off his rocker.

Murphy perceives the "imbalance" of the insane as a "self-immersed indifference to the contingencies of the contingent world" (*M* 168), a will-lessness more complete than that recommended by Geulincx in "beautiful Belgo-Latin": "*Ubi nihil vales, ibi nihil velis* [Where one is worth nothing, there one should want nothing]" (*M* 178). In a misguided way, it approaches the impassiveness that attracted Schopenhauer to the Hindu holyman: "The freedom of indifference, the indifference of freedom, the will dust in the dust of its object, the act a handful of sand let fall" (*M* 105).[54]

But imbalance can also denote an excess, on the individual and on the societal level. Murphy's irrational heart is immoderate, as is "his deplorable susceptibility to Celia, ginger, and

so on" (*M* 179). So also is his empassioned contestation of psy-
chiatric treatment that goes against his habital retreat from
any conflict. And the insane too are immoderate in this way,
giving vent to "frequent expressions . . . of pain, rage, despair
and in fact all the usual" (*M* 179). The principle of in-difference,
which Murphy believes will lead him to at-oneness with Endon, requires the stifling of all such "issues" and "outbursts."
It is not an easy matter, however, to fabricate such "a dungeon
in Spain," the narrator explains (*M* 180). It depends upon constant perversion of the evidence (*M* 178), and almost scandalous
domination of the resistant elements: "*Quod erat extorquendum*" (*M* 184).

Ironically, these are the same techinques that, as Michel
Foucault has demonstrated in his *Madness and Civilization*,
are used by inquisitive psychiatrists in their attempts to master
madness. They are also the techniques that make possible syllogistic logic, which is based on considering identical what are
in fact only similar propositions. Drawing abstract principles,
whether rational or empirical, involves a measure of violence.
Many proofs and conclusions are not self-evident; they are evidence that has been (de)formed.[55]

Nevertheless, it appears that abstractions do not and cannot
control life, which is constantly transgressing their limits. Even
Plato's ideal Republic, as closed and static as a totalitarian system could be, was unable to avoid being contaminated by the
issue of becoming: by the coming into existence that is being
born, or by the passing through existence that is dying. Life,
then, contains too much irregularity—both excesses and deficiencies—to be contained within any abstract system. This
does not, however, seem to be simply because, as Berkeley has
argued against Locke, abstractions are life experiences purified
of sense perception. The problem is more fundamental. As Derrida has argued, it is because abstraction—or the analogous
emphasis on the sensory, for the two terms are permanently
implicated—denies the movement of spacing or temporization
by which a term both differs from and differs with itself, and
thus always defers its self-identity. Abstractions, by determin-
ing the meaning of identity as "life without *différance*," thus

reveal a fundamental indifference to life.[56] They lead to the nihilistic belief, expressed by Belacqua in Beckett's short story "Yellow," that it all comes to the same thing in the end.

That such in-difference is really another name for death would not disturb Murphy in the least.[57] He is quite attracted to that "bijou edifice" covered with the "traveller's joy" upon being at home (endon) and the "ampelopsis" of "self-clinging" solipsism "set in a bay of clipped yews" (M 165). "Left in peace," he would be "as happy as Larry, short for Lazarus, whose raising seemed to Murphy perhaps the one occasion on which the Messiah had overstepped the mark" (M 180).

Nevertheless, Murphy, like D.H. Lawrence's Man Who Died, still needs the warmth of another. Although he would never admit it, *"il est impossible à celui qui vit hors du monde de ne pas rechercher les siens* [it is impossible for him who lives away from society not to seek out his kin]" (M 161). It seems, in fact, a part of the human condition to seek the company of similar beings, even if their similarity lies in the desire to leave the world. Yet, in this way a world is re-created, and the impossibility of ever fulfilling one's desire inadvertently revealed. Before, Murphy had tried to eliminate all that might enflame him, particularly Miss Counihan and Celia. He had rejected a Nelly in heat and a feverish Ticklepenny. Now, however, he is "drawn to" Mr. Endon (M 186). This is no wanton attraction, he believes, but rather "a love of the purest sort, exempt from the world's precocious ejaculation of thought, word and deed" (M 184). But had not Murphy after his encounter with Rosie Dew in the cockpit of nature (M 101-3) concluded that "pure love" was no more than a fiction, one of the synthetic forms of the understanding? The "Idea of Pure Love" does, nevertheless, have a regulative use in that it points to a love which it cannot constitute because it is limited to the realm of experience. In this realm we cannot know "love-in-itself," we can only know it phenomenally. Nevertheless, in the cockpit of the mental mercyseat, Murphy would find a way to truly "love" Endon, to be "one in spirit" with him through "vicarious autology."[58]

At the same time, however, Murphy would retain the impenetrable self-identity which he believes makes him as similar to Endon as Narcissus and his reflection (*M* 186). Such a "rare bird" as Murphy, it seems, desires simultaneously to stand by himself and with the others of his species (*M* 193). But is it really possible to have one's microcosm and also extend it out to another as Leibniz contended? Or is it possible that individuation survives in undivided unity, as Hegel and the Romantics argued?[59] Murphy, is seems, is as guilty as Celia, perhaps more so, of wanting to give his cake to the cat and have it too (*M* 202).

The narrator's opinion, at least, is clear: Murphy "could not have it both ways, not even the illusion of it" (*M* 189). What keeps two "monads" apart and yet draws them together is a "want" in the double sense of desire and lack. Striving to eliminate the space that separates them, they "cry out for extension" (*M* 163). What attracts, however, is not simply what is similar, but what is different. Murphy, for example, is drawn to Endon by his apparent will-lessness. But, even if Murphy manages to quiet his instincts, he still exhibits a will to be one with Endon. If he ever managed to eliminate this final desire and therefore to resemble Endon in his will-lessness, then there would no longer be any impetus for union with Endon; he would, according to the Leibnizian law of indiscernibles, be (identical to) Endon.

If, on the other hand, like the Hegelian *Geist*, Murphy ever attained to self-recognition in Endon, how could he know that it had happened? Would there still be a Murphy to know anything? When Murphy succeeds in coming alive in his mind, he is, of course, not aware of it, for he is improved out of all awareness. He only knows, for example, that he resembles Clarke, the catatonic, because of Ticklepenny's perception.[60] But that is also what brings an end to Murphy's trance. Perception, it seems, including apperception, can only occur across the space of difference and therefore, like the shuttered judas, betrays any attempt to redeem the divided self. The "space" between (and within) "monads," however, is not absolute, but relative. It expresses a relation between them that, like the gas to Murphy's garret, makes "heating" possible.

What exactly is this *gas*? According to its discoverer, van Helmut, the word derives from *chaos* (although it has been supposed that he modeled it on the Dutch for *spirit*). *Chaos*, however, is a very problematic word. Ovid understood *chaos* as formless matter. This paradoxical expression suggests a general blending of opposites, a blurring of distinctions, or a constant movement of one thing into another.[61] Chaos so upsets the closed system that it is often separated out generically: "Let there be Heaven in the midst of the waters, let it divide the waters from the waters. The Chaos and Waters Facilities Act. The Chaos, Light and Coke Co" (*M* 176). Or interpreted away, following Aristotle, as empty or unlimited space: "Chaos was yawn" (*M* 175). Or relegated to the irrational domain.

The Magdelena Mental Mercyseat illustrates both the means by which an institutionalized structure tries to dominate chaos and the ways in which chaos subverts these means. Beneath a façade of apparent identity, the M.M.M. conceals its crossed categories, the interplay of its excess and lack, and its irreducible relational spacing. Consider Skinner House, "the cockpit of the M.M.M." (*M* 165). Its passageways do not lead into the orienting light, but only onto a "decapitated potence." In the other direction, the "extremities developed into spacious crutch-heads" (*M* 144), known as "sublimatoria" to the "wittier ministers of mercy," but commonly called "wrecks."

Thus, it might be said that this Mental Mercyseat lacks both simple *arche* and *telos*. And these "wrecks," which the doctors of the soul would see as sublime, are the domain of reading, writing, and play, strenuous or otherwise (*M* 166). Here Murphy could observe the so-called insane. "Melancolics, motionless and brooding, holding their heads or bellies according to type. Paranoids, feverishly covering sheets of paper with complaints against their treatment or verbatim reports of their inner voices. A hebephrenic playing piano intently. A hypomanic teaching slosh to a Korsakow's syndrome. An emaciated schizoid, petrified in a toppling attitude as though condemned to an eternal *tableau vivant*, his left hand rhetorically extended holding a cigarette half smoked and out, his right, quivering and rigid, pointing upward" (*M* 168).

These activities are, however, interpreted by the institution as "doing nothing," and by Murphy as a "self-immersed indifference to the contingencies of the contingent world" (*M* 168). The chaos within the patients' psyche is thus seen as a void. This can only be done, however, by disregarding or muting "the frequent expressions apparently of pain, rage, despair and in fact all the usual, to which some patients gave vent, suggesting a fly somewhere in the ointment of Microcosmos" (*M* 179).

Yet these issues and outbursts, like the traces and residues left after Murphy's dream of chaos (*M* 175-76) can be neither totally eliminated nor evaded. They remain as premonitions and "postmonitions" of the calamity that inevitably befalls attempts to repress the gas within the system. If taken "seriously," this measure of structural chaos need not result in painful silence, not in destructive explosion. Like Murphy's "aposioposis" (*M* 164), it can instead open a variety of differing possibilities that do not, in the end, reduce to quite the same thing.

Now in chapter 10, the analogous thermodynamic system of Murphy's materialist doubles is similarly never closed, particularly not in London where there is an abundance of fuels, with differing levels of combustion, to keep it burning. "Jezabel" Counihan is "suck[ing] up to a Hindu polyhistor" (*M* 196) and "Judas" Wylie is keeping warm without her inferior Irish turf. Although they are "not living together" (*M* 195), they do meet now and then to "compare notes and ruts" (*M* 197).

Neary too has gone on to other delights, his quantum of wantum ever varying. Like the unredeemed Augustine, he is doomed "to scratch himself out of one itch into the next, until he shed his mortal mange, supposing that to be permitted" (*M* 202). Now his need is not for sexual gratification but for friendship; not for Miss Counihan's *fesses* but for Murphy's *face*. Is there no desire but once satisfied that does not engender new ones? "Is there no flea that found at last dies without issue? No key flea?" (*M* 201). As long as one believes that something somewhere could bring complete satisfaction, one is "doomed to hope unending" and, therefore, to a life of repeated disappointment, "the old endless chain of love, tolerance, indifference, aversion and disgust" (*M* 225). Murphy's self-love, the narrator indicates, attempts to end this eternal series of mews. Nevertheless, as a search for self (*Selbstsucht*), it is as selfish and willful as Neary's search for Murphy.[62]

Are then all human actions motivated, as Hobbes contended, by such selfishness? Cooper, for example, "did not try to reinstate himself with Neary, feeling it might be wiser to wait till Neary sent for him. He also felt a shade less wretched as the coadjutor of a pair of twisters, who not only knew next to nothing about him but seeemed in a fair way to being as crapulous as himself, than as the cats-paw of a hardened toff, who knew all, including much that he himself had contrived to forget" (*M* 198). Thus, he was able to serve two masters with "beautiful indifference . . . without infamy and without praise" (*M* 198). He manages to help all those who quest for Murphy that they might enjoy the fuller life promised by Wylie (although Cooper himself was skeptical). Does it not then seem possible to follow Cooper's namesake in arguing that self-regarding impulses can be harmonized with the common good? Perhaps. The cost is nonetheless the repression of all desire (e.g., Cooper's for Miss Counihan—*M* 204) that could ruin the most cordial relations, as even Cooper knew from painful experience (*M* 206).

Cooper's discovery of Celia's refuge, and therefore presumably of Murphy, manages to bring Neary, Wylie, and Miss Counihan together. "Sit down the two of you, there before me," said Neary, "and do not despair." Neary's Pythagorean description of their hoped-for salvation ("Remember there is no triangle, however obtuse, but the circumference of some circle passes through its wretched vertices") unsettled somewhat by the arbitrariness of Augustine's God ("Remember also one thief was saved") is repeated by Wylie, with some skepticism, in humanist terms ("Our medians . . . or whatever the hell they are, meet in Murphy"). Taken by Neary in a more metaphysical direction ("Outside us"), it is then restated in a materialist form ("In the outer light"). And stops when Wylie feigns teleological disdain. Their syncretic union is only possible if "they . . . agreed not to differ" on whether Murphy was found. They celebrate this problematic communion with an offering of Irish *eau-de-vie*:" 'To the absentee,' a tactful description of Murphy under the circumstances" (*M* 213).[63]

What results is a carnivalized symposium—"Let our conversation now be without precedent in fact or literature, each one speaking to the best of his ability the truth to the best of his knowledge" (*M* 214). Truth, propose Wylie and Miss Counihan, playing a series of internal variations, is harsh reality thinned down, brightened, sweetened, blunted, and falsified. Neary finds this "nihilism" too facile, easier on the philosopher's eyes. Might not truth be instead simply snarled, waiting for someone to undo its knotty problems? And this someone the Nearyean oracle reveals is, not the Master, but Murphy: "The end, my end, unique and indispensable" (*M* 216). The existence of Murphy, it appears, has passed from what Leibniz termed the domain of synthetic and contingent propositions to that of analytic and necessary ones. Since only existential statements about God fall into the second category, it seems that Murphy has now replaced the deity in Neary's philosophy, as he had already in his own. Wylie, the enlightened voice of Reason or Self-Love or both (*M* 216) counters with a preoration that reveals the hedonistic tendency of his Newtonian materialism. He quests for Murphy "half on the make and half on pleasure bent" (*M* 217).

Miss Counihan, however, is attracted to Murphy's peculiar "heating" equipment. Amid the carnivalizing comments of Neary and Wylie, she explains that in most men, the "infinite riches" of the mind are connected to the corporeal WC by a "psychosomatic fistula" creating at best a "crass and unharmonious unison" that defiles both mind and body (*M* 218-19). Murphy, on the other hand, is different. Because he lacks this "pipe," he plays "an ineffable counterpoint" in comparison with which Wylie and Neary come either too soon or too late. Miss Counihan's love song, an Occasionalist parody of Plato's *mousike*, is almost too "idealized" for Neary and Wylie to hear, although the latter is more attuned to "the bawdy innuendo of eternity" (*M* 219). Wylie, however, can only ironically speculate that it is from the ethereal realm of "pure smut."

Miss Counihan can now rightly ask what has been gained by this colloquium. If it is that they can now part, as Neary contends, then he must first prove that they have "met"—something their apparent lack of agreement both confirms and denies. If meeting is a question of "sight" as Miss Counihan will admit, then they are met (and Murphy will be [found] when he is seen: *esse est percipi*). If meeting is a question of love, however, then it has nothing to do with acts and (e)motions as Wylie contends. Rather, it is a purely intellectual operation of Murphy's "ineffable counterpoint." Love, here, is not that force that draws the subject to recognize the object as itself in the sublating moment of absolute knowledge. Overcoming Hegel's "arrested development," it is "the repudiation of the known" (*M* 222). (And Murphy will be found when Neary has followed him into Nothingness.)

If, however, their being held together is merely the occasion for meeting, then Neary will "count on the Almighty to pull off the rest" (*M* 223). In the abyss created when He says "Let there be darkness," Miss Counihan and Wylie may be brought to make contact, but Neary is left alone, his dark night of the spirit before him. Neary, does not have the strength to follow Murphy into that dark. Their quest toward Murphy next takes them to Brewery Lane—"All things hobbl[ing] together for the only possible" (*M* 227).

Only Celia's love now seems without the striving of selfish desire that causes the others merely to splutter blindly in search of their own pleasure. Yet perhaps for that very reason, she lacks the means of finding Murphy. Purified by her ascension into the Light, she can only wait to experience Murphy's presence. Having followed the way indicated by Murphy, Celia has already withdrawn from the world to seek, like Mallarmé's swan, "the panting syllable to rime with breath" (*M* 229). With "nothing to lose . . . therefore nothing to gain," she now faces her judges in complete peace. Before her own dark night is over, she must suffer to hear of Murphy's (supposed) betrayal and be defiled by Miss Counihan's jealousy. Yet once she has laid herself to rest, she reveals her comprehension of Murphy's quest, and of her own.

Although Celia was a necessary station on Murphy's way, "a piece out of him that he could not go on without," she now understands that she did not fundamentally change him but only confirmed his "csscncc." His cstrangcmcnt from hcr was therefore inevitable, since separation, suffering, and loss are essential to Murphy's progress toward self-actualization. More important, however, is her tragic realization that she may not be the last exile. Love, the narrator, explains, "is wont to end, in protasis, if it be love" (*M* 234).

Love, "passionate" love, for there is really no other kind, "ends," in other words, by stretching itself forward. It is not a closed circle; it is never complete. While representing a desire for a whole, its continuance implies both the awareness of a lack and the desire to exceed oneself into that lack which can never be filled. It is this passion that would have to be scapegoated in order for unitary love to be attained. Conditionally, then, Celia's afflatus comes to an end bringing only a very problematic "dim yellow light" to the day.

In chapter 11, while Celia lies entombed in the dark, Murphy begins his own *via dolorosa*. Murphy's path might be called circular, coming in the end back to where it began (or so he fondly hoped), like his rounds of night duty. Cyclicality, as yet another form of identity, has not been overlooked by *Murphy's* Menippean testing. Just as the celestial motion which the ancients believed repeated itself perfectly throughout eternity, has been shown to vary irregularly, so too do characters, relations, and even scenes reappear throughout *Murphy*, but with not insignificant variations. Neary is not exactly Wylie, nor Mr. Kelly, nor Murphy. Miss Counihan is neither Miss Carridge, nor Rosie Dew, nor Celia. Murphy's quest resembles Celia's, but not exactly. No more than the first "glorious gin-palace" that Cooper visits in London is identical to the last where he deposits Murphy's ashes. Thus, it is too that Murphy's second sit is far less pleasureful than his first (*M* 80), that Mr.

Endon cannot repeat the same pattern of chess moves twice, and that the next time around the Virgin is no longer one (and if she is Irish, the narrator suggests, even the first time is in doubt).

This irregularity would not be quite so unsettling if the varying patterns of characters, scenes, and relations that recur throughout the novel at least remained symmetrical, as do the changing designs produced by Mr. Endon as he moves his chess pieces. But in the play of time, unlike the work of God, the parts are distributed asymmetrically (like the halves of Cooper's face) and differences cannot be overlooked. So too does it become increasingly apparent as the novel progresses that identity cannot be found in the analogous form of the closed system either. The losses and gains simply do not cancel each other out. Murphy's continued existence, after all, depends on cooking rental bills and defrauding restaurants. Of course, an appeal can be made to an external force, God or Mr. Quigley, to perfect the terrestrial sphere, as in the Magdelena M.M. when a round exceeds its limits (M 237).

During the day this problem was less apparent; then the regularity of the routine made the M.M.M. stand for "music. Music. MUSIC." Night duty, however, makes Murphy aware of the difference within repetition, but also of the similarities between putative opposites:

Murphy's first round had shown him what a mere phrase was Neary's "Sleep and Insomnia, the Phidias and Scopas of Fatigue." It might have held good in the dormitory of a young ladies' academy, where quite possibly also it had been inspired, but it had no sense in the wards of the M.M.M. Here those that slept and those that did not were quite palpably by the same hand, that of some rather later artist whose work could by no means have come down to us, say the Pergamene Barlach. And in his efforts to distinguish between the two groups Murphy was reminded of a wild waning winter afternoon in Toulon before the *hôtel de ville* and Puget's caryatids of Strength and Weariness and the tattered sky blackening above his perplexity as to which was which. [M 239]

Moreover, Murphy, who by day could imagine himself at one with the patients and opposed to the staff, by night finds himself identified with the latter as tormentor. "It was as though the microcosmopolitans had locked him out" (*M* 240). Through the judas, the eye can violate the self-contained worlds of the closed cells. This Murphy must do, as his horoscope had predicted: "Magical Ability of the Eye, to which the lunatic would easy succumb" (*M* 32).

The logical problems discovered by Murphy might be expected to draw him even closer to the insane. On the contrary, the zone of oppositional interplay, a somewhat chaotic region, is interpreted by Murphy as empty space or void. He feels more painfully than ever an "unintelligible gulf" separating him and the patients: "that was all. All. ALL" (*M* 240).

But what of Endon who represents, at least for Murphy, the principle Other, the impenetrable *aliéné* with whom nevertheless Murphy still hopes to be reconciled. Can Murphy penetrate his solipsism? The result of their encounter is the curious game known as "Endon's Affence or *Zweispringerspott*," a kind of carnivalizing replay of man's attempts to bring himself into union with the Ultimate Monad. Mr. Endon, by refusing to play white, presents himself as the Prime Mover, the first cause of all change, though not subject to change himself. Murphy could prove that a harmony preexisted between him and Endon by moving first his knight.[64] By instead moving his pawn ("The primary cause of all White's subsequent difficulties"—*M* 244), Murphy reveals that he has no a priori knowledge of the game plan. He learns mimesis quickly, but it is already too late. Having fallen out of step, there is no going back. It seems, however, that Murphy's fault was not simply having made the wrong move, but rather having chosen chess at all. Any *telos* of harmony presupposes an origin in harmony. In chess, however, the field is so structured that the positions are skewed even before the pieces are put "into play." Consequently, it is impossible for one opponent to be in harmony with the other even in the stasis that precedes any opening.[65] *Initio et ab origine*, then, there is neither perfect repetition nor perfect symmetry; there is, in other words, no originary unity.

Nevertheless, Murphy continues his struggle to ape the symmetry of Mr. Endon's expanding and contracting patterns. The best he can manage is an imitation whose imperfection increases as the game progresses. Murphy changes to a more or less Neoplatonic mystical strategy (without, however, abandoning completely his tendency toward Platonic mimesis). He now tries to force Mr. Endon, by the folly of his self-sacrificing plays, to take notice of him. He will be satisfied with nothing less than a direct capture of himself by the One. He will appeal to no redeemer for absolution; he will not wait for Endon to send the word: "Check." He will refuse any *salut*(e) that would be adventitious (*M* 245).He will, in other words, play at all costs by the rules of the game as he understands it, despite Endon's silences, in the ever-renewing hope that Endon has finally chosen to engage him in a conventional manner.

Ready to surrender his most powerful piece, Murphy attempts with his forty-first move to create a situation in which Endon will have to manifest himself as in days of old. But after Endon's next two moves, Murphy despairs of ever receiving the answer he wants and submits to what he perceives as indifference. Like the Oriental holyman, he resigns himself to the "meaninglessness" of the game: "But little by little his eyes were captured by the brilliant swallowtail of Mr. Endon's arms and legs, purple, scarlet, black and glitter, till they saw nothing else, and that in a short time only as a vivid blur, Neary's big blooming buzzing confusion or ground mercifully free of figure" (*M* 245).

It is this absurd chaotic state that Murphy, here as elsewhere, comes to perceive as nothingness. His act of Schopenhauerian submission, which appears closely to imitate Endon's "Oriental" attitude, only makes explicit the underlying nihilism of his more classical-Christian perspective. Sitting opposite (*upani-sad*) Endon across the chessboard, Murphy acquires knowledge of what he is (*tat swam asi*) and what the One is (*net neti*): Nothing.[66] Unable to be One with Mr. Endon in the positive sense (as he was unable adequately to correspond with Mr. Quiddity), Murphy, by reversing the signs, decides to travel the negative way to the Unnameable.

The sound of the Abderite's guffaw, that pre-Socratic Joe Miller, however, disturbs Murphy's experience of the supposed primordial void: "No-thing is more real than nothing," or as the narrator puts it, "naught is more real than nothing" (*M* 246).[67] After surrendering in the chess game, Murphy swoons onto the board and begins "to see *nothing*, that colourlessness which is such a rare postnatal treat, being the *absence* (to abuse a nice distinction) not of *percipere* but of *percipi*." Murphy seeing "nothing" is Murphy not perceiving Endon (*non percipi*). It is also, however, Murphy not perceiving Endon (*non percipere*), or rather, seeing "that Mr. Endon was missing" (*M* 246). Seeing nothing, then, is seeing no thing, that is, "seeing" an "absence" of sorts, seeing that something is missing.

The traditional confusion between no thing and nothingness is signaled throughout the novel, for example whenever an expression like "not a thing escaped him" (*M* 23) is repeated several pages later as "Mr. Kelly missed nothing" (*M* 25). Murphy's quest for integral peace, whether positive or negative, is a quest after an illusion. What he may find is a becoming or a be-ing of sorts but never Being, an absenc-ing of sorts but never Nothingness. What he finds may be related to what Derrida has termed *différance* (or at other times, spacing, alterity, dissemination . . .): "the irreducible space constituted between two—as well as the movement of differentiation which interrupts any identity of a term to itself, any homogeneity or interiority of a term within itself."[68]

Mr. Endon's presumably closed ontological system appears no less problematic. Endon is not playing the traditional game of chess that progresses linearly toward an apocalyptic *telos* at which the master finally conquers his adversary (or that, at worst, ends with the Manichaean draw). Indeed, he refuses ever really to engage the issue; there is no *agon* here. (This is what had earlier convinced Murphy of his kinship with Mr. Endon—*M* 187-88). Nonetheless, Mr. Endon is not proceeding in a disinterested manner. Both the starting point (Endon always refuses to play white) and the patterns of moves are matters of voluntary choice. More important, he is not oblivious to Murphy's existence.

Twice during the game, in two knight-mockeries [*zwei Springerspott*] (moves 4, 17), Endon moves so as to taunt Mur-

phy, who is in no position to imitate him. It appears that Endon
both perceives Murphy and yet chooses not to perceive him.
And Murphy in turn may be said to be aware of being disdain-
fully perceived, but dissatisfied unless he receive a clear sign
of election. For Murphy, it is all or nothing.

Endon's affence makes a fool out of Murphy and mocks his
attempt to have his microcosm and share it too. Moreover, this
metaphysical joke is replayed when Murphy comes face to face
with Mr. Endon. The revelation he receives as he stares into
Endon's eyes is not that Murphy has taken the Other back into
himself and so is at home with him in his Otherness. Instead,
Murphy realizes that he is both seen and unseen by Endon and
by himself, and thus, in Heraclitean terms, that he both "is"
and "is not."

Returning to his garret "without reluctance and without relief" after this unsettling epiphany, Murphy felt "incandes-
cent," aglow with the interplay of contraries. Having lost all
feeling of conviction and yielding up gnosiological questions
in despair, he now must suffer his agony in the garden. He
cannot re-present any one to himself, not even his Father.[69]
His mind is full of a chaotic "flux of forms" that evokes no
rational, coherent thought, no complete object, and therefore
to him, evokes "nothing."

Earlier, after a series of temptations on the Jobpath, Murphy
had found the dead sleep of the self's annihilation healing and
soothing. From it he had awakened refreshed and reborn, ready
to return to the Celian music before entering the "new heaven
and new earth" of the Magdelena Mental Mercyseat. Unfortunately, the effect on Celia of the Old Boy's suicide had, by
removing the center of her universe, shattered his chiliastic
hopes. Now Murphy has suffered an analogous shock. After a
period of indecision, Celia had moved the rocking chair up into
the light, there to await the *parousia*. Murphy also returns to
the rocking chair from where he began his quest, with the
heightened awareness that the failure of attempted reconciliation with the Ultimate Other has brought. He still intends to
return to Celia after regaining his well-being, but now only
dimly, for others are less important now than ever.

Celia had found (at least the illusion of) paradisial innocence when the strands of her own personal history were untwisted and scattered until she was one with the cosmos (*M* 149). She does, however, come to understand that one cannot go back to the garden, or at least that it was no Eden. Murphy, on the contrary, feels he must stop the unraveling of his self "before the deeper coils were reached" (*M* 252). "Astir in his mind," he still believes that he can transform the "scraps of bodies, of landscapes, hands, eyes, lines and colours" into "the freedom of that light and dark that did not clash, nor alternate, nor fade nor lighten in their communion." If he cannot be one with Endon, at least he can be one with himself.

Unfortunately, the question of chaos and nothing(ness) cannot be decided so easily. They are not simply two poles: "At one of the rock's dead points he saw, for a second, far beneath, the dip and radiator, gleam and grin; at the other the skylight, open to no starts" (*M* 252). They are inextricably intertwined as the paradoxical meanings of chaos were to the Greeks; or the structural music and the playful rhythm of passionate love. The "superfine chaos" that will finally destroy Murphy's attempt at a closed system is the very undecidability of existence. But only when ignited by the ambiguous fire of Murphy's own mental candle.

Murphy is destroyed when the fire of the little world comes into contact with the gas of the big world. Or as Swami Suk predicted, when the passion produced by irrational and incommensurable conjunctions—"The square of Moon and Solar Orb afflicts the Hyleg"—meets with what disrupts the unity of the cosmic forms (*morphai*)—"Hcrschel in Aquarius stops the water."[70] Murphy's system simply cannot accommodate such a blow.[71]

Once the novel has reached chapter 12, the apocalyptic prophecy in Murphy's dream—"the Chaos, Light and Coke Co."—of the night in which the earth shall be burned up has brought Murphy's crisis of negativity to a fatal end. Will the earth now give way to "new heavens and a new earth" in the paradise regained of a second coming? The starless sky is blue again. Cooper, as if born right at last, finally takes off his *coif* and sits for the first time. Beyond this, however, the reform of the heavens cannot go.[72] The clipped yews outside the mortuary still announce that no resurrection should be expected. Celia, Neary, Wylie, and Miss Counihan, although they have been brought together by Murphy's death, are nonetheless still kept apart by their fundamental differences. More importantly, Murphy's identity still remains problematic, as it was in the beginning.

Marked with its peculiar stigmata, Murphy's "end," so to speak, confers on him his final form. In the ultimate carnivalizing gesture, he emerges "sublimated" from his last trial by fire in the form, not of Absolute *Geist*, but of (Im)pure Rump. Or rather his end exceeds its own limits, for the naevus that identifies him is really "an excessive capillary angioma of most unusual situation" (*M* 266). The Coroner will try to recuperate him for classical symmetry[73]; Neary to pardon him with Christian understanding; Miss Counihan will simply refuse to recognize him. Only Celia can accept him "as he now is," lumps and all.

Even after death, moreover, it seems that Murphy cannot be totally "will-less." Murphy's "will" or at least part of it, has also passed through the flames unharmed. It is addressed to "Mrs. Murphy" as if, in death, Murphy had wanted to signal by a semblance of marriage that his relation to Celia had been regularized. Celia's own quest for comprehension, however, has led her to believe that such a "sacred union" is impossible. Besides, Murphy's last moments suggest that it is perhaps "epigrammatic" or "paradoxical," both longed for and yet fled from, both partially possible and yet ultimately impossible. Similarly, Celia both is and is not Mrs. Murphy.

More parodically, Murphy's will calls for "the disposal of these my body, mind and soul" reduced to original ashes and dust, comingled in a paperbag and flushed into the waters of purgation in the lower ranges of the theatrum of the *Abba*, from there to be swept into the *dubh-linn*, or black pool, below.[74] "The whole to be executed without ceremony or show of grief" (*M* 269). (By thus denying the immateriality of both mind and soul, Murphy reveals a fundamental affinity with his materialist doubles.) Yet, in what could be construed as the ultimate profanatory gesture, Murphy's dirt, like all that exceeds the limits of propriety, is to be evacuated at the time and in the place where it will most disrupt communal representation.

Murphy's "last wish," however, is not respected by Cooper any more than his ultimate need was satisfied by Endon. Unable to find a dustbin in which to deposit Murphy's ashes, Cooper carries them into the New Jerusalem Bar, similar it might be assumed to the City of God Saloon to which he had rushed after seeing Murphy crucified upside down in his rocking chair.[75] There during a drunken brawl, Cooper mingles Murphy's ashes, not with the pure water of life, but with the vomit and cigarette butts on the barroom floor. Murphy, however, does not spring reborn from his ashes. Nor does he emerge sublimated. Nor, however, can he be said to disappear into the Void. Rather, Murphy joins the mess. It might be said, then, that Murphy's apocalypse, instead of restoring both man and the cosmos to the perfection of their original unity, merely confirms the alienation and fragmentation of the unredeemed.

These proceedings, of course, would appear highly irregular to the analytic Killiecrankie. This does not mean, however, that "life is all rather irregular," as Neary contends. Both remain, like Murphy himself, within the logic that insists on totalization or bust. Life includes perhaps a great deal of mess, but also a good bit of form. The problem is to find a form in which the mess can be articulated.

As Murphy's quest brought him back to his starting point in the end, but on a higher level, both in the physical and in the spiritual sense, before destroying him, so Celia's quest also brings her full circle in the final chapter. She is again a fallen woman, having lost all hope of salvation in the Magdelena Mental Mercyseat. Now she has only her crippled Will-o-be Kelly.

Murphy could not have his solipsism and share it with an "Other," perhaps because his "rocking-chair system" could not

adequately accommodate the flux of becoming. It knew only
of equilibrium leading to stasis. Consequently, it was bothered
by whatever might cause a draft (*M* 141), either in or out. Mr.
Kelly's system, on the other hand, is "self-propelled." Thus, he
finds a draft "not unpleasant" (*M* 276). Its aim is neither to be
completely seen nor completely unseen, as was Murphy's, but
rather to link the seen and the unseen. Like Rosie Dew, he
would mediate between the physical and the spiritual realms,
but while remaining in control himself.

In Kelly's system, Celia plays a fundamental role, for she
must set it in motion by "throwing up the kite."[76] Following
the path marked by Hegel in his lectures on the philosophy of
history—"out, back a little, stop; out, back a little, stop"—the
kite climbs upward. Then, after a "wild rush of line, say the
industrial revolution," it comes to the end of its line, creating
an effect that redounds to the glory of its "hypermetropic"
creator (*M* 179-80). Kelly is enraptured before his kite sublated,
not into Absolute Kite, but rather into a "nothing to be seen."
Kelly, it seems, has accomplished what Neary had only
dreamed of: "the repudiation of the known" (*M* 222). (Like
Murphy's experience of Nothingness, however, it is merely the
apparent "absence of kite.")

In order, however, to determine the point at which seen and
unseen meet, Mr. Kelly must reverse the process and draw the
kite *ex nihilo*. If only he can find the nodal point, he could
reconcile the unity postulated by reason and disunity taught
be experience into a universal order. Murphy, however, like all
true Platonists, denied becoming, so for him the transition to
the spiritual realm remained ungraspable. The more Hegelian
Kelly believes not only that he can find the link but moreover
that he is the link. He would simultaneously be the culmination of the system and be aware of it, in order that he might
consciously re-create it.

Murphy died in the process, as Mr. Kelly would have if Celia
had not restrained him. While the Child failed to break the
(kites') fall from union (*M* 281), Celia, like a second Eve despite
her sin in the garden (or perhaps because of it) prevents Kelly
from plunging into the Round Pond. Murphy's system could

not truly accommodate the fire of her passionate nature, nor the chaos of her stimulation. It could only make room for it in the form of its "senerade, nocturne, albada," and that only temporarily, preferring the more self-identical "music, Music, MUSIC." (It was, however, to Celia's rhythm that Murphy "dimly intended" to return after the Endon afflatulence ruined his dream of being at home with himself in his otherness—*M* 252). Mr. Kelly, more fortunate, having placed Celia at the origin of his system, also finds her at its *telos*. While the ambiguity of her nature may keep Kelly's system from either simple *arche* or ultimate totalization ("Celia, s'il y a"), it will also keep him from committing suicide.

Expelled from the Garden by the Rangers, Celia must, however, continue to toil up the hill "into the teeth of the wind," along the inclined plane back toward the point of "originary unity." "There [is] no shorter way home." Nevertheless, unlike Neary, she does not seem condemned to hope unending. Perhaps she senses that the goal can never be attained. Not because, as some Romantics claimed, "the realization of the goal is an infinite one which lies forever beyond the reach of man, whose possibilities are limited by the conditions of the infinite world."[77] It may be rather because lacking a stable center (after the deaths of the Old Boy and Murphy), she must follow what Hölderlin called an *excentrische Bahn*.[78]

And the expulsion from the whole may yet be understood as a *felix culpa* of sorts, for the continuous striving that results from it may provide a "form" that can accommodate or articulate the "want" of ultimate Form. Celia may close her tired eyes but her action will annihilate neither the objective nor the subjective world, anymore than they were destroyed when Murphy set out on the jobpath or Endon was found to be missing. The world will still "be there" when she opens them again. Her play may have come to an end for the time being, but the contest may still go on. Thus, Murphy ends, not with "Nothing," but with "All out."

When salvation through religious or philosophical means seemed impossible, romanticism turned to art. Schelling, for example, finds the "imagination" able to annul the ultimate contradiction "at the roots of the artist's whole being," namely, that between nature and intelligence (i.e., object and subject). For Wordsworth, this faculty, distinct from yet "each in each" with intellectual love, is "the first and chief" in which "we begin and end." It replaces the Redeemer as the indispensable mediator that saves the poet from a "universe of death." Blake went even further: "Imagination . . . is the Divine Body of the Lord Jesus, blessed for ever." Or in Wallace Stevens's formulation: "God and the imagination are one." The apocalyptic conflagration that brings Murphy to his end, however, comments ironically upon "how high that highest candle lights the dark."[79]

The unifying function of art may, however, also be conceived from a somewhat different, albeit analogous, point of view. In Schiller's formulation, an initial opposition between *Formtrieb* and *Stofftrieb* is postulated, which is united in *Spieltrieb*, of which the correlative is beauty. As in Neoplatonism, beauty is here both the way toward and the expression of reconciled opposition. It is a "middle state" that harmonizes "diametrically opposed" contraries.[80] Beauty is here personified as the Mediatrix: Mary, Magdelena, Beatrice. Or perhaps Celia. Yet, Celia could not save Murphy any more than he could save himself. Redemption through art does not here seem possible. It might seem that all that is left after *morphe's* demise is for art to return to prostitution, longing for that conjugal state it realizes it can never attain. Nevertheless, Celia may yet "save" Murphy from "a universe of death," nihilism, and silence, by offering not a means of totalization, but by pointing toward another "form" of *Spieltrieb*.

Celia, I have argued, is, by her very nature, an indeterminate creature—simultaneously the "Aphrodite of the heavens" and the "Aphrodite of the public ways,"[81] the heavenly *caelum* and the hellish *cavus*. She is rhythm embodied in an enflaming form that arouses a passion at once destructive and creative. Celia, then, is the scene of the systematic play of the differences, traces, and spacing by which elements are interrelated. It is through and in this "between," at once physical and spiri-

tual, passive and active as befits a woman, that the dissemination of signs which makes signification possible takes place.
The opposition between form and content that Schiller believed was overcome in and by the artist's aesthetic drive repeats a logic of domination that must scapegoat all elements
and aspects that exceed or in some way disturb its parameters.
"Art until now," Harvey reports Bcckctt as saying, "has sought
forms and excluded all aspects of being that there are no forms
to fit."[82] Celia, however, suggests a matrical form capable of
accommodating the exquisite confusion of that "superfine
chaos."

Nevertheless, the congruence of Celia's nature lacks the in-
trusive element that would allow her style to leave its mark
upon the traditional genres. She needs her own *entremetteur*,
the ironic narrator, who functions as Mr. Kelly could not and
Murphy would not.

This narrator occupies a between position of his own, both
participating in *Murphy*'s passion play and standing above it.[83]
His ironic distance, however, does not remain constant. It is
most pronounced in those chapters dealing with secondary
characters and least in the later ones in which Celia figures
prominently. Moreover, he reveals a sympathy for what he at
times openly mocks and mocks what he elsewhere deals with
sympathetically. This is particularly noticeable in his treatment of the protagonists. The strategic placement of epigraphs,
for example, puts Murphy at a distance when the reader might
expect greater proximity.

In *Watt* the ironic narrator himself becomes implicated in
the plot. The *Trilogy* introduces the narrator/protagonist. This
does not, however, mean that the narration is free of irony. Not
only is the narrator/protagonist's own irony directed toward
other characters, including those that are his own creations,
but it is also self-directed. For although he is fed up with
rationalist assumptions and cognitive modes, he cannot do without them, or even remain indifferent to them. This double-
edged irony is personified in the narrator/narrated of *How It
Is*. While this narrative irony appears increasingly somber and

desperate, its stylistic counterpart retains its carnivalizing qualities, incorporating "negative" irony into a larger context of carnivalized dialogism.

Carnivalesque irony is a way of describing that "passion" in which the ethical impulse of the classical-Christian tradition struggles against the Dionysian form of pathos. The desire for unity or identity, on the one hand, confronts active, conscious questioning, on the other, in a tense contest that is not only recognized as inevitable but also provoked and encouraged as fundamentally creative. This passion affirms the value of contestatory strife, as well as a complex of other specific values—for example, life, play, nondomination—and ideas—for example, the impossibility of a simple ground, origin, or *telos*, the necessity of undecidability as opposed to simple identity. This suggests an alternative worldview, a definitely "pathetic" one involving at least a partial affirmation of what is being criticized.

In its overall structure no less than in its constituent elements, *Murphy* contests the possibility of totalization. Instead of what Coleridge called "multeity-in-unity" that attempts to integrate multiplicity and diversity into a unified whole,[84] we find a continuous *agon* of the many. It is not a mere chaotic jumble of anecdotes and characters, nor is its structure, whether aesthetic, narrative, or thematic, totally unified. Despite its obvious similarities with the *Bildungsroman*, it cannot simply be reduced to that very Hegelian narrative pattern. Yet, it is not totally divorced from all traditional forms. On the contrary, as a Menippean satire, it tests the limits of genre classification while necessarily working or playing within, or on the boundary of, those limits. Like Murphy's lucky number four, it is a seemingly paradoxical form of the whole that, because it makes a mess, is often simply mistaken for one. Such agonistic play, by exhibiting the "law of becoming," and the "play in necessity"[85] makes room within a structure for a measure of creative chaos.

Variations on the Hermeneutic Theme

Murphy could still savor the repose of his mental mercyseat, hoping eventually to attain, by either positive or negative means, to the truth and plenitude of the "One." In *Endgame*, however, Hamm and Clov, are too aware of Murphy's failure to retain any illusions about their ever reaching such a meaningful *telos*. They have cast into doubt the criterion of meaning itself, at least in any absolute sense. Nevertheless, even after the destruction of their faith in eschatological hermeneutics, their will to signification remains. If previously man had been acting out his own earthly roles, believing them integral parts of the divine Author's play, Hamm and Clov can now only continue commenting on their own interpretations, painfully aware of their all-too-human nature. If, by a subsequent process of displacement, man had confidently proclaimed a humanist faith in himself as the ultimate source of meaning and value, they, the last men, can only struggle vainly against the implications, both natural and cultural, reaching after factors that repeatedly escape their anxious grasp.

The problem, then, is no longer the meaning and attainment of metaphysical unity, as in Beckett's first novel. *Endgame* broaches the question, how to interpret after the criterion of unity has become questionable. Sometimes, it is as if the characters would like to believe that the aesthetic dimension of their actions is enough, or that they need merely be diverting. Ultimately, however, the characters take seriously only those

interpretations that promise to bring an end, by putting all the
pieces together into an essential whole, with the rational interpreting subject as its center. But is this not once again Murphy's monistic quest, replayed self-consciously on the level of
humanist hermeneutics?

At the same time, the reader/spectator's effort to understand
Endgame repeats and varies Celia's effort to understand Murphy. Since it was first produced in London in 1957, this play
has received far more critical attention than *Murphy* (though
less than *Godot*). This is certainly owing at least in part
to the vogue for the "heroic" humanism of various quasi-
philosophical trends of the day. For *Endgame* has often been
read as an illustration of certain extremely popular themes,
particularly the "absurdity" of the cosmos and the "meaninglessness" of human existence within it. This approach has unfortunately overshadowed other possibilities.

Two critics who have reacted strongly to the existentialist
view, but from seemingly divergent perspectives, are Stanley
Cavell and Theodor Adorno.[1] Rather than presenting *Endgame*
as merely symptomatic of "modern ontology," both treat the
play as a critical response to this particular avatar of Western
metaphysics. They see the entire (or almost entire) philosophical tradition as implicated in the play's eternally frustrated
search for ultimate meaning. And both point in consequence
to the possibility of interpreting *Endgame* as a philosophical
satire, while nonetheless presenting its critique of the rationalist tradition in fairly negative terms.

Totally instrumental, Adorno argues, contemporary rationalism has suppressed the possibility of meaning by eliminating
all traces of the nonconceptual, namely, the material, the temporal, the historical. Only pure logic—empty technique or
form—remains. Reason has thus deprived itself of the means
of reflection upon both "what is" and itself. *Endgame* provides
no solution, but works to stimulate the elaboration of a new
theory capable of dealing critically with this irrationality or
"meaninglessness" of modern socioeconomic reality. Where
Adorno sees a challenge, however, Cavell discovers only an
essential equivocation. He considers the play stuck between

two equally destructive (and in his opinion equatable) possibilities: nihilism and the revaluation of values, with no exit in sight.[2]

Thus, each critic may in the end be doing more to confirm than to contest the dominant, humanist interpretation. Diverging from this view, I should like to argue that, by casting the satire in a specifically Menippean or carnivalized "form," Beckett does suggest an alternative to the paralyzing despair so often detected at the heart of the modern situation.

Historically, the carnivalesque has always coexisted alongside our sober rationalist tradition. It has, however, been increasingly confined and reduced. According to Bakhtin and others, an effort to control and ultimately to eliminate all that does not conform to the totalizing (and not infrequently totalitarian) presumptions of our cultural heritage has been operative on a fundamental level within the historically predominant hermeneutic perspectives whether philosophical, religious, moral, scientific, or literary.

For Beckett the task of creative thinking is now to conduct the search for "a form that accommodates the mess" instead of repressing it through an excess of rationalist order. The carnivalized satire comes to the fore in this context as a means of playing out "messy" relations such that the anxiety they engender may be engaged in a more positive manner. An affirmation of their vital importance within the relative structures of temporal existence is in fact basic to this phenomenon, in as much as carnivalization normally involves an open confrontation between contending forces, above all between those that strive for a full, harmonious unification and those that contest this desire.[3]

In *Endgame*, as perhaps in all of Beckett's work, the text itself reproduces such a contest on several levels. In the explicit narrative, Hamm and Clov struggle to deny the indeterminacy of their "messy" condition. Yet, it keeps returning to increase their anguish. At the same time, they endeavor to eradicate crucial aspects of the carnivalesque—the body, nature, time, history, laughter—whenever they manifest themselves. A similar act of double repression is repeated on the stylistic level, where an effort at straightforward monovocality and orderliness is countered by the processes of linguistic dissemination that cannot be contained. On all levels, the carnivalesque both counteracts the totalizing impetus and interacts with it in an agon that contributes greatly to the palpable tension of the play. *Endgame* is largely a comment upon similar confrontations that have repeatedly occurred throughout the course of Western history. By the very act of testing and contesting our familiar teleological hermeneutics, moreover, the play may, in the uncertainty of its own nature, be demonstrating and providing, not simply a critique, but an alternative as well.

Let us suppose, then, that *Endgame* takes place within the mind: not that of an individual subject like Murphy, but that of Western culture itself, centered as it is upon the human subject. Its "bare interior" is lit by a "gray light," that is, neither the true Light nor total Darkness, but the half-light in between. Here, on a mental stage, the cultural mind will replay in perpetual frustration its various interpretations of life and world. What had been for Murphy a moment of "Belacquan bliss" upon the threshold of purgatory has become for Hamm and Clov a dark night of longing at the gates of a paradise lost.

As often in the medieval theater, the opening tableau is a concrete representation of the end of days. The exit from the prison cell—of life, of mind, of language itself—is through the door stage right. The characters who are living there *huis clos* always remain nonetheless within sight of the door. Their being there is lived toward a passage that they hope will lead to a better situation, or at least to a different one. They hope to transform their inevitable finitude from a "simple" closure into a meaningful end.[4] Next to the door, however, there hangs a picture with its face to the wall, a traditional sign of mourning. Whose picture is it—the all-seeing deity of *Film*, the Old Boy of *Murphy*? Is the human mind in mourning after the death of that Being who created and gave meaning to the door, indeed, who was the Door?

The condition of Hamm and Clov might then be compared to what Pascal described as the "misery of man without God."

He can be satisfied with nothing less than the infinite and absolutely stable, and so can find no real satisfaction at all. The characters' attempts to forestall the inevitable may thus be prompted by a fear that there might in fact be no fully meaningful end. The complexity of their perception of this improbable way out will in any case contribute to the passion of their play.

Of course, the door could also be a way in: into a new earthly paradise (or is it only a new hell?). With the disappearance of the deity, man is left to his own devices. He must find another authority to give his life direction and fulfill his Pascalian "capacity for God," be it Reason, *Geist*, Will, the Natural "Laws" of science, or a Transcendental Ego. These and other substitute centers are produced by thought which, by itself, Pascal too considered man's greatest attribute. When man begins to search for a concept, or idea, to replace the divine Mind (*Mens*), it is accordingly not so surprising that he should find, sooner or later, himself. The new heaven becomes what it was already for Murphy: the human mind itself.[5]

On the left side of this opening tympanal tableau is a counterpart of the door, another way out (or in) as debris. The two dustbins standing there, like two funerary urns, are also signs of mourning, not for the heavenly Father, but for Hamm's own grotesquely earthbound parents. Like his (and man's) biblical ancestors, they are associated with the physical body. Man comes into life and departs from it as what *Murphy* called a "waste product" of the organic processes: ashes to ashes, dust to dust. They may also be associated with the social body and all its "organs": family, church, state. They evoke as well the historical body, including both the biological and the cultural heritage.

In both West and East, the physical body has normally been regarded as earthly detritus that corrupts the spirit and shackles its freedom (e.g., by Platonism and Christianity, but also by the Sartrean existential humanism in vogue at the time of *Endgame*). At best it is perceived together with the social dimension of life as a means to a higher (and therefore noncorporeal) end: as the tools of *Geist* or Proletarian Man on the dialectical march toward cultural self-realization. In positivism (including important aspects of the Marxist perspective) it functions as the mere object of scientific law. And when even this instrumental value was cast into doubt, organic life became, as it was for certain prominent forms of religion, simple refuse. In one way or another, by either assimilation or elimination, nature is mastered and its most "earth-bound" elements depreciated, deprecated, and finally denied.

Between the two extremes is Hamm, seated in his Faustian chair on castors, a pose that both repeats and varies that of Murphy, Mr. Kelly, Molloy, Moran, the Unnameable *et al.* Hamm as man (*homme*), man as soul (*âme*). Blind to the sensory world, his body immobilized, Hamm is man reduced, in metaphysical terms, to his most essential features: those of the mind or soul. At the center of this "theater of the world," he occupies a place of authority, with the power to separate the damned from the saved, the power of a man-God upon his mercyseat.

This center, however, is double. Beside Hamm stands Clov, his alter ego. Clov reminds us that man is by nature dual, both matter and spirit. Hamm and Clov might together represent man, the former as mind, the latter as body. Yet to be Clov(e) is already to be two, and not simply two, but simultaneously simple and dual. Even from within the Christian or classical framework, Clov, as man's material nature, would not be totally devoid of spiritual qualities himself. Although inferior or even hostile to spirit, matter is still regarded as part of divine creation.

Traditional metaphysics does, all the same, effectively bind one leg of the Clov(e). Reduced to the instinctual, that which is cloven represents all that is infernally "sinful" in man. Or his more material functions may be so tightly governed by "natural" reason and law that he is progressively crippled. In the idealist tradition (and some consider all of Western philosophy fundamentally idealist), the material leg is all but amputated, leaving only spirit to represent nature as a whole, at least in its "essence." To deprive the Clov(e) of its most corporeal member, however, is in a sense to destroy it.[6]

Not only is Clov cloven, he is also "in" Hamm, as Hamm is "in" him. Hamm himself is a form of Clov, albeit a more repressed and therefore enfeebled one. Man may be soul, but he is also flesh (ham). And the soul (anima), as mediator between pure spirit and pure matter, is also double. A portion (mens) participates in the divine intellect, while another (animus) experiences the sensory world. This problematically cloven nature has been a major thorn in the side of our classical-Christian anthropology. And it cannot be removed. Beside Hamm stands perpetually this devilish supplement: too material to be totally assimilated, too spiritual to be completely eliminated.

That which is cloven is fundamentally undecidable. It cannot be reduced to one leg or another of the complex relations of sameness with difference that it embodies. Nor does it "amount to" their totality. The problematic, impure "gap" in between is never quite closed, nor ever extensive enough to become a complete break. The cloven situation is therefore liminal, yet agonistic both in itself and with regard to the familiar "home" oppositions (matter/spirit, body/mind, object/subject, nature/culture, other/self, and so on), at once more reminiscent, more promising, of unification and less open than they to attainment of that end, a perpetual cleaving to and simultaneous cleaving asunder. The cloven thus engages the problem or process of différance. It is subject not to ultimate solutions but to modified repetitions and more or less successful accommodations. It points in this respect to the ancient but ongoing interaction of repression and displacement within our cultural context.[7]

It is Clov, this perplexing supplementary excrescence at the side of the central One, who sets the play in motion. For Plotinus, such an originary excess implied an overflow of limits that was also an expulsion, a casting out of that which cannot (or can no longer) be contained within the whole. It is, in sum, a form of cleaving and thus an act by "Clov." Clov sets the play in motion by breaking away from Hamm and setting off upon his own eccentric path. Yet, to cleave in this way would only be to obscure or even to destroy the nature of the cleft.

The "end" of Clov's action appears to be the end of the cloven itself. He is the agent, in some sense, of his own eventual elimination.

In the beginning of the play there is not the word but the deed, a rather Faustian notion. Or rather, the act—for Clov's activity is part of a routine, even a conventional comic routine. In the beginning, then, there is already both repetition and, in a sense, the act of interpretation. And here it is also an act of repression. The "beginning" (of the play, of the world, of civilization and culture) is thus marked by an effort to control the originary indeterminacy of (man's) nature. It is even the nature of/in man that is repressed. Thereafter, Clov will only repeat and intensify this attempt to cleave fully asunder.

What his act accomplishes amounts to a final uncovering of Hamm. Man, after the exclusive deed that establishes and maintains the dominant intellectual tradition (viz., the separation of mind from matter)[8] is himself reductively reconstituted in a spiritual mode, as soul. Physically, he is blind, paralyzed, moribund.

On his way out the door, Clov can therefore stop to announce that the process of repression has reached its culmination. To be finished—perfect and closed—is in this case to be soul alone, without the body, man without his cloven nature. It is fitting, then, that Clov as he leaves should repeat "Christ's Parthian shaft."

The first spoken word of the play is also *"fini"* indicating finality, in the sense both of finite and finished, and pointing therefore to the problem of teleology right from the start. It is a significant, albeit uncertain beginning. For what precedes the "word," on stage and in the text, cannot be dismissed as meaningless chaos, while teleology is at the same time the most obvious issue addressed by *Endgame*.

What exactly is implied in this statement, "It is finished"? Among other things, that one has, as Hegel observed, already placed oneself, in some (hyperbolic) sense, beyond finality and, paradoxically, become able to look back upon it. It is consequently a moment that, by exceeding its own goal, renders questionable the latter's status as *telos*.

Even the very simple grammatical structure of Clov's statement, like Murphy's expression of self-identity, reaffirms the notions of time, space, and movement, all of which dispute the finished, thinglike quality of that putative end in itself.[9] The reified state that Clov posits with his initial "finished" slips away even as he appears to grasp it: "Nearly finished, it must be nearly finished" (E 1) ["It will perhaps finish"—FP 15].[10]

Clov's opening sentences fall from his lips like the grains of "that old Greek" (Is it Zeno or Eubulides?), indicating "the impossible heap": a plurality of separate moments will never make a whole.[11] Clov transforms the pain of being "imperfect" into a sense of guilt at having fallen from a static state ("finished") into the indeterminacy of time ("it will perhaps finish"). Unable ever to atone for this "sin," he is condemned, like Sisyphus or Ixion, to perpetual frustration. "I can't be punished any more."

What is finishing will never be made clear. Indeed, the characters remain incapable of defining it, naming it, giving it an identity. In order to bring "it" to an end, the troublesome aspects ("*ça*") would have to disappear and be replaced by something completely knowable. There is no room for the undecidable in any perfect state, be it a republic, absolute knowledge, the well-adjusted psyche, or "ordinary language."[12]

Clov's response to this inconclusiveness is to retreat into a refuge of his own, analogous in its symmetry to the New Jerusalem. The door, we are told, leads into the kitchen. Now a kitchen, it is true, is a sort of domestic laboratory in which the old Greeks prepared their coction—the same coction they also associated with their ideal of balance, equilibrium, and harmonious proportions (cf. *Murphy*). Nevertheless, a kitchen maintains a strong relation to the bodily realm. Like the City of God Saloon, therefore, Clov's refuge is not without its carnivalesque dimensions. His kitchen is not so far from the garbage cans as he would like to believe.

In any event, Clov's retreat can procure him only a moment of solace. He remains at the beck and call of a higher authority. The latter—in his own eyes the Alpha of the play's system, though appearing only posterior to his own more fleshly coun-

terpart—is the egotistical Hamm. Like Mr. Endon playing
chess with Murphy, Hamm has "allowed" Clov to make the
first move. Now it is his turn to play. Clov, with his Galilean
telescope, methodological ladder, and artificial or deadened
specimens, will continually expend his energies in more or less
mechanical efforts to comprehend or systemically order the
world. He manages only to confirm his senses in their frustration and anguish.

Hamm, on the other hand, may create the illusion of having
clearer sight by repeatedly cleaning his glasses, but his eyes,
totally white, have no pupil through which to look into the
world. His knowledge of it, like that of all who dwell entirely
in the mind, must come from an inner sight. Still, even Hamm's
intuition requires at least a modicum of sensory information,
provided of course by Clov: a pupil of a different sort. The auto-
nomy of his insight may thus be a bit of a sham.

Clov's quasi-mechanical activity can be regarded as a response to the anxiety provoked by his cloven nature. Unable
to move his legs, Hamm is confined to his mind. He can only
play with words, creating fictions that counter, or compensate
for, the flux that surrounds and permeates him. With his "very
red complexion" (*E* 2), Hamm resembles Lewis Carroll's Red
King, whose dream may constitute the whole story.

The Tweedle brothers ask a question that greatly disturbed
the heroine of *Through the Looking Glass*: Who is more real,
the Red King or Alice? Which is the dreamer and which the
dream? The same question is implicitly posed in *Endgame*.
Whose activity is more authentic, that of the speculative
Hamm or that of the empirical Clov? Is the real world the realm
of everyday existence or that of ideas? From a materialist point
of view, the ideal world is a fiction. From an idealist perspective, the phenomenal world is an illusion. By himself Hamm
also suggests the problem of subjective vs. objective idealism:
Is the natural world merely a projection of the finite mind, or
should it be identified with the thoughtful activity of an encompassing *Weltgeist*? In the first case Hamm, like Alice, may
be understood in either individual or specific terms. In the
second, he brings to mind one view of the Red King.

But when is Hamm "dreaming"? When he is asleep, or when he is awake? When he is reconstructing the world from Clov's observations, or when is he inventing his chronicle? Perhaps it is the distinction itself—between dreaming and waking, between interpretation and fact, or even fiction and fact—that is at issue here. Neither Hamm nor Clov can be said to move in the "real" world or to know things as they "really" are. The point, indeed, may be that this is always an interpreted world, that the two characters are therefore fundamentally more alike than they seem, that we ourselves may resemble them both in this respect more than we should normally be willing to admit, though more as well—given their curious combination of sophisticated naïveté and unreflective technique—than need be.

If life is, in fact, a dream to be interpreted, hence an interpretation that can only be reinterpreted, we are faced with the problem of interpreting from the inside, as it were. How can we judge among interpretations? Are some "truer" than others? better? And what would this mean? Can interpretation ever constitute knowledge?

Hamm awakes from his deep sleep and, upon removing his shroud, prepares to "look" again at the world around him. But what exactly does he want? His desires seem contradictory. On the one hand, he wants to separate himself from Clov. Or rather, he wants Clov to separate himself from Hamm, either by leaving his "master" or by killing him (achever). On the other hand, he wants Clov to complement or complete him (achever). He seems, like Murphy, to want it both ways. His is the impossible humanist dream regarding all sensuous nature. Either by expulsion or sublation, however, the cleft that maintains Hamm and Clov apart, while nonetheless keeping them together, would disappear. Yet both means prove impossible. Clov can neither leave Hamm nor finish him. Instead, they continue, like the pulsating universe of certain cosmological models, alternately cleaving to and cleaving from one another.

Or is Hamm simply avoiding the end he desires, fearing an ultimate disappointment? Equivocation may be his reponse to the dilemma.[13] But it may also be a way of avoiding serious reflection about the problem, as well as the problematic in general. Are sterile equivocation, paralysis, bad faith, and so forth, the only possible attitudes when faced, like Neary, with a "deathless end"?

Why then do Hamm and Clov go on with "this thing"? Why are they still together? Are they simply "stuck" in their world ("There's nowhere else"—*E* 6)? They are "stuck" with one another, cloven together ("There's no one else"). Quite in the manner of a Heideggerian "identity," Hamm and Clov are held simultaneously toward one another and apart, facing one another, with an intensity that never lets up. The way they carry on their relation between the parts of man makes it a form of perdurance (*Austrag*): a way of holding out, but also of suffering, that heightens their anxiety (as it does with O in *Film*) even as it enables them to perdure.[14]

Clov would retreat from bothersome questions that Hamm repeatedly poses in order to retain him. Yet Hamm's compulsion may itself be no more than an attempt to defer rethinking these questions: "Ah the old questions, the old answers, there's nothing like them!" (*E* 38). His mode of repetition characterizes the course of Western rationalism as well as Hamm's journey. One may even know that it will not lead to the desired *telos*, yet find less distress in continuing along the beaten path than in the prospect of hauling oneself out upon less familiar ones.

To be sure, "new" paths need not, and in fact could not, be totally without relation to the old one. Yet tradition could still mean something other than thoughtlessly, compulsively repeating, à la Hamm and Clov, the same old questions and answers. A more creative form of repetition is possible, one that involves rethinking established patterns in an effort to elicit more meaningful variations. Precisely because of what Derrida has referred to as "solicitous" force, repetition of this sort is capable of playing a regenerative role. It cannot be understood in terms of the simple regressions and counterfinalities that Sartrean existentialism saw forestalling the progressively holistic self-realization of Man in freedom. Rather, it suggests that tradition provides us, as Heidegger maintained, with hidden resources, many quite strange, which may yet be recovered and employed in more or less unfamiliar, or even unsettling ways.

Repetition, then, may entail a "handing down" of actuality, but also of possibilities: of possibilities that have come down to us from the past, but are received and developed as our own, and not necessarily *as* they have come down to us. It may be seen as the return of a certain inventive potential.[15] In a sense, it is the return of this too often repressed force that, like the cloven in all its manifestations, both excites and perpetually frustrates the desire for a totally unified end, thus creating much of the tension in this endgame.

When Clov disappears from the scene, for example, he reappears in the form of Nagg (from *clou* to *Nagel*, as Ruby Cohn suggests).[16] The instinctual forces return from the garbage cans into which they had been cast. Nagg calls for a nourishing pap, that messy mixture which sustains organic life at its beginning and end. Clov can only produce a classic biscuit (*FP* 24): hard, dry, geometrical.[17] Its English version is the "natural" plainness of Bishop "Sprat's medium" for transmitting scientific information (*E* 10). Hamm would rather suppress this disconcerting reminder of his own physical nature. With an imperious gesture—"Bottle him!!"—he sends his infernal double against those very forces the latter so often represents (*E* 10).

Toward nature in general Hamm and Clov display attitudes that are complex and fraught with contradiction, if not outright confusion. For Hamm, who can only speculate upon the scanty evidence provided by his "pupil," nature appears as constant change, understood in entropic terms. He only regrets that he and Clov do not seem to be part of it: "Nature has forgotten us" (*E* 11). For Clov, their own deterioration proves that this is not the case. They are part of the natural process, but that process requires disintegration. In nature there is no gain without loss; indeed, everything is eventually lost. Every natural being is in time left behind as detritus. Disappointed, Hamm acquires a more simply negative, and even destructive, view of nature. If there is neither absolute gain, nor anything free of change (and therefore of loss), better that the natural process should not exist at all. Hamm, however, refuses to acknowledge the nihilistic implications when they are actually voiced by Clov: "You exaggerate" (E 11). Sobriety, as Adorno observes, is one proven means of sabotaging thought, and by this means Hamm manages to blind himself even further.[18]

Clov, on the other hand, would limit his knowledge of nature to what can be generalized systematically from observation, objective and precise, of his environment. The result is a devitalization of nature through reduction to abstract terms. A desire for domination through scientific knowledge, the humanist form of what Claude Lévi-Strauss calls "species imperialism," may thus conceal a desire to eliminate nature altogether: "There's no more nature (E 11).[19]

Awareness of the fact that the object of their study is subject to continued modifications and variations causes both characters considerable distress. Their efforts to comprehend and explain the natural world repeatedly go awry, generating a mass of fairly obvious distortions. "No one that ever lived ever thought so crooked as we" (E 11). Yet Hamm and Clov do not resort to critical reflection upon the way such problems have habitually been addressed. The one looks to control his anxiety with tranquilizers, while the other retreats into his cubicle. Both are growing impatient with the entire interpretative project: "This is slow work" (E 12). Clearly, it is not leading very quickly toward a final resolution.

That does not mean it is leading nowhere, however. The dialogue continues. From the problem of nature, we pass to that of knowledge. The kitchen, from Hamm's point of view, is not unlike Plato's cave. Like the chained prisoners in the latter, Clov passes his time there staring at the wall. Hamm offers two mocking descriptions of what Clov sees. "Mene. Mene," suggests that if Clov believes he can comprehend the world in numerical or quantitative terms, he is undoubtedly mistaken (E 12).[20] More importantly, Hamm appears to be suggesting that strictly quantitative methods involve something analogous to faith in a revelation.

The great pioneer scientists were all serenely confident of the mathematical (and therefore abstract) simplicity of nature.

To them it was not merely a methodologically necessary premise; it was a fundamental fact of the universe. Galileo believed that mathematics best represents the structure of the natural world. Whatever can be expressed in mathematical discourse is true, and God himself could have no clearer knowledge of the natural order it comprehends.

When Bacon took over and modified Plato's cave image, he incorporated it within a metaphoric complex, a portion of which could be turned against Plato himself. The philosopher's dependence upon deductive reasoning a priori and the ideal of pure mathematics were included among the "idols" that lead to erroneous conclusions.

Following Bacon, much empiricism continued, in Heine's words, to "run about sniffing at things, to collect and classify their characteristics," until Kant appeared. Taking up the cave metaphor once again, Heine concludes: "Kant proved that we knew nothing of things as they are in and for themselves and that we can have no knowledge of them except as far as they are reflected in our own soul."[21] Thus, in helping to reestablish the possibility of science in the wake of Hume, Kant also sought to establish its fundamentally subjective limits. Scientific knowledge could henceforth be predicated upon the existence of certain basic categories and procedures of the human mind. One could no longer hold any act of perception to be completely objective, an unmediated vision of the world as it really is. Kant attempted to describe the conditions of the cave and to refute Plato's conviction that science can provide a way out.

Hamm, then, who would mock Clov by pointing out their differences, has at the same time uncovered similarities. Clov too is "dreaming" when he takes his empirical observations for a straightforward image of the real world. Hamm's ironic description of Clov's activity simultaneously obscures and calls attention to the fact. Clov peers at "naked" bodies: a crude and vulgar sort of knowledge deriving from a mode of viewing that remains necessarily improper. Clov appears at times to realize that he is interpreting and experiences the waning of his confidence in the absolute status of scientific knowledge: "I see my light dying" (E 12). With his greater degree of self-consciousness, Hamm would even now retain superiority. How can Clov, whom he cynically calls his "dog," possess any light of his own? Is not Hamm the ultimate source of Clov's illumination? Is not his decline therefore more significant? "Take a look at me and then come back and tell me what you think of *your* light" (E 12).

The impotence behind Hamm's aggressive posture renders him incapable of genuine domination. On the other hand, his persistent arrogance makes harmonious relations difficult. He tries again by returning to the problem of nature. What of Clov's grain? If an increasing heap cannot make a mathematical whole, perhaps a sprouting pile can make an organic one. Hamm would still believe that, in the world's vast seedbed, physical change is evidence that a larger, metaphysical Force is working itself out in time toward self-realization. Clov, however, has no faith in any such teleological design: "They'll never sprout!" (E 13).

Is it impossible, then, to understand what is happening? Can we ascribe no meaning to change and to the passage of time? An inability to comprehend it all by means of a rationally totalized scheme is a source of Hamm's anguish, an anguish that Clov does not appear to share. The latter merely concludes that "something is taking its course," believing he has made an impartial, objective statement (E 13). He cannot of course know that there is such a "thing" or that it has any "course" to follow. Moreover, he too still dreams of abstracting a final all-encompassing system: "I love order. It's my dream. A world where all would be silent and still and each thing in its last place, under the last dust" (E 57).

Thus even if he at times openly disdains Hamm's desperate desire for meaningful purpose, Clov too aspires to full comprehension. In itself a perfect whole, the world would not need—it could not have—any other purpose or end. Traditionally, in fact, the fully self-consistent, unified system is its proper *telos*. The fact that his "dream" rests upon a network of conventional presuppositions, and not upon inductive conclusions from sensory experience, creates another similarity between the speculative Hamm and the ostensibly more empirical Clov.

Clov's somewhat reluctant accommodation to teleology is enough to bring temporary agreement while advancing the dialogue to another stage. Having "met," like Miss Counihan, Neary and Wylie, the two characters can now separate, Hamm pretending to expell Clov, Clov pretending to leave freely. "We're getting on" (E 14).

Once each has withdrawn into his own abstract dreamworld, the refuse they have left behind comes to life. Nell and Nagg emerge from their garbage cans to replay the dialogue between spirit and matter in a more organic mode. Like the most problematic element of a dream, the cloven is repeated and varied, now condensed into composite figures, now dispersed into manifold manifestations. These displacements are not unrelated to the act of repression. Concealed or occluded in one form, the repressed element always returns in another.

First Nell and Nagg attempt to consummate a union. "Their heads strain towards each other, fail to meet, fall apart again" (E 14). Why do they continue this comedy of frustrated conjugal love? Perhaps for the same reason they daily remember their tandem accident and catalog their losses. In a manner reminiscent of Clov's opening act, they would deaden the pain by recasting it as a vaudeville routine. They too would master anxiety by compulsively repeating the actions that provoke it. Beginning again, this anxious play again begins with an act of repetition.

The bicycle accident outside Sedan in which Nell and Nagg lost their "legs" might be described as a carnivalized condensation of Taine's catastrophic history of modern France: from Enlightenment through Revolution to the final impotence of Napoleon III. The tandem alignment of classical spirit and a belief in scientific progress set up human reason in the driver's seat of civilization, but only by first depriving mankind of its historical sense. "Deprived of [its] precious legacy [legs]," the nation succumbed to Rousseau's call for a return to "nature."[22] The significance of Nell and Nagg may thus have less to do with what Georg Lukács saw as Beckett's doctrine of bestial irrationalism,[23] than it does with a criticism of our smugly rationalist tradition for its inclination toward something analogous to precisely that sort of reduction. The fact that Beckett may also be having critical fun with Taine's quasi-castration theory does not by itself invalidate this line of interpretation.

The resurgence of the corporeal Nell and Nagg keeps Hamm from mental peace within himself. In good Freudian fashion, their burlesque intercourse may remind him of a childhood scene when he, like his Old Testament namesake, beheld, as it were, the means by which he was conceived.[24] For his transgression Noah's son was cursed. Nagg's son curses his father for the latter's original sin of the flesh: "Accursed fornicator" (E 10).

To displace the distressing primal scene, Hamm attempts an imaginary re-creation of the sensory world he has denied. Like Fichte he would derive the objective "Not-I" from the purely spiritual "I." Nagg finds it a ludicrous enterprise. His own world—that of the bodily desires that require satisfaction, of the mange that needs to be scratched—is for him the true world. Nagg therefore counters Hamm with a materialist reworking of the mental re-creation myth: "the world and the trousers" (E 22-23).[25]

The comparison calls to mind Herr Teufelsdrockh's magnum opus. Nagg, however, presents the Divine Tailor as a careless craftsman who rushed through the job in order to rest on the Sabbath: Genesis as a bad Jewish joke. In recent decades it has been the absurdists who have, with a sort of arrogance, regarded the cosmos as "botched." Yet, the idea has a long genealogy. In Nagg's burlesque rendition the human tailor, by working from Christmas to Easter, manages to save his creation, but only by concealing "the hollow" beneath the smoothly tailored lines of an artificial bottom: a humanist, and to some extent existentialist, rewriting of a bad Christian joke.

Nell too is obsessed by the bottom: in this case the bottom of Lake Como, that draws her down to the depths of nostalgic reverie: "It was deep, deep. And you could see down to the bottom. So white. So clean" (E 21). Her own retreat from materiality involves an act of negation, of "nelling." Hers is the death knell of the body that longs for a return to the more basic, more nearly static condition of the inorganic world. Here too the desire for the bottom is ultimately a desire for the end. More overtly corporeal than either Hamm or Clov, Nell and Nagg nevertheless suggest still other ways of either overcoming or undermining the life of the flesh: "By rights we should have been drowned" (E 21). Nell's negativity, however, is more profound. The dull, gnawing pain of living is too much a part of Nagg for him to give it up.

The couple's continual prattle, so similar to his own conversations with Clov, disturbs Hamm's solipsistic dreaming. It draws attention to his residual facticity, those nagging remains of "Not-I": physical aspects, his heredity, his past in general. And therefore to their, his, and "its" imperfection: "Will this [ça] never finish" (E 23). All must be expelled and carted away. Hamm's putative self-sufficiency is lost if he cannot rid himself of that which limits his spiritual freedom: "My kingdom for a nightman! . . . Clear away this muck!" (E 23).[26] This is, as usual, a job for Clov.

Fundamentally, however, it is Nell's own nihilism that explains her demise. If her mortal itch stops ("She has no pulse [pouls/poux]"—E 23), it is not really because of any power Hamm might have, whatever he might say. ("Oh for that my powder is formidable"—phrase eliminated from the English version—FP 39, my translation). Her existence was "bottled" before Clov put the lid on her.

Hamm and Clov seem more reluctant to cut all the ties that bind them in material ways to a more vital existence. Rather than take responsibility for freely willing his end, Clov would prefer it be determined for him. For example, he restates as exile—"She told me to go away, into the desert"—Nell's dying exhortation—"Desert" (E 23). And Hamm refrains from permanently obstructing Nagg's reemergence. The psychologically related decision to postpone eliminating his own bodily waste would, on the other hand, be physiologically counterproductive in the end.

His subsequent efforts to circumscribe the limits of his domain belong to this complex of retentive inclinations, for it promises to give Hamm a surer comprehension of his powers vis-à-vis the physical world. Can he eliminate it entirely or must he struggle merely to dominate and thus control it? The walls mark his limits and they embody the basic building blocks of modern epistemology: space, time, number, causality, and so on.

Like the philosopher in the "Preface" to Nietzsche's *Twilight of the Idols*, Hamm would sound out these fundamental concepts. "Do you hear? (He strikes the wall with his knuckles.) Do you hear? Hollow bricks! (He strikes again.)"

What if the bricks were, as Hume suggested, merely the products in the mind of mere perceptual habit? Or what if they represented the innate mental categories with which Kant responded in an attempt to describe the a priori conditions of legitimate scientific rationality? Hamm's wall would then resemble Clov's cave. What happens if these categories are themselves understood as interpretation rather than pure truth? If "all that's hollow" (*E* 26), then at the limit one would be thrown back. The dream of a full comprehension remains unfulfilled: "That's enough. Back!" "We haven't done the round" (*E* 26). But need this imply simply that all is devoid of meaning?

Reduced to the hollow, both here and in Nagg's joke, the "cleft" now reappears thwarting anew the desire to rebuild the world on an absolute foundation. Hamm would fill it himself. Yet, he relies upon Clov to place him at the center and must continue to endure the troubling proximity of this all too necessary adjunct.

Hamm senses that the security of his own small domain might be enhanced through nihilation of the outside world. His authority, however, ought not to depend upon any empirical evidence of it. Clov's (Galilean) telescope ought only to confirm Hamm's speculative insight. Clov himself eventually objects to the way it is used to maintain him in a position of subservience. Even the most accurate observation, however, is inadequate by itself. True knowledge requires what Bacon describes as a methodological "ladder." Hamm's displeasure at the thought—"I don't like that" (*E* 28)—derives in part from a suspicion that his assistant would thus acquire the means of displacing the master. A Baconian Clov might succeed in uniting the rational and empirical aspects of knowledge rather like a Hamm cured of his sensory blindness.

Indeed, the prevailing tendency of Western science has traditionally been to seek after that coordination of observation and method that would enable mankind at last to comprehend the world as a systematic whole. With Clov this excess of expended energy turns into a comic routine: "Exit Clov with telescope. . . . Enter Clov with ladder, but without telescope. . . . He sets down ladder under window right, gets up on it, realizes he has not the telescope, gets down. . . . He goes towards door. . . . Exit Clov. . . . Enter Clov with telescope. He goes toward ladder. He gets up on ladder, raises the telescope, lets it fall" (*E* 28-29). Yet, modern physics has been no more successful than Comtian positivism in achieving Bacon's Great Instauration that many, if not all, men of science still seem to desire.

In a moment of self-conscious theatricality, Clov decides to gage the reaction of the audience: "(He gets down, picks up the telescope, turns it on auditorium.) I see . . . a multitude. . . . in transports" (The French version reads simply "en delire": delirium, in a frenzy—*FP* 45. The English specifies "in transports . . . of joy"—*E* 29.) No one in the theater finds this joke amusing, but its "serious" dimension need not be simply negative. A public that accepts uncritically the propositions of a conventional science—propositions emanating in good part from principles, or impulses that are fundamentally hostile to its own material existence—is delirious, if not mad.

In *Dialectic of Enlightenment*, Max Horkheimer and Theodor Adorno seek to demonstrate that Baconian scientific and technological enthusiasm, with its ethos of instrumentalism and exploitation, contributes importantly to the alienation and repressive standardization of modern society. Heidegger, following Nietzsche, goes further, arguing that both rationalism and positivistic empiricism belong to the same metaphysical, hence fundamentally antinatural, tradition. Clov is accordingly right to stress the farsightedness ("*longue vue*"—*FP* 45) of those who have attempted to see through the popular delusion.

Clov's seriocomic self-parody—"I did it on purpose" (*E* 29)—thus suggests the insufficiencies of his own habitual procedures. His playfulness also helps to recover the possibility of a different sort of science, one that displaces the desire for systematic unification and technological mastery of the world in favor of a renewed openness to nature and its capacity for continual (self-) contestation, a transformation, but also a restoration, of science: "Things are livening up." Is this a serious proposition? "Well? Don't we laugh? . . . I don't. . . . Nor I" (*E* 29).

From the instrumental observation he finally does make Clov agree that the world outside is "*mortibus*" (*FP* 46). This allusion to the liturgy of death may be at once accurate in some sense, and a way of mocking the desire—Hamm's of course, but Clov's too by implication—to play the destroyer God. If everything has indeed been "corpsed" (*E* 30), either by Hamm's thoughtful desire or Clov's unthinkingly technical way of representing it, each is as curiously inept as Nagg's Divine Tailor. Clov may also be "corpsing" Hamm in order to arouse anxiety with regard to his desire for speculative certainty: "Never seen anything like that!" (*E* 30). Even apparent precision, moreover, can produce uncertain results that make classification difficult: "Gray . . . Gray! . . . GRRAY! . . . Light black [*noir clair*]" (*E* 31-32; *FP* 48). At worst the sensory data received from Clov is treacherous. At best it remains fundamentally paradoxical.

Why then does Hamm continue to rely upon it? "Why this farce, day after day?" (*E* 32). Hamm suggests it is habit. Routines at least make it possible to continue. But if it is really only a question of "killing time," Hamm may be right to find such repetition deadly.

In his desire to "see" and thereby master what is going on, Hamm eventually runs up against the problem of meaning. "We're not beginning to . . . to . . . mean something?" (*E* 32). Clov's ironic answer goes beyond Humean skepticism toward the view that life has no ultimate purpose and is therefore devoid of real meaning. Common enough in the late nineteenth century as a response to developments in natural science, this despairing "absurdism" has affinities with the frustrated rationalism found in both Schopenhauer and certain forms of mid-twentieth-century existentialism. Ignoring Clov's insinuations, Hamm continues his hermeneutical meditation. A transcendent Intelligence could certainly comprehend all human activity: "(Voice of rational being [*l'intelligence*]) Ah, good, now I see what it is, yes, now I understand what they're at!" (*E* 33; *FP* 49) Might the human mind not still hope to achieve something similar, albeit on a rather reduced scale? "(Vehemently) To think perhaps it won't all have been for nothing!" (*E* 33).

Suddenly, a flea disrupts the illusion of phenomenological mastery. "Clov starts, drops the telescope and begins to scratch his belly [*le bas ventre*] with both hands" (*E* 33; *FP* 50). Any itch "in the trough" is distressing since "humanity might start from there all over again!" Like Neary's "key flea," this one must die without issue, "lying doggo" [*coïte*] rather than "laying doggo" [*coïte*], or the creation that Hamm is trying to finish would be as open-ended—as "bitched," if you will, as God's. Clov is again required to be the agent of repression.

Hamm prophecizes that, as a result of entropic or negative evolution, Clov too will ultimately become like him "a speck in the void, in the dark, for ever, like me" (*E* 36). Unlike Murphy, however, Hamm realizes that a mote in nothingness is forever separated from the (w)hole. "Infinite emptiness will be all around you, all the resurrected dead of all the ages wouldn't fill it." Pity might overcome such isolation and create at least the illusion of a bond. This would, of course, be the end of Clov, subsumed into a universal Hamm, if it were not for his irreducible otherness: "And there's one thing you forget. . . . I can't sit down" (*E* 36-37).

It is significant that the nature Clov fabricates for Hamm is no more vigorous than what the latter envisions. The process of scientific "reconstruction" leaves out all that is "natural." The result is Hamm's artificial dog. Doubly gelded, its physical mutilations repeat its symbolic value. Overdetermination,

moreover, suggests the difficulty, even for technology, of finally eliminating the truly problematic.

Having "mastered" both the inanimate and lower animal
realms, Hamm moves on to the human. He may compel Clov
to exterminate the flea, but he cannot compel his success. He
failed completely, moreover, to keep Mother Pegg alive. He can
have Clov make him a silky toy dog, but he could not keep
Mother Pegg's beauty from fading. Hamm does not have the
power to prevent "ça" from taking its course. Even his own
life remains in some sense a fatality: "I'm taking [suis] my
course" (E 42; FP 60)—but it is one which nature has determined for him, whether he will it or no. To be master still,
Hamm would have in some existential sense to coincide with
his course—"I am [suis] my course"—in the manner of Hegel's
Geist, for whom neither nature nor will had in the long run
any reality. Then he, causa sui, would necessarily set himself
in motion toward self-actualization.

The obvious question is whether Endgame allows us to believe that such an end would ever be attained—whether it could
ever again be anything but a more or less useful fiction. And
once it becomes clear that purely instrumental means are basically a worn-out gaff, that Hamm's cloven alter ego is a necessary other, one may wonder whether even so masterful a form
of self-delusion is really the most desirable way of confronting
the problems that time and tide pose to each, as well as to every
society.

Hamm and Clov play out the complex relation between
speculative rationality and empiricism, a relation which is itself an epistemological version of the spirit/matter opposition
from classical ontology. No clear distinction can easily be
drawn between the two characters, although they are different.
Hamm commands; Clov (usually) obeys. Yet the master depends upon his servant. He may formulate questions and hypotheses, elaborate histories and systems to describe events,
but sensory perception must inform and verify his theories.
Clov the observer baulks at having to express what he observes,
complaining in almost Kantian terms that he can only observe

by means of the concepts and categories that Hamm has taught him.

Like Mephistopheles, however, he can also use words to tease, trick, and torment the maladroit Faustian Hamm, even interpreting in his own polyvalent ways the reality he "objectively" sees. What, for example, is that "*morpion*" really (that Clov discovers with his telescope in the French version [*FP* 103] but not in the English)—a flea, a small boy, or just a game? And what of the word *yesterday* that so angers Hamm? What could it mean to a mind that would be eternal and immutable, but finds itself caught up in the flux of existence. "Yesterday! What does that mean? Yesterday!" (*E* 43). Clov responds with an allusive invocation of Humpty Dumpty's naïvely subjectivist doctrine: a word means just what the mind has determined it to mean. But what if the terms no longer seem appropriate? "Teach me others. Or let me be silent" (*E* 44).

Hamm comes back with a parable whose conservatism anticipates certain existentialist interpretations of the play. Without faith in the conventional view of time, space, causality, the beauty of life turns through madness to ashes and dust (*E* 44). Art can no longer offer salvation by perfecting the world, like the pants of Nagg's tailor. It only expresses the despair at having been left behind to witness the destruction. But since the artist is "mad," how should we evaluate his vision? Is it the cause or a result of his alienation? Or is he only said to be deranged because of it? The significance of the matter lies in the fact that, as Hamm observes, this madman's situation is scarcely uncommon. His fundamentally Judeo-Christian conception of earthly existence (see, e.g., Genesis 18:27) still in fact underlies the dominant tendency of our entire culture. Again the question returns: Hasn't this lasted long enough? "All life long the same inanities."

Yet, the dialogue continues, playing further variations on its theme: the elimination of the "cloven," of that which is divided without being cleanly split apart, in which fundamental sameness comes marked by "essential" differences. The conflict between (and within) the characters could be "resolved" if Clov would simply leave. But how could the sightless, immobile Hamm ever know the Other had really gone? Clov comes up with a battery of characteristically practical, sensuous, quasi-Aristotelian solutions. Hamm should rely upon smell and hearing. The former is useless, however, because a strong odor of things long dead and decaying pervades the scene. Recourse to hearing suggests a paradoxically "mechanistic" device. Clov will set an alarm clock to ring when he is gone. Unfortunately, Hamm finds he cannot quite take in the decisive moment. It is "unheard (of) [*inouï*]" (*FP* 67). Salvation from Clov remains as remote as the Last Judgment. Unable to accommodate his infernal double, unable to attain his true end without him, Hamm opts for the relative security of a familiar middle.

Having repeatedly failed to find a fully satisfying solution to their dilemma, each character seeks relief in a state of equanimity: Hamm by returning to his painkillers, Clov by retreating once again to his kitchen. They are attempting to follow the advice of Alcmaeon, "that old doctor," who held that by self-harmonization through atonement, making one again by inwardly "joining the beginning to the end," at least the passion of human finitude could be eliminated. Hamm has doubts, however, and tries to keep Clov from leaving with his own version of the salvation story, a variant of Clov's more mechanistic one. Clov himself is uninterested, but Nagg can still be bribed into listening with the promise of either a baptismal bonbon [*dragée*] or a Christmas sugarplum.

The latter's resurrection at this juncture signals the fact that Hamm's story is also another son's attempt to retailor the work of the father, conceived in terms of bungling and recuperation. As a more humanistically oriented tale of salvation, it belongs as well with those of the mad painter and Mother Pegg. Why so many variations? Perhaps the real point is that even the greatest story (ever told?) will finally be debased by fundamentally unthinking forms of repetition, by revisions that are more like reversions, and that even the parodic aspects of this essentially retentive project will not necessarily save it from final exhaustion.

Hamm's story begins, however, somewhere in the middle,

though not in the just middle that he is always seeking. This "beginning" parodies Clov's opening words and thus also the words with which Christ consummated his own work of atonement. Hamm's words invert their import. "There'll be no more speech [*voix*]": no more *Logos*; no more Way (*E* 50; *FP* 70). The very possibility of a way out through full identity has been lost. Hamm's story, in other words, opens with a prologue in which all real hope of true ending is already forsaken. As with the mad painter, to be saved now only means to have been spared, that is, to have been forgotten.

The prologue is a false start. The next attempt is not a true beginning either. For he begins by repeating something he has already said. The third time he simply proceeds. Hamm has as much trouble beginning his story as he has in finishing. In this sense, *Endgame* points forward to *How It Is*.

Hamm's story is a Christmas carol reaching for, but never quite reaching, its proper conclusion. Certainly, it offers no remedy for the disease of life from which the characters suffer. There will be no rebirth, either sacred or profane. But without it, [his]story cannot really go forward. Hamm does not want it to stop before his own life's story is finished. Ideally, the two must coincide. And, like Moran, he will only accept an ending that brings everything together into a classical whole. What if he runs out of material before his time is up? He may then have to continue reworking, revising it, perfecting the story as best he can, striving to make fiction a meaningful expression of life, searching for the satisfying, the consummate end for both. Or he might generate new characters. But from where?

Clov, whose natural member has been crippled through contact with Hamm, can only bring forth a half-exterminated rat. The episode replays the perspective of Hamm's chronicle on a concrete level. Trapped in a milieu out of which he would like to flee, the rat cannot save himself. Yet his end is not really an end. He, like Hamm and Clov, will be finished only later.

If there is no salvation on earth, Hamm and Nagg can still appeal to heaven. Their hope of an answer, however, is unfounded. "He doesn't exist" (*E* 55). Not, at least, until they have reinvented Him in order to fulfill their need. Without a divine Father, there can be no rebirth, no return to an origin. Only an essentially external Source can create an oasis in the desert of life. Without the divine *Logos* it provides, man cannot slake his thirst for an Ultimate Word. Thus, he cannot attain what he wants most of all from the world, and perhaps even more than the world: a final, certain answer to all questions, a solid foundation or core of Truth, sure and unchanging, a stable point of reference on which he may rely, the lasting security, the peace this would bring. Because this desire is so strong, man himself eventually steps forth as a replacement for the lost center of meaning and value, stepping into that crucial space He has managed to leave behind. That in this role man is a charlatan, unable to deliver what the tradition has promised, is a suspicion that may nonetheless arise.

Even the mind that would be God finally finds itself alone before the darkness of death. It then calls for a Way out, for a different end to the chronicle of life. This is the more worldly Nagg's curse upon his son, the gnawing doubts about one's own self-sufficiency. Setting himself apart from and above what he perceives to be radically other—nature, body, "in-itself", object, "Not-I"—expelling, as it were, all that from his presence, he will find that he cannot stand alone in the end. He earlier needed Nagg to listen to his story. Earlier still the child Hamm had cried out to his father. He will again cry out to him during his final soliloquy. An impulse that waivers between conventional religious and more secular interpretations becomes more mundanely humanist when, in much the same way, Hamm repeatedly recalls Clov to his side (as Nagg recalls Nell to his). In the end, however, there is no response from the Father, and no full reconciliation with the other is ever achieved. Knowledge knows no way out, and neither pity, nor love, nor mastery through physical, psychological, or cognitive means, ever enable the self fully to possess the other or effect a perfect union between them. The nagging double curse of finitude and incompletion, or nontotalization, will continue to hang upon man.

Hamm then tries to arrive at a satisfying consummation by himself. All attempts at a union with Clov have failed. His moves in that direction have produced only a strange *jeu d'é-checs*. If his consequent solipsism seems ludicrous, so perhaps must every attempt at a genuinely teleological interpretation of life in this world. Yet, man insists on taking these failures seriously, believing that through their very failure his efforts in some way reveal, not the questionable, almost comical, nature of the project itself, but the grim truth about the human comedy. Where Democritus could not help laughing, the tradition has preferred to weep: "You weep, and weep, for nothing, so as not to laugh, and little by little . . . you begin to grieve" (*E* 68).

Exhausted, Hamm would like to have reached a genuine end in the classical sense, one that would bring at last the peaceful rest implicit in the full realization of a completed state of being: "Ah let's get it over [*Ah y être, y être*]" (*E* 70; *FP* 93). Instead, he has something nearer to the Heideggerian sense of being-in-the-world, one that necessarily involves awareness of that cloven state which is never complete. Hamm experiences this awareness with profound reluctance, and anxiously tries to master it—or at least to control his anxiety—by compulsively playing the *fort-da* game with Clov(enness).

Having sent Clov away, Hamm would like to be certain he is really alone. Clov, however, returns with the frustrating news that his bestial analogue, the rat, has escaped annihilation and will therefore continue, like Murphy's, his troublesome fidgetting. Hamm's distress is so intense that only a painkiller can allay his fears. Clov has tricked him. Now it is his turn to play the master. Replacing the turned-over picture with an alarm clock, Clov makes his own attempt to wind things up (*E* 72).

He wants to remove himself from Hamm's speculative authority, claiming it is both irrelevant and irresponsible. He also tries to put aside the instruments he employed to bolster Hamm's insight. Clov intends now to see things with his own eyes instead. Trying, he loses his equilibrium and nearly falls from his methodological ladder. Moreover, the dog, his only direct outlet for aggression, has by now been domesticated in Hamm's service. In place of open confrontation, there is only sterile frustration: "Let's stop playing!" "Then let it end! . . . With a bang!" (*E* 77).

The game's gradual winding down, its approach to what has traditionally been regarded as the ideal state is suddenly complicated by the reintroduction of procreative potential. Repeatedly repressed throughout the play, the disturbing element reappears in yet another displaced form (*E* 78). This time, however, Clov does not set out after it. Hamm no longer wants his assistance. The little mite, like the rat or the flea, will die there or here, if he exists at all. For he may not exist. Empirical observation no longer seems relevant or trustworthy from the perspective of philosophical reflection. The end has accordingly been reached. "It's the end, Clov, we've come to the end" (*E* 79). The timing of their routine is perfect. Hamm no longer needs Clov just when Clov is set to leave.

Still, a fully satisfying end requires a true consummation. The play cannot simply stop. To conclude there must be a final judgment, an illuminating evaluation of all that has led to this terminal state. The last speeches of Clov and Hamm, however, only seem to provide this. More like the chess game between Mr. Endon and Murphy than the epilogue of a traditional morality play, their summary conclusion is merely a replay in miniature of the entire endgame problem.

Clov opens with a prefacetious ditty, *amour emmerdé*, that expresses the plight of his unhappy consciousness. He had been told—"they said to me"—that reason would provide all the answers and, through "skilled attention [*science*]" (*E* 80; *FP* 108), eventually enable us to avoid our natural end. On the other hand, his own inherent skepticism—"I say to myself"— which perceives life as irrational suffering borne through resignation and habit until a welcomed death provides relief. Clov's self-conscious theatricality, however, both underscores and undercuts the romanticism of his supposedly empirical interpretation. "This is what we call making an exit" (*E* 81).

Sensing that it is now all up to him, Hamm takes his turn at the articulation of ultimate significance. He thus returns to his opening line: "Me to play" (*E* 82). Once again he picks up the threads that have dropped along the way—the means for reaching the desired end—and tries to weave them into a unified text. The result is more a catalog. Like the grains in the paradoxes of Clov's old Greeks, these bits and pieces never add up to a whole life. The same could be said of *Endgame*. It plays repeated variations on a set of complex themes. But these, because they are also scenes fraught with internal tensions, interplay, and indeterminacy, do not and could never constitute a totalized work.

First Hamm abandons his vain hope of becoming the Prime Mover of his world. *Receuillement*, in the poetic translation of its religious sense, is aesthetically pleasing but does not attain the desired end. Hamm's attempt to rewrite history is inconclusive. Reconciliation with the other is attempted three times without success.

Hamm in fact has known all along that his quest for totality must fail. All the means at his disposal amount to little enough: "Moments for nothing, now as always . . . " (*E* 83). Perhaps they may yet be recuperated as moments of negation, aspects of an inverted desire for pure void, a negative totality. Insofar as it seeks to deny the dynamic flux of life, or bring it to an end, the idea of totality is always nihilistic at bottom. Yet, even negative points never quite add up to a (w)hole. The final count cannot be made, nor the history brought to a true end.

Hamm has led the play through a series of renunciations on up to the last, a renunciation of the (humanized) *Logos* itself: "And speak no more about it . . . speak no more" (*E* 84). Even despairing silence fails, however, since Hamm must add another word, another deed, or as in the beginning, another act. Just as Clov "began" the play with an act of repression, Hamm now attempts to end it with another. He would simply stop the flow of interpretations in an arbitrary manner, employing "the old stauncher." Yet, as always, the repressed reemerges when Clov returns once again to decenter Hamm's deadly solipsism and close the play *more or less* as it opened.

For Hamm and Clov the game of life acquires true significance only insofar as it can be described in terms of a comprehensive system or goal. Like the all too Sartrean hero of *Nausea*, they are faced with the fundamental problem of excess and lack. On the one hand, the characters are unable to provide an interpretation that is fully adequate to empirical reality. In one way or another, life seems constantly to go beyond total conceptual comprehension. On the other hand, their desire for perfect order and propriety may itself become excessive. The world is then inadequate to their expectations. In both cases, the characters take their own desires and aspirations as the measure of all things. This is what authorizes existentialist interpretations of *Endgame.*

I am not, then, trying to argue that they are irrelevant to the play, but that their relevance is of a different sort than the predominant view of Beckett would allow. Existentialist humanism, I have tried to show, is itself critically situated within the play and cannot, therefore, provide a complete explanation of it. To deny or overestimate the significance of Beckett's relation to the Cartesian *cogito,* or human subjectivity in general, would be difficult. It forms one of the more prominent departure points in most, if not all, his fictional and nonfictional work. His "subjects" are usually engaged in endless struggles with the more or less irrational "others" that constitute their natural world. By repeatedly destabilizing the various anthropocentric structures that the subject erects, these natural forces continually frustrate the desire for rational mastery.

Yet, regret or despair at disorderly conduct of the world is not the "essential meaning" or "message" of Beckett's own "play." It is merely one tempting response to the situation— a response, however, his work normally treats in a demonstratively critical, or at least parodic, fashion. *Endgame* is typical in this respect. Indeed, Beckett's writing tends forcefully to convey the impression that humanism, including its existentialist variant, has exaggerated the extent of our freedom, the nature of its relation to human subjectivity, and the degree of dignity which the latter has granted him.[27]

Endgame suggests ways in which humanist ideology may actually have debased mankind along with the entire natural world to which we inevitably belong. Both the "idealist"

Hamm and the more "technocratic" Clov desire a simpler, a neater, and less troublesome world, a world in which comprehension can be related to security through one-sided processes of domination and control. It is a desire rooted in humanist—and at bottom, other-worldly—ideas about man and his relation to all nonhuman beings. Beckett's play may thus imply that human dignity would be enhanced if *homo rationalis* were to see himself less as master of the world, the focus of its meaning and value, than as one vital element in a decentered world that can never be securely placed under the dominion of any.[28]

The end-problems that plague the narrative of *Endgame* may reappear during its interpretation. Sharing their fixation, the reader is likely to become impatient with Hamm and Clov. The play repeatedly proffers situations that both excite and frustrate the desire for final comprehension.

One of the difficulties of confronting any reader of the play is that interpretive handholds seem so scarce and obscure, whereas Beckett's earlier work features a chaotic proliferation of cultural references. The difference has often been explained as a consequence of Joyce's influence and Beckett's later attempt to overcome it. Yet, it may also be argued that Beckett did not so much abandon Joyce's style as translate it into another mode. And here the attraction of Flaubert's highly problematic aesthetics should not be left out of the account.

The perplexing combination of starkness and obscurity so characteristic of Beckett's later style often gives the impression that he is striving for a monadic, or closed, system of language. This would suggest stylistic analogue of the quest for self-identity and totality that is lampooned on the narrative level of the text. The idea of a closed text may nevertheless be detected behind the progressive paring away of extratextual references as Beckett moves, for example, from *Murphy* to *Endgame*, and from *Endgame* to later works. This can be interpreted in at least two ways.

First, one may say that the words are increasingly shorn of their connotative qualities and reduced, as Cavell puts it, to "declarative utterances, ones of pure denotation." Cavell considers that Beckett shares with both existentialism and positivism the desire to "escape connotation, rhetoric, the noncognitive, the irrationality and awkward memories of ordinary language, in favor of the directly verifiable, the isolated and perfected present." Cavell thus points to the ontological nature of the common philosophical and scientific quest for the purely cognitive statement.[29] Implied here is an understanding of being in terms of presence and of language in terms of adequation. If, then, the text were in fact "closed" in this way, the quest would have been successful. Although the characters fail to attain their end, the text would have succeeded in attaining its linguistic analogue.

There are, however, several problems with this view. Even the ordinary words that remain, like *telescope, bicycle, ladder, dog,* are never simply denotative. Without the restrictions imposed by explicit metaphoric expression or cultural allusion, Beckett's usage may become more, rather than less, charged with possible meaning, since it may then carry a wider, though less certain, range of connotations. The empirical fact is that language is always marked in this way by the vast structure of contemporary and historical contexts to which it inevitably relates. This is not, of course, to say that all connotations are equally possible or appropriate. There remains the limiting context provided by the text itself. Each word or phrase is meaningful only as part of the particular network of relations that actually make up any given textual fabric.

Yet, simplicity of expression is no guarantee of simple, determinate meaning. It may well create a situation in which an uncommon degree of interpretive reflection is possible, or even necessary. In any case, it has yet to be shown that *Endgame* has anything like a unique denotation or straightforward meaning. Even Cavell would perhaps admit that the play means for him something different than it does for Adorno or Martin Esslin, and that none of these interpretations is simply wrong.

The desire for a purely denotative or literal language may, moreover, actually be caricatured within the play itself. Here I would merely signal its relation to "Sprat's medium" for transmitting information, that classical regimen preferred by the "scientific" Clov and no one else. Nagg finds it quite unsuitable to his all too human needs.

Alternatively, the ideal of pure self-referentiality has also been imputed to Beckett.[30] This would be a special reflexive instance of the perfectly denotative language. The linguistic signifier here becomes in principle its own unique signified. To the extent that it could be cut off from every extratextual referent, whether historical, cultural, social, or political, language would become an *ens causa sui*: autonomous, both means and end in one, the Alpha and the Omega of its own semiotic world. As smooth as Christ's seamless garment, as blank as Flaubert's wall, it would exist for itself. From his own more critical perspective Lukács treats Beckett's work as an embodiment of such an alienation from, or even rejection of, every temporal, material context.

This idea of a pure language-in-itself is, of course, subject to the same problems as that of a purely denotative language. In addition one may ask whether true self-referentiality, the absence of all external reference would really be possible. Opponents often proceed as if it were, but that in itself proves little. Just as there is no domain completely "outside" of language, there could be none completely "inside" it either. For language in general is the scene of an often tense interplay of meanings, wherein a variety of contexts are necessarily implicated. A language devoid of contextual reference would be a language without meaning. And a language without meaning would be no language at all.

One may of course argue that this is precisely the point, for silence is Beckett's ideal. This is a critical commonplace. But silence attained through perfect self-referentiality or self-containment would also be the end of language, of signification in general, through the realization of perfect self-identity or totality. As a linguistic ideal it is therefore related, or even analogous, to the goal of the dominant ontotheological tradition of the West. Its affinity with certain well-known varieties of neurotic-obsessional personality formation and behavior is what opens it to the carnivalizing critique of *Endgame*.

Furthermore, absolute self-referentiality can be viewed as an

ideal form of that almost hyperbolic degree of self-consciousness apparent in Beckett's work from at least the *Trilogy* on.
The theatricality of Hamm and Clov has repeatedly been noted
and analyzed by critics. Yet, it is this very self-consciousness
that reveals a fundamental problem in the concept of self-
referentiality, a problem it shares with the concept of apperception.

To regard oneself as a character in a play is to recognize that
the self is not entirely at one with itself. The theatrical distance
between self and role becomes explicit. To know oneself as
conscious of being conscious, as referring to oneself, is also to
make explicit the paradoxical play of excess and lack inherent
in every conception of self-knowledge and identity. Insofar as
one *knows* oneself, one cannot *be* one self. Knowledge, as it
endeavors to plug the implied existential deficiency, or gap,
seems inevitably to shoot it as well. Thus, a self-referential
text that would know itself to be such could never be a closed
monadistic system.

Self-consciousness might also be seen as a form of internal,
multivoiced dialogue that replaces the ironic narrator of *Murphy* and approaches the free indirect style of Flaubert. In *Murphy* the ironic narrator served as a more or less stable point of
reference. Still the central figure of authority, he commented
upon the characters and their actions as if from above. *Endgame*
is also permeated with irony, but of a more diffused and unsettling sort. There is no stable reference. A reader/spectator
can never really be certain of the "vantage point" from which
he or she is viewing the play. The very idea of a stable reference
is subjected to critical scrutiny. The interwoven strands of the
textual matrix "itself" limit the proliferation of interpretations,
but it never fixes them, much less reduces their number to one
which could be called proper.

Viewed as a kind of "cultural anarchy," this might seem to
imply that the text is ultimately meaningless: a tempting interpretation for many. No single meaning emerges, and the many
subjective and objective references might even appear to cancel
one another out. A plurality of meanings is often regarded as
chaos and chaos as the void. Certainly, mainstream classical

philosophy in general has seen it this way. It is also the way Hamm and Clov habitually reason. Without such formal or ideal perfection they are overcome, like Bouvard and Pécuchet, by a nausea of discouragement and despair.

This reaction is symptomatic of the anxiety that uncertainty tends to induce. Those who long for a secure universe, completely under control, at least cognitively, are not always inclined to waiver under the impact of the doubts aroused by recent developments in science and philosophy. Every possibility that does not conform to traditional modes of apprehension, or at least hold out the hope of satisfying the desire for a familiar idea of good order, then appears in a threatening light. It upsets and may well destroy the fragile "perfection" of the various models they employ. What modern science has come increasingly to think of as an inherent degree of relative insecurity in the universe, a universe in which man participates as a vital, but no longer central, element implies, however, that the carnivalesque with its proliferation of grotesque "forms" need not be evaluated simply in terms of its destabilizing potential. Indeed, destabilization itself need not be taken simply as a threat to every form of order.

The absence of a unique, ulitimate meaning is open, I think, to another interpretation, one that regards it with less apprehension, regret, and gloom. In this case, the demise of the one implies not chaos or significative void, but a virtual cornucopia of relative or partial forms, meanings, and values. Beckett's seemingly fragmented and dispersed cultural references then become a network of signifying elements that never coalesce into a total interpretation, but are not on that account devoid of all significance. This understanding of regulated interpretive play would contribute to the possibility of new structures of meaning more open to self-contestation and for that reason better able to withstand the anxiety and internal pressures that have contributed to the breakdown of older, more repressively humanist ones.[31]

Dialogues with the Double

The double is often considered an organizing theme in literary criticism. As such it is usually studied from a mythological, or psychological, or even mythopsychological perspective. Such investigations tend to obscure certain fundamental problems by not giving sufficient attention to the ways in which the double plays with the peculiar logic of identity and difference. Consequently, although implicitly pointing to it, they usually fail to relate explicitly the double to a search for unity or totality. By not confronting these issues, they remain blind to the ways in which the double may, in fact, work to undercut any final integration, implied or explicit, as well as the very logic on which such integration depends. I will, therefore, begin by considering the problem of the double from a somewhat more philosophical point of view and then discuss two of Samuel Beckett's shorter dramatic works, *Film* and *Krapp's Last Tape*, that investigate the confrontation between man and his doubles. Each work involves a dialogic encounter on some level with these provocative supplements. The two works, however, develop different aspects of this confrontation. The former shows him attempting to flee his doubles (this flight amounting to a form of repression), but failing; the latter shows him attempting to recover his doubles, but also failing. In both cases, the protagonist is trying to be one with himself, either by eliminating the disturbing supplements, or by integrating them. Although the tactics are certainly different, the goal appears to be the same: the integral, totalized personality.

Self-identity seems in Beckett's works, however, a futilely

sought-after chimera. Even if man's doubles, his past selves as well as the multiple aspects of his present character, are all similar, they are nonetheless not identical. Some differences always remain that cannot be integrated into an all-encompassing whole. The doubles, in other words, "belong together" in a supplementary, rather than complementary, relationship. At the same time, Beckett's texts themselves are doubled by other literary or philosophical works with which they enter into dialogues, amiable or contestatory. But while nonidentity on the narrative level appears to lead to the characters' sterile despair, on the textual level it leads, on the contrary, to renewed artistic vigor. These intertextual doubles, like their intratextual counterparts, are, of course, neither to be completely refuted nor totally assimilated. There is a degree of give and take between, or among, them that leads to continued creative interpretation.

The theme of the double, then, poses the problem of identity. The word *double* itself is fundamentally ambiguous on this score. It first suggests a perfect duplication, repetition of the identical (from *duplex*, twofold)—"a thing that is an exact repetition of another" (OED). As such, the double calls into question the commonly accepted idea of simple self-identity, that is, the unity of a thing with itself.

This traditional view finds early expression in Plato's *Sophist*: "Each one of them is different from the (other) two, but itself the same for itself." Thus, if the double is understood as an exact copy, it contests this Platonic formulation in which the identity of a thing is established through its self-containment and clear distinction from any other thing. For Plato, then, two things can never be exact copies of each other; if they were they would be one and the same. There can be no exact repetition. Between *two* entities there must always be a difference, however small.[1]

Consistent with this idea is the way this first dictionary definition of the double becomes representable by the equation $A = A$. Upon closer inspection, however, we find that even this mathematical formulation has obscured something important. It appears from the equation that A is separated from

A by a distance of both time and space. The copula, indeed, marks a difference within that expression of sameness. Beckett also suggests as much in his analysis of *Remembrance of Things Past*: "The most ideal tautology presupposes a relation and the affirmation of equality involves only an approximate identification, and by asserting unity denies unity" (*P* 52). This difference will undercut every traditional understanding of the double as an exact repetition.[2]

A second definition might then be proposed. The double might be thought of, and indeed has often been thought of by writers, as an entity sufficiently similar to another to be considered identical. The double, then, is like the "original," yet still somehow unlike it. If a true identity between doubled elements is to be established, if the two are ever to become one, the difference between them must be confronted. The problem becomes how to relate to this double with a difference, to the difference within the double.

The difference may be treated in a number of ways. The double may be regarded as a complement of the "original," so that the two together might be said at some point to form a basic, unified totality. This very common approach will often involve a denial (most often implicit) of all similarity between the two elements and an at least tactical effort to treat them as dichotomous opposites. The double is thus rendered completely different so that the opposition may subsequently be overcome by a logical synthesis with the original. Each brings what the other lacks; no awkward overlapping or superfluous ingredients appear. It is, of course, a line of argument that will depend, in one way or another, on the familiar notion of identity as a transcendent union. Prevalent since the era of speculative idealism, the latter reminds us that the concept of identity has often been related to that of idea or essence. The identity of an object or person, whether in the Platonic or Hegelian sense, is here said to be its essence or ideal form. The essence of an object is therefore only manifest when it is reunited with its double(s). Certain tendencies in modern psychoanalysis that strive, through a process of familiarization with the unconscious, to totalize the fragmented self, seem to share this view of the double as a mere complement.[3]

One might ask, however, whether this notion of complementarity is really compatible with that of the double. To fit together as a perfectly unified whole, that is, without overlap or remainder, elements must complete one another without replicating any components. But to what extent could such complementary opposites without shared traits ever be seriously considered doubles? It has been suggested that the theory of a double is based on sameness that nevertheless implies an irreducible degree of difference. By subsequently turning around and attempting to eliminate similarity, the notion of perfect complementarity ends by actually eliminating the double itself.

Alternatively, the double may be considered a genuine supplement, something never fully capable of being completely integrated into a harmonious whole. A different problem then appears: what is to be done with the left-over, with those frightening elements, however small or few, that resist complete assimilation, thereby thwarting the ancient desire for integral self-identity and perfect self-perception? For these stubbornly resisting elements of difference will be nonetheless *related* to that from which they differ. How, then, in history's quest for the integrity of the "self," can such awkward remainders, the double among them, be handled? One way is to remove or subjugate them in some manner, to "kill" them, as it were. The double thus becomes a kind of scapegoat that must be suppressed—eliminated or marginalized, either entirely or in part—if the purity and authenticity of the self is to be won. Whatever can be seen as a threat to perfect integration, in other words, either because superfluous and therefore destabilizing, or else because actively subversive of integral harmony, must ultimately be filtered out.[4]

Historically, this has been the most widespread manner of treating a twin or rival claimant to an inheritance. When dealing with racial or religious minorities, it has been at least as common as the process of assimilation of which it often forms a necessary step. Frequently, only certain characteristics of the double require suppression, and an individual or people may be integrated more or less easily, according to their ability to conform to the needs and desires of the dominant (and dominating) "original" who defines social life. The double is transformed into a complement, or complementary addition. Many times, however, the degree of difference or the embarrassment of similarity is felt to be too great, and the double is suppressed altogether.

All these more traditional means of coping with the double have at least one thing in common: each aims at integral totality. What distinguishes them is the amount of suppression deemed necessary to attain the goal: little in the case of similar entities more or less willing to conform (e.g., most ethnic and racial minorities in the United States, or women entering the business world—both cases in which differences may be retained provided they are basically trivial and the general shape and character of the society in question remains unaffected), a great deal wherever the double is wholly or largely resistant to unproblematic absorption (e.g., twins in many primitive cultures, Jews in Nazi Germany or under the Inquisition, etc.). In each case, however, there is an attempt to do away with significant difference in order to attain the ideal of pure, harmonious identity.

A more creative approach to the double may be to consider it a member of a pair or couple, something that always comes along with the "original." Such a relationship presumes an unspecifiable bond or tie of similarities and differences.[5] It might be said that the "original" only becomes present in the interplay with the "double." But this is not to say that the "original" came first or once existed without its double. The "double" is always already there along with its partner. In revealing itself, the "original" also reveals the "double," and vice versa. This is indeed to suggest that there is no "original" but always only "doubles." No single element ever appears by itself alone.

And yet, as Heidegger and others insist, neither is completely revealed; something always remains concealed or dissembled (dis-[as]sembled). And that something is the difference, that

part which can neither be totally assimilated nor totally suppressed. That something is also deferred by the spacing which
holds apart the "original" and the "double." This irreducible
distance, as well as the movement of differentiation, interrupts
any quest for identity and at the same time renders problematic
the traditional notion of double as transitory phenomenon, destined for oblivion in one way or another.[6]

The use of the double in this sense of dynamic supplement
would then in literature create a pluridimensional work in
which several unmerged strata meet interpenetrating and overlapping from various dialogical angles.[7] This contestatory dialogue would attempt neither mastery through suppression nor
unity through totalization. It would necessarily be open-ended,
unfinalized, never ultimately determinable.

The double becomes two-faced; in its concealing and unconcealing, in its similarity and difference, it acts in a double
manner. This nonidentity in sameness, this creative strife between a hero and his adversary who is also his double (agon),
has been considered, by Heidegger, the origin of the work of
art.[8] The two short dramatic works to be considered here investigate this relation between man and his doubles, between
a text and its doubles. Each work involves a contestatory dialogue on some level between these provocative supplements.
This meeting is staged, not in traditional modes of duplication
or fragmentation, but by technological means: in Film, the motion picture camera; in Krapp's Last Tape, the tape recorder.

Film presents us with a protagonist "sundered into object
(O) and Eye (E), the former in flight, the latter in pursuit. It
will not be clear until the end of film that pursuing perceiver
is not extraneous but self" (F 11). The general introduction to
the screenplay goes on to specify that "E is the camera." Taken
together these statements suggest that the writer has already
begun to play with traditional principles of identity and difference. E is both part of O and not part of O; E is also the
camera and, through the camera, the eye of the spectator as
well. But E is also self, not merely O's self but also the self of
any person or people, specifically that of the other characters—

the elderly couple and the flower lady—who respond to its stare with that look of horror. And as O's self it is also an eye, that wrinkled eye that opens the film and stares at the spectator, an eye that belongs to O's double who is only seen in the last episode. Already E is not simply O. Nor is E merely the camera or the spectator. It should be added that O is not simply E, nor in fact merely O. The seven photographs of moments from his past, like Krapp's tapes, present other O's that are similar to, yet different from, the present self of O.

"Throughout first two parts," continues the screenplay, "all perception is E's. But in the third part there is O's perception of room and contents and at the same time E's continued perception of O" (F 11-12). In order to distinguish between the two perceptions, objects seen by O were shot through a lens-gauze, blurring O's perception while keeping E's clear.

O believes he is fleeing from all *extraneous* perception, from perceivedness or *percipi* in general; this is the search of "non-being" (F 11). He abandons the street, where he jostles the elderly couple, for the narrow passageway where he avoids the flower lady, finally arriving in a room from which he removes or obscures all perceiving "eyes"—windows, mirror, dog, cat, parrot, fish, print of God the Father, photographs, even a manila envelope with eyelike clasp and a "staring" rocking chair. But he has been mistaken; his pursuer is really his own uncanny double—his self.[9] Irrepressible, this latter must eventually be encountered, it seems, "face to face." Perception, in the form of self-perception can never be totally eliminated.

Now E is never seen at all until the final scene, and O is only viewed until then from behind and at an angle not exceeding forty-five degrees. The convention is established that O only enters the state of perceivedness when that angle is exceeded. Only then does he experience the "anguish of perceivedness." But why forty-five degrees? And why should self-perception, being perceived by one's internal double, be so painful?

Ernest Fischer has suggested one explanation. The angle of forty-five degrees creates an isosceles right triangle, a symmetrical figure, symbol of reassuring regularity and Pythagorean harmony. The widening of the angle destroys the balance. "The elegant order of the squares drawn on the sides on the triangle, the trinity of the two equal and one double square $[c^2 = a^2 + b^2 = 2a^2]$ collapses."[10] Or perhaps it might be suggested that forty-five degrees is exactly half way between the x and y axes that correspond to two ways of looking at time (diachronic/temporal and synchronic/atemporal) and matter (excess and lack). Forty-five degrees would be the just middle, the angle of stasis, or perfect being. A movement in either direction would destroy perfection. More likely, however, forty-five degrees was chosen because an observer standing at such an angle (or at one more acute) to a mirror can no longer see his own reflection. By analogy, *Film* may be suggesting a point at which man does not reflect on himself, that is, is not aware of his own existence as conscious being. To exceed that angle is to focus consciousness on the self. Forty-five degrees is, in any case, "the angle of immunity"; any other causes O anguish or pain. The immunity to pain provided by un-self-consciousness can moreover be destroyed whenever E wishes (*F* 11).

In the third part of the film, E corners O and retains him within the "anguish of perceivedness." This besieging of O (but not his capture, for E always remains at a distance, is termed "investment" (*F* 39). It is, however, more than a military operation; it is also a (Berkeleyian or Sartrean) investiture, a clothing with attributes and qualities, a doubling by the "other."[11] But it might also be seen as a Heideggerian appropriation, an appearing as one's own. E and O catch sight of one another for the first time; they seem to stand face to face. For they belong to each other. E appears as the double of O and O as the double of E.[12]

"Investment," in this sense, then, is what O flees, and what he momentarily experiences in the anguish of perceivedness. But why anguish? What causes that look of horror when O (and before him the elderly couple and the flower lady) sees his double as he perceives himself (i.e., realizes that he is both perceiver and perceived and, therefore, capable of self-perception)? A number of critics, among them Ruby Cohn and Martin Dodsworth, have understood O's attempt to suppress all perception as a search for nonbeing, for the peace of Nothingness.[13] In other words, this is how they interpret the phrase "search of non-being" (F 11).

The clues in the text that seem to substantiate this claim are so flagrant that they render the entire notion suspect: the rocking chair (Murphy's, of course, but unfortunately it too has eyes); the destruction of the photos (mother's "must be on tougher mount for he has difficulty in tearing it across," F 38); and the return to his mother's room/womb/tomb ("to look after the pets, until she comes out of hospital,"—F 59n. 8). For them, E is what keeps man from attaining this annihilation.

Charles C. Hampton, Jr., on the other hand, understand O's flight as a search for an identity, or rather as an attempt to escape "the discovery of one's nothingness reflected in the eyes of another person." Self-perception he argues, finally brings the realization that the self has, after all, no existence. Hampton, then, sees O as a nonbeing in search of "lasting existence."[14]

Different as they are, both views suggest that without E, that troublesome double or supplement, O would have an impression, at the very least, of self-identity. But E does not go away, so that, as far as *Film* is concerned, no unification of the self is possible. Not by any means. I should like to propose that it is this unconquered and apparently, for Beckett, unconquerable difference between E and O—which I have earlier referred to as part of the supplementary nature of the double—that, once understood, causes the character's anguish. That nonidentity seen in E's stare—the stare, we must remember, of self-perception—is suffered by the characters. They must endure that stubborn "belonging together" of E and O, for it cannot be resolved into unity.

Thus, *Film* seems to present a quest for unity (at least on the level of the narrative) that is blocked by an irrepressible, unassimilatable double. The protagonist, however, never interacts with his double; in fact, he seems to avoid every possibility of it. There is no dialogue between any of the characters. All have indeed elected to be silent, as the elderly lady's "Ssssh" indicates. The confrontations are consequently sterile and lead to an evident impasse. Yet there is a dialogue here after all, though it takes place on another level and with another double. *Film* is not closed upon itself. It both differs from, and defers to, other texts, and within that peculiar historical "space" it opens the possibility of dialogue that will challenge the characters' (and any other) quest for final unity or perfect identity. It is itself inscribed, that is, by and with other texts—literary (e.g., Sartre's *Nausea* and Beckett's other works), cinematographic (e.g., Keaton's other films), philosophic (e.g., most obviously Sartre's *Being and Nothingness* and Berkeley's *Principles of Human Knowledge*)—with all of which it may enter into, or among which it may provoke, something like a genuine conversation.

This is not, of course, to suggest that *Film* is merely in some ways a simple repetition of these texts. Neither can it be seen to complement them by providing some ultimate meaning or conclusion, nor even totally to confirm, support, or refute them. Beckett refuses to allow any philosophical meaning or thesis to be attributed to his work, including the significance of that very refusal.[15] Consider, for example, the statement that follows a series of apparent philosophical references at the beginning of the screenplay: "No truth value attaches to above, regarded as of merely structural and dramatic convenience." (*F* 11).

Beckett has elsewhere written that what interests him is the "shape" (rather than the "truth") of an idea, and his comments on Proust's explanations might be applied to his own: "His explanations are experimental and not demonstrative" (*P* 67).[16] Neither repetition nor completion, confirmation nor refutation, *Film* is, on the contrary, at once similar to, yet also always different from, all its textual "doubles." And it is this special difference that creates the possibility of somehow going beyond the impasse that Beckett's characters (here and elsewhere) appear to experience.

The general introduction to the screenplay begins with the words *esse est percipi*, signaling the importance of *Film*'s relation to Berkeley's *Principles of Human Knowledge*. One might, then, begin by following the course of this particular dialogue with one of Beckett's historical "doubles."[17] It will quickly become apparent that, whatever else it may be, *Film* is also an effort to work through the logic of Berkeley's chief thesis. This is not to say, however, that Beckett is a Berkeleyian or that *Film* merely repeats the latter's ideas. Rather, we shall see that Beckett is taking Berkeley seriously here in order to point up the weak spot in his generally fascinating work.

Now, Berkeley's *Principles of Human Knowledge* argues that "the absolute existence of unthinking things without their relation to their being perceived . . . seems perfectly unintelligible. Their *esse* is *percipi*, nor is it possible they should have any existence out of the minds of thinking things which perceive them" (*PHK* 23 sec. 3). Therefore, to the extent that *Film*'s O is a sensible thing (or "idea" in Berkeleyian terminology, i.e., a body), he cannot ever actually succeed in fleeing the perception of others—not, at least, without fleeing into absolute oblivion.

Indeed, from Berkeley's point of view, O can exist at all only *because* he is perceived. It is only in the act of being perceived that O is invested with sensible qualities, thereby coming into existence (*PHK* 60 sec. 78; also *TD* 186-87). Were he to escape perception altogether, he would no longer be. Hence, apparently taking Berkeley up on his proposition, Beckett shows that to attain (or maintain—Beckett's text is here ambiguous, *F* 11) a state of nonbeing, O must first suppress all extraneous perception, animal and human. He must remove or obscure whatever might perceive him.

Shutting out the everyday world, however, is not by itself enough. He must also eliminate God, for as Berkeley insists, "all objects are externally known by God, or which is the same thing, have an eternal existence in his mind" (*TD* 99). Beckett, then, continues to take Berkeley at his work and is visually working through the argument in its most forceful form. Yet, even after O has symbolically eliminated God the Father by tearing up the print, he remains anxious about the blank spot created on the wall by the representation's absence. And with good reason, for this is the spot into which E steps at that crucial moment of investment.

Self-perception replaces divine observation, it seems, and

maintains O in being. Following Berkeley's line of thought forward into the modern world-without-God, Beckett can reason that, from the perspective of our dominant subjectivist philosophy, one might still maintain with Berkeley that to be is to be perceived, since even when everything else has been successfully avoided, there is always perception by the self.

By thinking Berkeley's argument through in this fashion, Beckett has clearly carried it further. In fact, he has apparently felt able to distill the Irish bishop's principal thesis into a simpler form. For Berkeley's complete thought was actually: existence is perceivedness or perception or willing, that is, doing (*PC* 356 #429, 429a). Perceiving, he believes, is as important to existence as being perceived. Further, as one who perceives (however poorly), O must also be what Berkeley calls a *spirit*, his word for whatever entity is capable of perception (*PHK* 34 sec. 27; 22-23 sec. 2). Spirit, for Berkeley, is an active, indivisible substance, distinguishable from others by its sole possession of this unique power. Only spirit can perceive; whatever can perceive is, *ipso facto*, spirit.

In order not to perceive, then, (and therefore not to be), O must not only cut himself off from the world, but also shut his own eyes. This, however, proves unsatisfactory, since he is nevertheless still obliged to have awareness of himself in one way or another.

Beckett seems here to respond to Berkeley's two-part thesis by suggesting that the latter has failed to take account of self-perception. Given the way the perceiver of other entities may also become aware of himself as perceived, the two parts of Berkeley's formula can be reduced in the end to that single assertion with which Beckett chooses instead to begin: to be is to be perceived. The fact of self-perception means there is no entity to which this revised formula might not be applied.

It might be argued that Beckett has forgotten the part of Berkeley's complete statement that the Bishop later added on the back of his notebook page: "or *velle* [willing] i.e. *agere* [doing]" (*PC* #429a). To be is to be perceived or to perceive or to will, that is, to act. The writer, however, has not forgotten. O, in his attempt to find nonbeing, retreats into a state of inaction—seated in a rocking chair in the middle of a deserted room, alone and immobile, his eyes closed and his mind as blank as the walls. He would like neither to will nor to act, in order not to be. But the inevitable presence of his self, E, engaged in the act of self-perception, makes that total retreat impossible. (For how would one ever know that one was attaining it, except by being conscious of one's act, which in turn makes the attainment impossible? And how could the attempt be made except by an act of the will?) The self that perceives itself (or is conscious of itself), that is both perceiving subject and perceived object, is, at the same time, inevitably both willing and acting. Consequently, perception, perceivedness, willing, and doing are all comprehended in self-perception and, where self-perception is at issue, as it is here, Berkeley's position can once again be stated as "to be is to be perceived."

Both Berkeley and Beckett would agree that *Film*'s O can appear as both sensible object and "spirit." Berkeley, however, would understand this to mean that O is a sensible object in that he is perceived by others and, at the same time, "spirit" in that he is capable of perceiving others. Beckett seems willing to accept this, but then goes on to add that spirit itself is a twofold thing in its turn because it is capable of perceiving itself. That part of O which perceives him as a perceiving spirit is E. Beckett, in other words, has invoked the phenomenon of everyday self-consciousness—the mind's awareness of itself qua mind—and asks, in a sense, what Berkeley can make of it.

This, Berkeley would not find easy to do. His texts do indeed appear to suggest that the make-up of mind mirrors that of the world, and that mind will consequently have two aspects: "as it perceives ideas it is called 'the understanding' and as it produces or otherwise operates on them it is called 'the will' " (*PHK* 34 sec. 27). Understanding resembles an "idea" in that it is passive (like the Aristotelian substratum), while will, like spirit, is active, having the qualities of *velle* or *agere*. Will may therefore be called the "real" mind, and as an active force, said to be (like the Aristotelian substance, or essence) closer to the Divine Mind than mere understanding. The passive O, who simply perceives worldly ideas but is acted upon by E, may be seen as the understanding. E, the cause of the "agony of perceivedness" and the earthly substitute for God, would in turn be functioning like Berkeley's will.

E, as will, would consequently be capable of acting upon O so as to produce self-perception. Berkeley, however, specifically rejects this conclusion drawn from his own conception of the mind. Spirit, he asserts, although it has two aspects, is actually indivisible (*PHK* 34 sec. 27; also *TD*, 176). Without a distance or difference between the two aspects, no self-perception is possible. Furthermore, despite the resemblance between understanding and "idea," the former is not an "idea," but rather pure spirit. Berkeley insists that spirits and "ideas" are so "wholly different" that "there is nothing alike or common in them" (*PHK* 93 sec. 142; also 65-66 sec. 89). "That this substance which supports or perceives ideas should itself be an idea or like an idea, is evidently absurd" (*PHK* 90 sec. 135). Now, only "ideas" are sensible. So, if no aspect of mind is like an "idea," then mind itself cannot be perceived to any extent at all, and self-perception is, according to Berkeley, a consequent impossibility.

Film, of course, raises certain major objections to these concepts. If spirit and sensible "idea" are completely distinct and unlike one another, if will and understanding are perfectly indivisible, how then does spirit ever come to know itself? Only "ideas" are perceptible. How, then, do I know that spirit exists? How do I know that *I* exist? Again and again Berkeley returns to these obvious difficulties. The nature of spirit, he insists, is "that it cannot be of itself perceived," since it is not an "idea," "but only by the effects that it produceth" (*PHK* 34 sec. 27). Arguing from cause to effect is never very satisfactory, however, as Berkeley himself shows elsewhere. It does not seem sufficient to say that spirit necessarily exists, simply because man is capable of perception, willing, and understanding.

In the second edition of *The Principles of Human Knowledge*, Berkeley has felt obliged to introduce the rather puzzling term "notion," by which he intends to designate something resembling, yet at bottom entirely different from, ideas. He then feels he can meet the objection that results from his stubborn insistence on the impossibility of our having any idea of something [mind] that is entirely spirit, by arguing that "we have some notion of soul, spirit, and the operations of the mind" (*PHK* 345 sec. 27; 65-66 sec. 89; 90-92 secs. 135-40). Berkeley then went back and substituted "notion" for "idea" in every passage that discussed our knowledge of mind.

Yet, the problem does not actually disappear with this new usage, for Berkeley seems unable to explain very well exactly what a "notion" is. Indeed, although obviously disturbed by the implications of his originally wider use of "idea," he has trouble making its replacement here and there by "notion" seem a genuine change. Though the distinction, if it is to be effective here at all, must necessarily be a radical one, it is never very well established, being not so much argued as merely asserted. And, as a result, the insertion of "notion" has the appearance of a sleight of hand. The change seems a merely nominal device, more a disguise than a solution.

Berkeley took up this problem again in *Three Dialogues*. Philonous, the Berkeleyian immaterialist, asserts that "the being of my Self, that is, my own soul, mind, or thinking principle, I evidently know by reflexion" (*TD* 177). So we come to have a notion of self, not through *perception* but by "reflexion." But what then is "reflexion"? Earlier Philonous had explained that "my own mind and my own ideas I have an immediate knowledge of" (*TD* 176). "Reflexion," then, is "immediate and intuitive knowledge," an "inward feeling," while perception is knowledge mediated by the senses (*PHK* 65-66 sec. 89).

Spirit knows it exists because it "reflects" upon itself. And what it reflects, or mirrors, although always extremely inadequately, is itself an image or likeness of the Divine Mind (*TD* 176). Through its knowledge of itself, the mind has, *ipso facto*, intuitive knowledge of the divinity. Beckett then responds by positing a world in which God is no longer felt to exist, a world, that is, like our own, in which the mind's immediate knowledge of itself continues, but without bringing anything like a certainty of the presence of a divinity. Beckett leads us to consider, in other words, whether Berkeley's solution to the problem of the mind's self-understanding—his appeal to "immediate intuitive knowledge"—relies upon our belief in a Divine Mind of which our earthly minds are a more or less distorted reflection.

The answer, I think, is no, but Berkeley cannot feel himself entirely off the hook. Rather, it seems his theory of the mind's capacity for self-reflection never really met the basic difficulty in the first place. *Film*'s repeated emphasis on the staring eye is almost certainly intended as a visual metaphor for the more general problem of apperception. Whether or not we feel able to believe that God is the ultimate source and support of the mind's existence, the fact remains that the mind can have a conscious awareness of its consciousness, and he is asking Berkeley how this might be explained. Berkeley, for his part, has appealed to intuition or immediate understanding: the mind simply *knows* itself, and that is all there is to it. This he calls "reflexion."

Beckett seems to be suggesting that this remains unsatisfactory for at least two reasons. First, because self-consciousness is not something we just have, immediately and intuitively. The act of "reflexion" that produces it is, in *Film*, the result of a struggle. O is not normally aware of himself. In fact, his "immediate," "intuitive" action is to flee from the E(ye) of apperception, by covering over his "reflecting" glass and keeping E, his mirror image, at a non-"reflecting" angle (less than forty-five degrees). E must actively pursue his double, track him down, and force him into a confrontation. Reflection, Beckett is saying, is an arduous, active process that does not at all come about naturally or by itself, without effort. Our knowledge of the mind must be fought for and attained against our natural inclinations. On Berkeley's telling, there should be no difficulty to self-knowledge, everything about the mind should be at once accessible to itself.

For Beckett, this is manifestly not the case. We have managed to learn little and that only by dint of our great effort. In this sense, then, the mind's self-understanding is after all mediated knowledge, for it is attained through the process of that struggle. And second because, however that knowledge is attained, and whatever the name we give to the process of attainment, the fact remains that when the mind is conscious of its consciousness, the mind has knowledge of itself qua mind.

This makes the mind (a "spirit" in Berkeley's terminology) both the knower and the known. It is at once the subject and the object of the act of knowing. We see this suggested, of course, in *Film*'s presentation of its protagonist as two "distinct" bodies, E and O. And, however he may struggle to escape an acknowledgement of the dilemma, Berkeley with his doctrine of spirit and idea, each a unified, indivisible whole, absolutely unlike the other, has no very sound way of accounting for this sort of awareness.

Film then goes on to raise a second, related issue. When the mind reflects on itself, what does it see? Berkeley, often considered a Platonist in some respects, believes that sensible things have an "archetypal and eternal" existence within the Divine Mind, as well as an "ectypal or natural" existence within our merely created minds. Although only referring in this way to "ideas," his comments on how we have knowledge of God suggest that a similar distinction, archetype/ectype, might be applied to spirit (*TD* 176). From Berkeley's point of view, then, E's vision would be so clear because, like the Divine Mind, into whose place he steps in the modern subjectivist world ("E" at this point might also suggest the modern Ego), he knows and comprehends all things. O, on the other hand, as an ectype, could only know his own "archetype" (i.e., E)— and, indeed, all other ectypes—in a distorted and incomplete manner. His vision in *Film* is therefore always hazy and blurred.

When O and E, as archetype and ectype, finally confront one another at the moment of investment, the result, for Berkeley, could only be total (self-)knowledge, or perfect self-identity: an attribute of God. If E has taken the place of God, and is therefore, like that deity, all-seeing and all-knowing, then O's coming face to face with him should establish man's status as the being privileged with total self-understanding and, as a consequence, a genuinely complete identity. This is, of course, an equally traditional goal of Western metaphysics. "We see now through a mirror in an obscure manner but then face to face. Now I know in part; but then shall I know even as I have been known" (1 Corinthians 13:12). At this unique moment the ec-type/archetype distinction should disappear as the two are merged. Only a single united entity could remain (cf. *TD* 195).[18]

Now, is this what occurs in *Film*? Critics have often affirmed as much, for the closing scene, by bringing E and O into direct confrontation, certainly does suggest a moment of conscious self-perception. And, while the figure of E remains immobile and impassive, his features fixed in an intent stare, the figure of O appears to undergo a change. A look of astonishment comes into his face as he recognizes E before him. Open-mouthed, he starts from his chair, then sinks back, hands covering his eyes. There he sits, face covered, slowly and silently rocking back and forth as E continues to gaze at him.

One might well argue, as critics have, that in this prolonged moment of piercing self-perception, the protagonist, man, has come to know himself perfectly; the barrier between the parts of the mind has been broken, the two now coincide, E = O, and a whole self has at last been created.[19] *Film* ends, they imply, with the attainment of that longed-for state of perfect identity, oneness, fulfillment, the final realization, peace, Nirvana, nothingness.

But is this really what *Film* shows us? Is it really the case that Beckett agrees with the implications of Berkeley's logic and here offers us an image of precisely the sort of conclusions all his other work withholds and in fact does its utmost to undermind? Not likely. Closely examined, the final scene of *Film* makes such pleasing impressions impossible. There is indeed what seems a moment of astonished self-perception. But, as O sinks back into his rocker, the covered eyes do not suggest the satisfaction of fulfillment, of full identity. Rather, they suggest a continuation of just that desire the entire short movie has been built around: the desire to escape perception. O, by shutting off his vision, would like to escape the stare of E, the stare of *self*-perception and hence, of self-consciousness. Yet, he cannot. The camera cuts back to show us E still there, still with eyes fixed on O. In fact, the camera has moved in, and the image is larger, the stare still more intent. Despite the effort to avoid it, the degree of self-awareness has only increased. The camera reverts to O, who sits as before, face still covered, then back to E for what is in fact the closing shot. The camera has moved in so close that the screen is now filled by a giant, staring E(ye): self-perception remains.

At this point, it must be remembered that Beckett has, in *Film*, gone to extraordinary lengths to emphasize the fact that perception of any sort presumes at least two elements: perceiver and perceived. He has used this logic to point up the difficulty Berkeley would therefore have in explaining apperception. The significant thing to note about *Film's* closing scene is that the distinction between E and O is preserved. There is no merger or unification.

This brings to mind the title of the work, *Film*. A film is a piece of celluloid on which images are fixed and which produces an illusion of the presence of something else. It is, therefore, not the thing-in-itself, but merely an illusory representation. A film is also a haze, or mist, or any translucent material like the lens-gauze itself, that partially veils, making a direct view or contact impossible. The confrontation between O and E always occurs through a glass darkly; vision and knowledge are only indirect and partial. This is not only because O's vision is blurred. Both E and O are discovered, moreover, to be partially blind. Yet their visions do not add up to a whole, since each is blind in the same eye. This vision is partial for the spectator as well. Raymond Federman has argued as much (while, at the same time, seeming to misunderstand somewhat the overall implications). "Conventionally, the viewer of a film sees more than the characters in the film. One might say that the spectator has a total perception of the action whereas the characters have a partial perception. In *Film*, however, since the field of vision of the camera-eye never exceeds that of the protagonist, the viewer is denied total perception".[20]

Perhaps this is why Beckett thought unsatisfactory "any attempt to express the two separate perceptions in simultaneity (composite images, double frame, superimposition, etc.)" (*F* 59n. 8). Indeed O and E never appear together within the same frame; they are always separated by a "filmic" distance. Anything else would have been to introduce at least the illusion of totality. And it is this unconquered and apparently, for Beckett, unconquerable distance between E and O that, once understood, causes anguish. That *non*identity seen n E's stare is suffered by the characters.

Some critics imply that a unification is possible, but that both human vision (whether internal or external) and the film medium itself (or any medium for that matter) are tragically limited. *Film*'s efforts to make E and O "coincide" must, therefore, remain, they say, regretably "ambiguous."[21] Such a conclusion depends on the assumption that a realm of essential identity exists from which man is barred by his corrupted nature, a thoroughly traditional metaphysical assumption. If this were the case, then Beckett would appear to share some of the conventional aspirations of those thinkers with whom he is usually so often at odds.

Finally, the belief that E and O are at least supposed to merge, depends on a willingness to ignore the structure of the last scene's close. Here we see the camera cut, three times in succession from O to E, positively emphasizing the distinction between the figures and the fact that it is preserved. There is no reason to believe their failure to be united is merely the result of a flawed medium. E and O remain apart, even in the moment of self-perceivedness, because, for Beckett, all perception requires two, and this is true even of apperception. Hence, there can never be full unity of the self, nor any perfect self-identity—not, at least, that we would ever be aware of. This is Beckett's point against Berkeley's understanding of both the mind and its knowledge, as it is his point against the entire Western philosophical tradition.

While *Film* may, then, in certain respects be considered a dialogue between two humorous Irishmen, similarly involved in the perpetration of what might, and indeed has been, seen as an elaborate joke, it may also at the same time address one often ponderously serious Frenchman, Jean-Paul Sartre. Only a few elements of this second "dialogue" can, however, be suggested here. Returning to the general introduction to the screenplay, for example, we find the statement: "Search of nonbeing in flight from extraneous perception breaking down in inescapability of self-perception" (*F* 11). In "Sartrean terms," it might be said that the people in the opening scene (later cut from the movie) live in bad faith, content in their simple perception and perceivedness.

O, on the other hand, is different. Trying to maintain his own liberty, he shuns the Medusa-like stare of others that would turn him into a mere object. O might then be seen as attempting to preserve the pure and total freedom of the for-itself by flight from the world that objectifies man and imposes upon him the will of the Other. Beckett's first question would then appear to be, whether this ideal of absolute freedom, maintaining itself only through a complete self-sufficiency and independence of others, does in fact imply the perfection of a nullity (O, void, nothing, "non-being")?

A second question would seem to be, whether such a freedom could ever in fact be achieved at all? Alone in his room, rocking in his chair, and staring for a time at the blank walls before him, O does seem at last to have established his freedom from the impositions of the Other. He does appear to exist at this point in the perfect wholeness and self-containment of the in-itself-for-itself, no longer threatened by extraneous determinations or will. (Cf. *Nausea* and, of course, *Murphy*).

Now, Sartre does admit that such perfection is only man's impossible dream, but *Film* would seem to emphasize that point, to ask if it does not call into question the entire Sartrean project of human existence. Beckett indeed suggests that there can be no attainment of an integral harmony and absolute freedom to live in and for oneself alone. For, given the fact of self-consciousness, there is no possibility of an integral self-identity. One is always both consciousness (for-itself) and that "object" of which one is conscious (in-itself). The confrontation of the two in self-perception does not bring about their transcendence in some higher unity (in-itself-for-itself), but rather means that the self can never really escape the stare of that ultimate Other which is at once one's self.

This is not to say that the E of *Film* merely represents those demands and expectations of the world that have been accepted by the self, that is, that internalized Other that Sartre condemns as obliging us to live not in freedom but for-others. Rather, it is to argue that the Other is always already there within, prior to any subsequent internalizing of this or that external norm. E represents for Beckett the gaze of the self-conscious consciousness, and given its experience, he seems to be telling Sartre, one is always to some degree already an Other to oneself.

But *Film* may be playing with the Sartrean categories in yet another way. E might be seen as the for-itself, far freer than O, whom he pursues and torments. And O might then be the pre-self-conscious *en-soi*. The problem then raised is that Sartre maintains these are entirely dichotomous opposites, having in themselves nothing at all in common. *Film*, however, appears to be arguing that E and O are, in fact, doubles—different, yet in many ways similar. Dominick LaCapra, in his *Preface to Sartre*, raises this objection to the categories of *Being and Nothingness* in more explicit fashion:

The treatment of transphenomenality suggests a relationship between consciousness and being (or between the for-itself and the in-itself) in terms of an overlapping interplay between excess (*de trop*) and lack (*manque*). The for-itself is added to the in-itself in a way that indicates a lack in the in-itself which the for-itself simultaneously marks, creates, and attempts to fill. The for-itself is in this sense the in-itself as "differed" or displaced. And, in this sense, the for-itself is not pure and total freedom. It is "characterized" by an internal alterity, for it is the same as its "other" but as "differed."[22]

During most of *Film*, this "overlapping interplay" between E and O is hidden by the convention of the angle of immunity. It was suggested earlier that forty-five degrees might represent a point of balance between excess and lack. Whenever E desires however, he may increase the angle, thereby disrupting the equilibrium. At those moments of agony, the supplementary relationship between E and O is perceived, and the dream of integral unity shattered. *Film* might then be said to agree with *Being and Nothingness* about the impossibility of reconciliation in the in-itself-for-itself, but at the same time, to take issue with the sharp analytic distinction Sartre there tries to establish.

Finally, *Film* seems to imply that the impossibility of ever attaining the in-itself-for-itself—and it might be the understanding of this impossibility that causes the characters such suffering—need not always be paralyzing or encourage a Sartrean sense of the hopelessness of the human enterprise. On the level of the work itself, for example, we certainly do not find evidence of the sort of freezing horror that leads to sterility or despair. Here, on the contrary, the dialogue with *Film*'s textual doubles leads to creative discussion and to a rejuvenation of ideas and men (e.g., Berkeley and Buster Keaton). And if artistic sterility is avoided, it is not only because *Film* was made at all but also because the work, in taking stock of its doubles, does not merely rehearse their arguments in empty, repetitive mimicry; it also differs from them, contesting their conclusions as well as the distinctions on which they are based.

In turning now to *Krapp's Last Tape*, it seems possible to say that it repeats, but also develops and varies that confrontation with the doubles in the photographs O destroys toward the conclusion of *Film*: the doubles that are past selves. Krapp's doubles are, in this case, preserved on the magnetic tapes he has recorded for so many years on his birthday. Two of them are partially reproduced here. The sixty-nine-year-old Krapp listens to the tape (or parts of the tape) recorded thirty years previous. On that earlier tape, Krapp-39 comments on his replaying of a still earlier tape, one from "at least ten or twelve years" before (*KLT* 16). At the same time, *Krapp's Last Tape* seems to provoke a dialogue with its own past textual double, Marcel Proust's momumental work, a dialogue mediated through Beckett's early critical momograph on Proust. Although critics have long seen Krapp as a derisory Marcel, the extent of the possible "conversation" between them has, to my knowledge, never been sufficiently investigated.

The Krapp of today, like his textual doubles—his younger selves as well as the narrator of Proust's work—appears to be in search of things past. Not that he ever acknowledges that search to himself, however. On the contrary, at every stage he insists he is glad the past is past. "Thank God that's all done with anyway," sighs Krapp-69 (*KLT* 24). Indeed, the play ends with the voice of Krapp-39: "Perhaps my best years are gone. When there was a chance of happiness. But I wouldn't want them back. Not with the fire in me now. No, I wouldn't want them back" (*KLT* 28). "False ring there," Krapp-69's closing silence seems to respond, just as Krapp-39 had in fact responded to a similar statement made on the tape to which he was listening (*KLT* 17). Marcel would agree, for, at sixty-nine and wearing, like the guests at the Guermante's matinee, the ridiculous disguise of the aged clown, Krapp seems acutely aware that "night is drawing nigh-igh" (*KLT* 17). And approaching death brings with it the renewed desire to step out of time altogether, that is, to immortalize oneself by (re)capturing the past. "Be again in the dingle on a Christmas Eve, gathering holly, the red berrie. (Pause.) Be again on Croghan on a Sunday morning, in the haze, with the bitch, stop and listen to the bells. (Pause.) And so on. (Pause.) Be again. Be again. (Pause.) All the old misery. (Pause.) Once wasn't enough for you" (*KLT* 26-27).

So there is an element of truth in Krapp-39's reproach. For how else should one interpret the effort to record each year's high points and then listen to them repeatedly, except as what Marcel calls "the long resistance, disparate and daily, to fragmentary and successive death as it inserts itself into the entire duration of our life, detaching from us at every moment shreds of ourselves upon whose mortification new cells will multiply" (*RTP* 1: 671-72).[23] Thus, like the aging Proustian narrator, although in a very different spirit, Krapp attempts to re-member himself.

Proust's narrator did not have the assistance of the tape recorder, so that "in the light of habitual memory, the images of the past fade little by little, are effaced, nothing remains of them, we will no longer find it" (*RTP* 1: 643). For Krapp, however, each spool of tape, secure in its own little coffinlike box, preserves a portion of the past, a time dead and gone. Before "embarking on a new . . . (hesitates) . . . retrospect" (i.e., of the current year), Krapp finds it "a help" to replay the old "postmortems"—his pejorative term for any previous "retrospec-

146 BECKETT'S CRITICAL COMPLICITY

tive" (*KLT* 16). In this way, he can examine the causes of the death of his old self and the changes produced in his current self by the disease (or dis-ease) that is living. But the ravages will appear so great, Marcel might have warned, that Krapp will barely recognize himself, just as Proust's narrator had barely recognized Odette in the Avenue des Acacias at the end of "Swann's Way" (*RTP* 1: 427). Indeed, the entire project—the preservation of past experiences for purposes of a life's ultimate re-membrance—proves a dismal failure. Proust's narrator could, have told Krapp as much, if he had cared to listen. Krapp, however, is probably listening; he has to go on anyway, despairing, yet somehow still nostalgically hopeful.

The tape recorder—like every mnemonic device or the voluntary memory they are meant to assist—can at best only reproduce or "represent" past thoughts, dreams, and events as they were understood by the intelligence at the time they occurred. It cannot by itself derive any new meaning or ultimate significance from them. Marcel might add that, not being able to retain the affective or sensuous aspects, it forgets what is essential in any experience. (We will see that Krapp would take issue with that statement.) Besides, the listener changes over time, as does his relationship to any recollected data. Perhaps in this, his last tape, Krapp will arrive at an ultimate summation at last, bringing all his previous selves together. Unlike his protagonist at any age, the younger Beckett has already realized that "the multiple aspects . . . do not bind into any positive synthesis" (*P* 13).

Krapp at sixty-nine is not every younger Krapp simultaneously preserved, negated, and elevated to a higher combination (27-29 years + 39 years ≠ 69 years). There can be no summing up. In fact, it appears that Krapp, despite the aid of the tape recorder, is no better off than Marcel; he no longer even recalls the events to which earlier tapes refer. Their significance is now lost to him, beyond hope of recollection—what, for example, does the black ball mean? (*KLT* 13)—even when he can hear his earlier selves describe what once was fresh and real. "A small, old, black, hard, solid rubber ball. (Pause.) I shall feel it, in my hand, until my dying day" (*KLT* 20).

(Marcel might here interrupt to assure Krapp that he would remember were he to feel a similar black ball, just as the Proustian narrator had seen the entire world of Combray emerge from the teacup into which he had dipped his madeleine. Krapp would perhaps gruffly brush him aside.) The very words of the earlier tapes are no longer entirely comprehensible to him. His earliest hopes and dreams, first mocked at thirty-nine, are merely passed over in irritation at sixty-nine. "The aspirations of yesterday were valid for yesterday's ego, not for today," agrees the younger Beckett in his monograph. "We are disappointed at the nullity we were pleased to call attainment" (*P* 2-3). At sixty-nine, Krapp reflects on the past year and has "nothing to say, not a squeak. . . . (with relish) Revelled on the word spool. Spooool! Happiest moment in the past half million" (*KLT* 25).

Krapp's use of the tape recorder has not only failed to remember the ultimate Krapp, it is actually actively dismembering him. The stops and starts, pauses, fast forwards, and rewinds, fragment and distort time and have the same effect on Krapp's understanding. He is thoroughly unsettled, destabilized by the withdrawal of every fixed reference point in time and space. It is impossible any longer to establish any certain chronology. There is no longer even a definite idea of where to begin. And the play comes to a close with Krapp's replaying the end of the tape he had recorded at thirty-nine. Time, in *Krapp's Last Tape*, does not merely move linearly from A as beginning to B as end, neither is it merely circular, returning to where it began. But neither is it dialectical, suggesting some higher synthesis of beginning and end.

Like its Proustian double, *Krapp's Last Tape* presents time as moving both backwards and forwards without either clear chronological beginning or ultimate closure. Proust's narrator, for example, insists that a strict chronology would have deformed the novel, "our life being so little chronological, so many anachronisms interfering in the sequence of days" (*RTP* 1: 642). The time of conscious life is discontinuous. This is not to say, however, that time is mere chaos, a random jumble of moments without any order. Choice is involved in the selection of the fragments of tape Krapp plays, a choice that brings him back several times to a moment of particular importance—his farewell to love.

Nevertheless, to emphasize the differences between Krapp and his younger doubles (as between Odette, for example, and her other selves—the lady in pink, Mlle Sacripant, Mme de Forcheville, etc.) is to risk overlooking their similarities. "Yesterday is . . . irremediably part of us," the critic of Proust points out, "within us, heavy and dangerous" (P 2-3). Ruby Cohn catalogs these similarities well.

We see before us unkept Krapp at the age of sixty-nine, addicted to bananas that constipate him, to alcohol that he drinks offstage, to desire for women in fact (Fanny) and fantasy (Effie Briest). Sixty-nine year old Krapp listens to a tape made on his thirty-ninth birthday, in which he laments his addiction to bananas and alcohol and lingers over his farewll to love. In that tape Krapp speaks of a tape made ten or twelve years earlier in which he recalls his constipation and his addiction to alcohol and sex. Each age is scornful of those that precede it: in his twenties Krapp sneered at this youth; at thirty-nine Krapp finds it "hard to believe [he] was ever that young whelp" in his twenties; at sixty-nine he begins to record: "Just been listening to that stupid bastard I took myself for thirty years ago, hard to believe I was ever as bad as that." Each age has its ambition: in his twenties Krapp spoke ironically of "the opus . . . magnum"; when he was 39, we hear fragments of his vision of darkness, impatiently interrupted by Krapp; sixty-nine year old Krapp comments sardonically on what may be the magnum opus resulting from his vision; it has sold seventeen copies. Each age has its love: in his twenties Krapp lived off and on with Bianca; at 39 Krapp recalls the eyes of a nursemaid, but he dwells longer on a nameless woman in a boat; at 69 Krapp has to be content with a "Bony old ghost of a whore" whom he perhaps moulds into a fantasy of Effie Briest in Fontane's novel.

Cohn goes on to list linguistic repetitions that suggest Krapp has not even completely lost the vocabularly of his past.[24] The voices on the tapes, his doubles, now become strange to him; yet still with their occasional familiarity, they are different and similar at once.

Proust's narrator would certainly insist that we have forgotten the magical powers of the involuntary memory. That "immediate, total and delicious deflagration," as Beckett's own younger double remarks, "restores, not merely the past object, but the Lazarus that it charmed or tortured, but more because less, more because it abstracts the useful, the opportune, the accidental because in its flame it has consumed Habit and all its works, and in its brightness revealed what the mock reality of experience never can and never will reveal—the real" (P 20).

Like an "unruly magician," he continues, involuntary memory "will not be importuned. It chooses its own time and place for the performance of its miracle" (P 20-21; cf. RTP 1: 643). But the tape recorder has not forgotten, Krapp-39 remembers "that memorable night in March, at the end of the jetty, in the howling wind," that moment of apocalypse in which the "whole thing" was suddenly, unaccountably revealed to him.

The vision, at last. This I fancy is what I have chiefly to record this evening, against the day when my work will be done and perhaps no place left in my memory, warm or cold, for the miracle that . . . (hesitates) . . . for the fire that set it alight. What I suddenly saw then was this, that the belief I had been going on all my life, namely—(Krapp switches off impatiently, winds tape forward, swtiches on again)—great granit rocks the foam flying up in the light of the light-house and the wind-gauge spinning like a propellor, clear to me at least that the dark I have always struggled to keep under is in reality my most—(Krapp curses, switches off, winds tape forward, switches on again)—unshatterable association until my dissolution of storm and night with the light of the understanding and the fire—. . . . [KLT 20-21]

The great, involuntary revelation lasted only a brief moment, outside time and space. It was, like every great apocalypse its description invokes, a break in monotonous chronology, a tear in the fabric of mundane time. What, however, did Krapp see; what enlightenment did he receive? This "whole thing" that Krapp "saw," unlike the complete world of Venise that reappeared when Marcel stepped on the uneven cobblestones, is refused to the reader or spectator. Krapp-69 can tolerate hearing only portions from the tape that was meant to preserve the account of that revelatory "memorable night in March." As he now understands, life's "whole picture," particularly if it exists only as shattered associations and dissolution, cannot be captured and re-presented in a coherent discourse. Consequently, the whole idea makes him impatient, and he refuses to play the entire passage.

The involuntary memory, transporting the Proustian narrator outside time and space, allows him to recapture the stable part of things, events, and people, particularly himself, that is not subject to change. At thirty-nine, Krapp "sat before the fire with closed eyes, separating the grain from the husks. Jotted down a few notes, on the back of an envelope. . . . The grain, now what I wonder do I mean by that, I mean . . . (Hesitates) . . . I suppose I mean those things worth having when all the dust has—when all *my* dust has settled. I close my eyes and try and imagine them" (*KLT* 14-15).

The "grain," that core of valuable, meaningful experiences and qualities, is further explained by the younger Beckett, as "the essence of ourselves, the best of our many selves and their concretions", "the pearl that may give the lie to our carapace of paste and powder" stored in what Proust called the "gouffre interdit à nos sondes" (*P* 18-19). (Elsewhere Beckett ironically compares it to "the heart of the cauliflower or the ideal core of the onion"—*P* 16.) The snatches from the "memorable equinox" tape suggest that, at thirty-nine, Krapp perhaps discovered that there was only darkness at the heart of being.

Krapp-69, however, appears to reject even the possibility of such a negative essence. He finds only husks and no grain, only crap (late Middle English *crappe*, chaff). He no longer believes in an essential core curriculum for life, a series of vital experiences that shape the "inner" self and which, when isolated and totaled up, might reveal the true, the real, the essential meaning of existence. Krapp, unlike Marcel, no longer believes. His search for a totalized and totalizing essence has become for him nonsense, and its results mere crap. Despite the apparent awareness that neither voluntary nor involuntary memory can ever really unify the various doubles of the self that the stages of any life produce, a certain longing for such unity remains.

The thought of love, that sentiment which to the critic of Proust "represents our demand for a whole" (P 39), continues to exercise its attractive power over the aging Krapp, long after it has been dismissed by Marcel and the young Beckett as a "desert of loneliness and recrimination" (P 38). Indeed, long after Krapp himself has called it "hopeless" (e.g., KLT 22). Krapp does not need to hear Marcel warn him of that powerful seductress who offers such ecstasies of total identity with another only to leave the jealous lover alone and miserable. He knows it all too well. Nevertheless, he replays two or three times the "farewell to love" passage of the Krapp-39 tape. It is, in fact, this very taped recollection that follows the fragmented memories of "illumination. "My face in her breasts and my hand on her. We lay there without moving. But under us all moved, and moved us, gently, up and down, and from side to side. Past midnight. Never knew such silence. The earth might be uninhabited. Here I end—(Krapp switches off)" (KLT 21-22).

In a moment of love, in a moment of silence, the lovers seem to be one with each and the world. Marcel, as he watches Albertine asleep in her room, experiences a similar feeling of total and ideal possession, of her and of himself (RTP 3: 70). "I asked her to look at me and after a few moments—(pause)—a few moments, she did, but the eyes just slits, because of the glare. I bent over her to get them in the shadow and they opened. (Pause, Low.) Let me in" (KLT 22). If only it had ended there in total harmony and contentment. But no, time had not really stopped. Albertine had to wake up and Krapp had to carry on with living, with change and the impermanence of any "perfect state"—"winds tape back, switches on again." Indeed, the very act of carrying on, of beginning again, of replaying the tape (each replaying is, after all, a little different because of where it stops or starts) gives the lie to any apparent totalization.

The passage of time is not, however, the only enemy of unity. Turning again to Beckett's early work on Proust, we find a fuller explanation. "No object prolonged in this temporal union tolerates possession, meaning by possession total possession, only to be achieved by the complete identification of subject and object. . . . All that is active, all that is enveloped in time and space, is endowed with what might be described as an abstract, ideal and absolute impermeability" (*P* 41). "Impermeability" makes the "complete identification of subject and object" impossible. Krapp, in other words, cannot "get into" the object he loves. And the way in is through the eye—" but the eyes just slits, because of the glare. I bent over her to get them in the shadow and they opened. (Pause. Low.) Let me in" (*KLT* 22; cf. the tribute to Bianca, *KLT* 16 and to the nursemaid, *KLT* 19). The eye is the window to the soul, but it is also, as in *Film*, the source of perception that reminds one of the distance forever separating the lovers.

Krapp-69 has abandoned the active search for union with another in love, and yet the longing—weaker now, but seemingly never to be entirely extinguished—is still there with him, even in the depths of cynicism, disillusionment, and despair. He still reads *Effie Briest* with tears in his eyes at the thought of such an ideal lover (*KLT* 25). At the close of the play he returns to the "farewell to love" passage in response to that despair felt at the way his memory project implied a desired to recapture a past that seems only "old misery." Unlike Marcel, Krapp turns to nostalgic memories of love, rather than art, as night draws nigh.

I have suggested that Krapp cannot have any experiences of the involuntary memory because he does not believe in the existence of anything like an essential core of being. But the replaying of the farewell to love sequence does bring to mind the central passage of *Remembrance of Things Past*—the intermittences of the heart. Marcel had lost any living contact with his gradmother because of his egoism, so that her death had meant little to him. As he stooped down to unbutton his shoes in Balbec, however, remembering how she had helped him do that very thing at the time when he was ill, he felt profoundly, and for the first time, the depths of her love. But more importantly he realized for the first time that she was really dead—absent and lost forever. Through his experience, he became acutely aware of death, and of guilt, and of the need to redeem himself through the act of writing (*RTP* 2: 751-63). Similarly, it is the replaying of the farewell-to-love passage that

makes Krapp aware of all that he has forsaken. It is this sense
of irretrievable loss that colors the closing words of Krapp-39.
Love fails for Krapp as it failed for Marcel because he is "self-
centered." Would not Proust's narrator, like La Rochefoucauld,
insist that "love is self-love"? *Remembrance of Things Past*
may be read, not as a quest for reunion of the world or of others,
but ultimately as a quest for a center, for a true self, an unchanging I. *Krapp's Last Tape* is also, after all, the monologue
of a man constantly watching, or rather listening to, his doubles. Its protagonist, seated in a strong white light at the middle
of the stage is its center. "The new light above my table is a
great improvement. With all this darkness around me I feel less
alone. (Pause.) In a way. (Pause.) I love to get up and move about
in it, then back here to . . . (hesitates) . . . me. (Pause.) Krapp"
(*KLT* 14-15). Here, as before, Krapp's name serves as a comment
on his own statement. Not surprisingly, then, self-love brings
Krapp no nearer his goal of full, harmonious totality; he and it
are merely crap.

A masturbatory love of bananas doubles this narcissism.[25]
And bananas lead to constipation, that "unattainable laxation"
(*KLT* 17). Traditionally, this malady has symbolized both a rejection of interrelation with the world and with others, and the
attempt at perfect self-containment—to keep oneself whole by
refusing to relinquish a part of one's body (i.e., to be dismem-
bered).[26] But constipation is unnatural, uncomfortable, and generally impermanent. Where prolonged it brings sickness and,
eventually, an untimely death. *Krapp's Last Tape* seems to suggest the same may be said about our stubbornly enduring insistence on self-identity, on the reconciliation or retention in
unity (and hence, the ultimate eradication) of every conceivable
double, that self outside the self. (Perhaps, too, it is a comment
on love and sex seen only as a "desire for a whole.")

Just as Krapp is physically constipated, he is also literarily
constricted. He is a failed writer, having produced only one
poorly received book in his lifetime: "Seventeen copies sold,"
he remarks somewhat bitterly, "of which eleven at trade price
to free circulating libraries beyond the seas. Getting known"
(*KLT* 25). His writing, in short, is crap. This analogy brings us

back to *Remembrance of Things Past*. In his art, in the novel he narrates, Proust's narrator strives to make permanent his experiences of involuntary memory. But art does not offer Krapp the salvation it did Marcel. His own narration—found not in the published book to which he refers above but rather in the old ledger in which he records the contents of his tapes— does not lead to remembrance. Indeed, it must fail, not only for all the reasons previously suggested but more importantly because the creation of a work of art—even one based on self-recollection—remains always a form of self-alienation. The work is expelled from the writer; it stands away from him; it confronts him like a double.[27] The dialogue between *Krapp's Last Tape* and its doubles, *Remembrance of Things Past* and Beckett's *Proust*, then, opens onto the problem of art.

Like the people in the street scene that opens the screenplay of *Film*, content in simple perceivedness and perception, everyday life is unaware of the difference that makes self-identity impossible. Beckett's own earlier self once again reinforces the point. "Habit is a compromise effected between the individual and his environment, or between the individual and his own organic eccentricities, the guarantee of a dull inviolability, the lightning-conductor of his existence. Habit is the ballast that chains the dog to his vomit. Breathing is habit. Life is habit" (*P* 7-8). Or as *Godot's* Vladimir puts it: "Habit is a great deadener." When, however, something happens to alter that existence, like the sudden awareness of the nonidentity (implied, for example, by the fact of self-perception), man is shaken out of his boredom. "The periods of transition that separate consecutive adaptations (because by no expedient of macabre transubstantiation can grave sheets serve as swaddling-clothes) represent the perilous zones in the life of the individual dangerous, precarious, painful, mysterious and fertile, when for a moment the boredom of living is replaced by the suffering of being" (*P* 7-8)

In those moments of transition, of doubling, of the difference within sameness, the spacing or clearing of life (rather than its vacuity) is experienced. Man and his "doubles" are, as Heidegger has argued with regard to the entire problem of identity between elements, held toward each other and yet held apart facing each other, with an intensity that never lets up[28]—like O and E at the moment of investment in *Film* or Krapp before his unnamed love or his younger recorded selves. This carrying out of the relation between doubles might be described by the term *perdurance (Austrag)* used by Heidegger in his discussion of Being. It is this holding out that provides the anxiety of O in *Film* and the cynicism or nostalgia of Krapp.

But the "suffering of being" caused by nonidentity need not lead to sterile despair. Rather than being a pretext for hopelessness and the desire for death, it can be a source of renewed vitality. Beckett has described the "suffering of being," this *agon* within the self, as "the free play of every faculty" (*P* 9). Bakhtin goes even further in asserting that "the genuine life of the personality is played out in the point of non-intersection of man with himself." To attempt to unify life and, in one way or another, to put an end to all conflict and strife, is to opt for a condition of oppressive monotony and concord, the peace of stasis, the deathly silence of total agreement. "Never knew such silence," says Krapp at the moment of his most nearly perfect harmony with the world (*KLT* 22).

To sustain the conflict, however, is to keep open the possibility of a positive interplay of forces. This does not mean that all forms of conflict and struggle are desirable. But it does suggest that conflict in certain forms is quite clearly preferable to the frozen expression of conformity, or the totalitarian implications of the perfectly unified self or society. The suffering of life's conflict will, of course, involve pain, anxiety, and often worse; but it also keeps alive the hope of growth, of course, of an affirmative give and take between opposing elements. "To be," says Bakhtin, "means to communicate dialogically. When the dialogue is finished, all is finished." And no dialogue is possible where integral unity has been imposed or where dissidence has been silenced. Where dialogic strife has instead been maintained, there art and all creativity are possible. For, as the early Beckett of *Proust* observed, the suffering implied by the disharmony of existence "opens a window on the real and is the main condition of the artistic experience" (*P* 16).[29]

This nonidentity in sameness that causes the suffering of being—this interinvolvement of similarity and difference—is then also what gives rise to creativity. The work of art fixes within its design that dialogic relationship between doubles. It maintains them apart while nevertheless holding them together, so that the spacing experienced in those moments of interplay between elements is contained within it. Art is an arrangement of forces so as to bring about what Heidegger calls an "essential striving." By this he means that antagonists are encouraged to close in such a way that they "raise each other into the self-assertion of their natures. . . . In the struggle, each opponent carries the other beyond itself. . . . The more the struggle overdoes itself on its own part, the more inflexibly do the opponents let themselves go into the intimacy of simply belonging to one another."[30]

In this creative conflict, the adversaries behave in a double manner, at once concealing and unconcealing each other. Through comparison they reveal each other to the extent that they are similar and, in contrast, to the extent that they are different. Yet, at the same time, that difference can never be completely reduced to the knowable. Something is always denied or refused, if only because, in bringing one aspect or quality forward into the light, others must necessarily be for that moment relatively less important, played down, or even absolutely obscured. When any element is brought to stand in the light, it necessarily casts a shadow. The stronger the light, the darker the shadow. Even the sameness that seems to have been revealed will often in fact conceal the remaining degree of the double's irreducible alterity. The concealing/unconcealing, this creative strife is, for Heidegger, what occurs in the work of art.

And what I have called the dialogic encounters between Beckett's works and their textual doubles may be seen as such a creative strife. These discussions are not mere rehearsals of previous ideas. *Film* cannot be said simply to repeat either *The*

Principles of Human Knowledge or *Being and Nothingness*, or perhaps *Murphy*. Nor does *Krapp's Last Tape* merely illustrate *Remembrance of Things Past* or Beckett's own *Proust*. They differ from their doubles in marked ways that call into question underlying assumptions and conclusions. Neither, however, do they break completely with these earlier texts. Beckett is not Krapp merely replaying the tapes of great works, nor O simply destroying them. Nor is he a Proust or a Sartre attempting to sum up and transcend the past in an *opus magnum*. His way is similar but not identical—more painful but perhaps more fertile as well.

Beckett has described the creative process as "a step forward" that is "by definition, a step backward." Heidegger has expressed a similar thought: "The step back points to the realm which until now has been skipped over, and from which the essence of truth becomes first of all worthy of thought."[31] Such a step back necessarily involves an encounter with tradition(s) and what tradition has repressed. It can provoke a dialogue with one's predecessors, the "doubles" of one's text. And by dialogue we mean a certain give and take, a struggle from which one learns and thereby profits, a relation that at once brings out and heightens the degree of both similarity and difference with the double that is the opponent. By denying the possibility of total re-memberment, of perfect wholeness or identity, the confrontation with tradition's doubles—alike yet different— affirms the possibility of renewal, of continued reinterpretation, of new perspectives on our world. It is the affirmation of a living tradition and, hence, of life itself.

Art, then, might be described as an expression of man's inability ever to attain unity, full presence/absence, (w)holeness. It falls outside him; it stands at a distance from him; it doubles him and is his ultimate double. As such, art is a failure (*fallere*, "to escape the notice of," "be concealed from"). It is never perfect, either in its revelation or in its obscurity. And Beckett concurs when he explains that "to be an artist is to fail, as no other dare fail . . . [F]ailure is his world and the shrink from it desertion, art and craft, good housekeeping, living." But that is not to say that the artist's hands are necessarily tied by the "certitude" that "pure" expression is an impossible act. Nor, as Beckett's ironic formulation makes clear, should "this submission, this admission, this fidelity to failure" be turned into "a new occasion, a new term of relation and . . . the act which unable to act, obliged to act, he makes, an expressive act, even if only of itself, of its impossibility, of its obligation."[32]

Neither *Film* nor *Krapp's Last Tape* attains unified integrality on the level of the narrative. But this does not mean that they celebrate the supposed impasse of everything less, offering us only sterility and despair. On other levels, by exploiting the conventions of medium (film or play, camera or tape recorder)[33] and by engaging in dialogue with other texts, indeed, by the very fact of its existence, Beckett's work demonstrates that creativity is not only possible in a less than totalized world, but that a perpetual deferral of totality, or completion, may be the very condition of its possibility.

Perhaps then art really is a failure, for it leads the reader astray, causes him to be mistaken, even deceives and deliberately cheats him of that sought-after self-identity. And the artist is a deceiver, a liar, and a joker (has not Hugh Kenner called Beckett the "comedian of the impasse"?).[34] By pursuing a winding and tortuous course, full of evasive turns and shifts, Beckett-the-artist has overcome Krapp's malady. His works slip out of the impasse into creativity, giving the reader, the critic, even the writer himself, the double.

CHAPTER 5

The Solicitation of Science

In *Endgame* the protagonists act out on a mental stage various scientific and philosophical attempts to elaborate a totalizing interpretation of temporal existence. *Le Dépeupleur* [*The Lost Ones*] takes the hermeneutical process a step further in the direction of abstraction, presenting the reader with phenomenological analyses of a closed system. The analyses themselves are, however, neither static nor internally unified. They represent a constant struggle to describe with precision phenomena that repeatedly threaten to transgress the rational boundaries and categories employed. Moreover, a number of possible models are provided. As they begin to play variations on one another, rehearsing as it were the history of our traditional mode(s) of thinking, it becomes apparent that they can never be clearly distinguished, for they share certain basic presuppositions. They both illuminate and obscure one another, like Krapp's tape-recorded doubles, revealing unexpected overlaps and deficiencies. It is these troublesome areas that the narrator works to eliminate in his search for a comprehensive overview.

Similarly, the narrator's style, while carrying objectivity to almost autotelic extremes, is time and again confronted not only by its own subjective aspects, but also by the historico-philosophical context that it would bracket out. In order to complete his project and the "system" it is tracking, the narrator must rely increasingly upon repressive measures that ultimately even he cannot condone. Furthermore, his critical inquiry leads him in the end to question the validity of his proposed final solution.

We are evidently within the realm of science, broadly understood. The task is to investigate the nature and behavior of objects ("bodies") moving within a circumscribed space. At the start, several explanatory models are juxtaposed. One is anthropomorphic and teleological,[1] another geometric and static. The former describes the contained "bodies"; the latter, the container. The two models can, however, be related in the familiar terms of Platonic-Christian dualism.

The narrator observes the motion of numerous bodies within a container. He presumes that they are not moving randomly, agitated by heat or some unsatiated "desire." In an anthropomorphic gesture, direction and *telos* are attributed to them. Each is on a sort of quest, searching for means of release from this curious mode of existence. More specifically, every body is looking for something (or someone) to deliver it from the life it is leading: a savior, un *dépeupleur* (the text's untranslatable French title).[2]

But what or who is this longed-for *dépeupleur*? The most obvious answer, perhaps, is death, which in the classical-Christian tradition brings deliverance from the futile effort to find ultimate fulfillment in this world.[3] By removing the accidents of human materiality, which are bound to time and space, death restores man to his true or essential nature: spirit.

The Platonic foundation of the Christian (and to some extent the Schopenhauerian) form of this quest for true being also underlies the more optimistic Aristotelian worldview that has been fundamental to natural science, at least through the eighteenth century. Each body strives to realize fully the specific form that it always embodies in a virtual sense. This end still functions as a *dépeupleur*, insofar as all individual differences and particularities are eliminated on the level of the species, and each member is considered essentially identical with every other.

From the narrator's perspective, however, there is scant hope of any body finding the one thing needful within the cylinder: "Vast enough for search to be in vain. Narrow enough for flight to be in vain." (*LO* 7). Truly, all is vanity. The "one" they are searching for cannot be found, and the seekers are accordingly doomed to remain "lost ones" forever. The impossibility of reaching their desired goal is reflected in the shape of the abode itself. The cylinder brings to mind Dante's conical world, except that the vertex of final atonement has withdrawn to infinity.[4]

Internal agitation is not simply a bodily condition. All physical aspects of the cylinder contribute to it. The light, though omnipresent, is as inadequate as natural reason has repeatedly seemed whenever thinking is dominated by thought of an ideal realm. Without more illumination, or a better illuminated guide, every body appears condemned to restless dissatisfaction within this cavernous domain.

Both the temperature and the light, moreover, are in perpetual oscillation. When the latter is calm, so is the former— "more or less hot or cold" (*LO* 8)—inspiring some hope of stability. But that hope too is never fulfilled. As often as a stable mean approaches, it eventually moves away again. We might say that, although it may seem paradoxical, natural reason and the passions cooperate, the one growing dimmer as the heat of the other declines. Neither, however, remains at rest for long.

The instability of "light" and "temperature" makes it impossible for the bodies to attain that degree of self-integration that might serve as a substitute for the "lost one." Despite repeated disappointments, their desire for corporeal union, like their will to search, remains irrepressible. If only their mucus membranes had not dried out, but had remained soft and padded, they would have been able to absorb the blows that their more excessive agitations engender. Then, as on the rubbery surfaces of the cylinder itself (or *Murphy*'s padded cells), no trace of these irrational drives would have been perceivable, even if they could not have been entirely eliminated. The repeated return of these more-or-less skillfully repressed factors, their refusal to remain within the bounds of rational control and moderation, causes problems on all levels of cylinder life.

The only objects within the abode are a number of ladders varying in size and type. They suggest the various gnosiological schemas that men have employed in an effort to scale up to a commanding position from which they could explain the world and so bring it under at least cognitive control. Here they are used to reach niches in the cylinder wall or simply to leave the ground. Although they are in great demand, only the courageous dare to use them because they are incomplete. Their deficiencies are a consequence of unruliness within the cylinder society. The ladders have deteriorated as various components were taken for use in attack or counterattack among bodies. Moreover, no new ones can be fabricated or improvised and the old ones can only decay.

A desire to climb above the teeming arena is extremely widespread, indeed fundamental. Not to feel it is "a rare deliverance" (LO 10): a deliverance because the desire to climb upward can never finally be satisfied and is therefore a source of anguish to every body within this cylinder world. Their solution is to focus upon the means rather than the end, upon the mechanics of the climbing rather than upon the moment of arrival at one or another of the little niches they are able to reach, or upon the (perhaps only imaginary) way out that always eludes them. It is not, however, a very satisfying solution.

The niches, or alcoves, found in the upper half of the wall are of different sizes. Large enough to lie down in, they resemble the *loculi* of the catacombs, where the dead were laid to rest when their earthly searching was over. There, like the early Christians, the bolder bodies can find momentary refuge from the turmoil and violence of the arena. Some of the niches are linked by tunnels, though most have only one issue, not into a transcendent world, but only back into the cylinder. The narrator suggests that the tunnels were constructed by some bodies, and that the project may have been abandoned when they grew discouraged.

Tunnel making, like ladder building, is in any case not part of the present activity. No body actively seeks a way out any longer. At most the climbing ones retrace and investigate the established channels, even though it is fairly clear that these can lead only to dead ends or fruitless conflict. The tunnels suffer from the same dim illumination and murky climate as the cylinder itself. They too offer neither true clarity nor perfect stability.

Thus, the "first aperçu of the abode" (*LO* 13) blends together variations upon the traditional theme of longing: longing for a way out, for a proper end, for complete (re-)integration. More precisely, it reinterprets this theme in terms of a specifically post-Enlightenment sense of futility and despair. Suggestions of the more simply nihilistic longing at least for an end to longing are readily discernible.

The second paragraph introduces the reader to the organization of the bodies within the system and describes the psychosocial consequences of their teleological despair. The narrator distinguishes categories of bodies. The categories are then modified in different ways. The narrator in fact has trouble maintaining his neat distinctions. At first there are four groups: bodies that are always in (circular) motion; bodies that stop occasionally; the sedentary; and the nonsearchers. The last two are the most problematic. The sedentary have "conquered" a place of their own, only leaving it when chased and then only to find another. But, as the narrator must admit, "that is not quite accurate" (*LO* 13). The sedentaries are not truly so, for they occasionally experience a renewal of the desire to climb. Paradoxically, they are also the most violent. The nonsearchers mostly sit apathetically against the wall in the typical Belacquan pose: "the attitude which rung from Dante one of his rare wan smiles" (*LO* 14).[5]

These nonsearchers are really ex-searchers: bodies that have simply given up. To counteract the searchers' enervating example of hopeless dejection, the narrator supposes that the need to search may be resurrected (*LO* 15). The nonsearchers have in fact sunken into a fixed state analogous to death, and initially the hope of resurrection seems little more than a wishful thought with which to sooth the still searching. Elsewhere the narrator explains that a remnant of the desire to search does indeed remain in the nonsearchers (*LO* 32). It is, however, unclear what we are to make of this emendation. It may be a testimony to the appeal of that resurrection fiction. His initial neglect of the remnant may also testify to the narrator's eagerness to establish clear and distinct categories of being within the cylinder.

Death is not perceived, for it takes the form of a progressive decline, weakening, or languor. No body can imagine the final state, "when every body will be still and every eye vacant" (LO 15). At that point, the light will be extinguished and the climate fixed at (about) zero: the dark coldness of immobile matter. The light and heat of the cylinder system are linked to the life force within it.

This section of the text concludes with a qualification calling attention to the fact that all the narrator's observations, analyses, and predictions are hypothetical at best ("if [this notion] is maintained", LO 16). Variant, or even alternative interpretations, are evidently possible. The narrator may even be soliciting them. His commitment to "scientific honesty" requires that he retain a degree of ironic distance upon his own formulations and even modify them from time to time.

Although the third paragraph resembles a summary, it is also a second beginning. There is a strange almost desperate quality to the sentences, which are now more encumbered with technical information. One has the impression that the narrator is elaborating a more narrowly empirical description in order to shore up or even replace his bolder teleological interpretation. To some extent, then, his renewed approach to the cylinder involves the narrator in a double movement with somewhat paradoxical overtones. His technical exactitude brings him nearer to the phenomena he observes, but also takes from him a sense of their real significance.

This second description supplements the first, both adding and deleting information. The most important deletion is the *telos* of the search now no longer mentioned. The sense of unity that has been "lost" along with it is replaced by a mechanistic framework provided by the narrator's emphasis upon the regulation of the conditions within the cylinder or the methodical order of the searching. Bereft of his faith in a higher, otherworldly purpose, he finds consolation in a concern for technique analogous to that which, in his search for knowledge, has compelled him to abandon the presumption of ultimate ends. Gradually, the means, which had only secondary interest and value, become the supreme reality, truth, object of knowledge, but only insofar as they themselves form a perfect system.

Previously, we had regarded *le dépeupleur* as one who (re-) establishes a state of oneness by eliminating from life all its incongruent, inconvenient corporeal elements. He ab-stracts. In that case the narrator to the extent that he analyzes with the surgical precision that was Kant's (and also presumably Murphy's) is himself a sort of *dépeupleur*. His narrative shares that deadly, deadening quality that characterizes every attempt to elaborate closed systems purporting to account for life's complexities in purely "objective" terms.

But while the narrator becomes a *dépeupleur*, the text itself also criticizes that aspect of the analytic method. Exact empirical observations, the positive "laws" of the mechanism of the search, do not remain constant. Problems arise within the closed system of the cylinder, and we learn that the mathematical/scientific explanations of its processes and structure often include mere approximations. Without the certainty of a *telos* there can be no absolute knowledge. And now even the bits of knowledge, the little "truths" discovered along the way, prove so unstable and indeterminate that they could never add up to a complex, mosaic version of absolute knowledge. Eventually, the narrator reveals the existence of a fundamental conflict between the passion for searching and the ethos of the search. In practice, the aspect of need or desire always threatens to exceed or transgress the laws that control and regulate it.

The abode, for example, is a cylinder, but one that tends as much as possible in the direction of a cube or a sphere: sixteen meters high and approximately sixteen meters in diameter, "for the sake of harmony" (*LO* 16). Not, this time, the harmony of *Murphy*'s foursquare New Jerusalem, but that of the cylinder-inscribed-sphere that Archimedes favored. Of course, this degree of formal perfection can only be attained in fact by removing every excess and filling in every deficiency. One recalls the fact that *Le Dépeupleur* always provides dimensions only "in all round numbers" (*LO* 13). Here, as always, the problem is *pi*. The sixteenth (or 4^2) letter of the Greek alphabet, *pi* is itself a means of containing factors that disturb all linear calculation and thwart the desire for the purity of whole numbers. The geometric descriptions of the cylinder turn out to be idealizing fictions (like those of the *Timaeus*) that attempt to provide a sense of security and control by masking systemic disharmony.

An analogous incommensurability exists between scientific precision and moving bodies. The population is said to be one body per square meter, or two hundred in a round number. Just as the base area of the cylinder cannot be a whole number, the ratio of space to bodies cannot be perfect. There are either too many of the latter or too little of the former.

The twenty niches in the upper half of the wall are arranged in four groups of five, also "for the sake of harmony." Yet, these groups form "irregular quincunxes . . . cunningly out of line" (*LO* 11). The lack of regularity is deliberate, or at least is interpreted as such. The narrator would restore the symmetry that seems necessary by insisting that each side is "roughly" ten meters. He subsequently admits, however, that this is "a perfect mental image" (*LO* 12) that no body is likely ever to attain because of their imperfect predilections. Their empirical perception must be corrected by his incorporeal intellect. Irrationality, both in the structure and in its inhabitants, again appears as an obstacle to the pure analytic form.

This double irrationality reemerges in the discussion of the ladders. Material ancillaries of the organic bodies, the ladders share with them a fundamentally discordant relation to the cylinder's formal order. They lean against the walls "without regard to harmony" (*LO* 9). Their relation to the curved surface of the walls is formally irrational.[6] Moreover, the ladders are themselves asymmetrical, lacking rungs "without regard to harmony" (*LO* 10). These missing rungs are signs of violent excess within and between bodies. The function of these ladders—escape from the ground—creates a final paradox. They themselves exist in irrational relation to the cylinder, and their components may be used for irrational ends, but they are intended as a means of fleeing the unreasonableness of others.[7]

Paragraph three presents a stripped-down version of important but problematic statements made earlier. Because it leaves out so much, it might appear to be simply a reductive summary: an abstract. Yet, it adds more technical information. More precise knowledge, however, also brings new difficulties (e.g., the fact that temperature extremes converge) and irregularites (e.g., in the rate of temperature change and the intervals between ladders).

The irrational elements that the scientific formulations tend to obscure, return as well on the stylistic level, disturbing the mode of analytic precision. At this stage the desire to convey information manages to keep the puzzlement and self-doubt in check, but they are still apparent. John Pilling points out that "whenever a sentence exceeds a very short breath-pause, an awkwardness and potential ambiguity (quite foreign to the lapidary clarity striven for) begins to affect the surface of the prose."[8]

We might go further. There is an interplay of certainty and questioning, order and indeterminacy, whose intensity varies throughout the text. This interplay and its variations can be linked analogically to the Second Law of Thermodynamics as well as to a critique of that law, both of which play important, semiparodic roles in the functioning of Le Dépeupleur as a textual "system." In more literary terms, one may speak of a dialogic relation between different "voices" that reminds us less of Dostoyevsky's poetics than of Flaubert's "aesthetic" ability to be at once both clinically cold and ardently engaged.

Pilling astutely observes that "as the work proceeds the oscillation between dispassionate description and passionate involvement increases to the point where one is no longer certain quite which is which, and one begins to ask oneself whether the former is not in fact a more genuine commitment to the "lost ones" situation than the latter. But the personal note is kept to an absolute minimum in order that the times where it does intrude may strike with maximum force." It seems in fact that a reversal occurs; the "dispassionate description" of the value-neutral scientist becomes empathetic, while "passionate involvement" grows increasingly ironic and distant.[9] The convergence of opposites, or murkiness of categories, which is found on the level of plot is thus repeated on the level of narration.

If the cylinder world is a closed system, nothing can cross its boundaries in either direction. There can be no passage through its walls, from either the inside or the outside. The narrator therefore maintains that all hope of escape is vain. Nevertheless, many bodies continue to believe that there is a way out. And even those who do so no longer might again, so tenacious is their desire. The more scientific narrator scorns their faith in what is, for him, mere fiction.

Opinion is divided about the nature of this supposed issue. Some, the more materialist, believe that there is a hidden passage in one of the tunnels leading to "nature's sanctuary," "in the words of the poet." Like the Epicurean Virgil of the *Georgics* or certain of the Romantics, these bodies seek a way out of their predicament in a return to an immanent domain. Union with nature would return them to that "lost" state that (as perhaps a mythopoetic analogue of death) would bring freedom from the need to go on with their existence and provide them with an asylum.

Others put their faith in a trap door at the center of the ceiling leading to a chimney "at the end of which the sun and other stars would still be shining" (*LO* 18). Echoing in this way the last words of Dante's *Inferno* and *Paradiso*, they link this view with Christianity and all hope of transcendental refuge. The inhabitants vacillate between the two views in a movement analogous to that of the temperature and light. Such a philosophical "vertiginous tremelo between contiguous extremes" (*LO* 16) underscores the similarity between earthly and celestial sciences. Nevertheless, the more speculative position seems to gain ground. "This shift," we are told, "has logic on its side" (*LO* 19).

The "logic" of the cylinder involves a move away from the material toward the ideal. The narrator interprets it as an attempt to displace the sought-after issue to an inaccessible location rather than admit its nonexistence. So great apparently is their need to believe in salvation that every body avoids the very possibility of having it disproved. The narrator's irony increases and becomes a condemnation of all those who refuse to accept that their condition is without issue (i.e., without children, sterile, unproductive, etc.).

The shift also parallels the movement from the activity of the searchers to the contemplative posture of the nonsearchers, a move with which the narrator seems to have more sympathy. Here, one wonders whether the grim "end" that the narrator anticipates for the cylinder world is not a way out as mythical as those in which the bodies believe and does not presuppose another that is at bottom not really so different from the delusions he scorns in them.

The fictional nature of that end is first implied by his words—"always assuming they are darkward bound" (*LO* 20) as well as by his description of what he takes to be the cylinder's general entropic process: "all should die but with so gradual and to put it plainly so fluctuant a death as to escape the notice even of a visitor" (*LO* 18). Only someone "in the secret of the gods" (*LO* 19) or with "a theoretical perspective" ("une vue de l'esprit"—*LD* 11)" could know how it is all going to work out, for this cannot be ascertained from within the cylinder itself. It depends, in other words, upon the attainment of a perspective outside the system, upon the discovery of a way out.

The narrator next develops the implications of his belief that, extended vertically, the longest ladder would permit somebody to explore the otherwise inaccessible zone of the ceiling. This would, however, require cooperation and here there is only the violence of Babel after the failure of a similar project. Curiously, it is the need to maintain the hope of a way out that prevents concerted effort. No body wants the myth to be destroyed by being proved either true or false. Possibly every body already suspects it is false but wishes to continue believing. What is important for these somewhat violent "amateurs of myth" (*LO* 21) is, as Sorel might have said, the belief in an ideal and not the way out itself.

Once the way out has been dismissed as a fiction by the narrator and put safely out of reach as a necessary myth by the cylinder's inhabitants, the discussion turns to the method of the search, just as attention had earlier shifted from a teleological interpretation of the cylinder to a mechanistic one. The prime aspect of the search is its conventions, now rigidified into laws, governing the use of ladders. The "system of justice" in the cylinder dictates that some infractions will pass virtually unnoticed while others will lead to unrestrained reprisals.

These conventions were established to maintain a certain level of intensity. Some keep the system from stagnating; others keep it from slipping into pandemonium. Either too little or too much activity would be detrimental to the cylinder's continued functioning. Those actions that would reduce the amount, however, are considered less offensive than those that threaten to intensify it. The former are easily pardoned, the latter violently punished. It should be noted, however, that although those who indulge in moments of quiet, either in niches or on ladders, are viewed with understanding, in general the conventions work to keep the maximum number of bodies in motion and encourage movement back into the arena of society rather than out of it.

Paragraph 7 adds another law to the code of the ladders. When moved from one niche to another, they must be transported in a clockwise direction along the wall within a track one meter wide. Nevertheless, it is only those who carry the gnosiological ladders who must follow the temporal arrow. The searchers-watchers move counterclockwise and the searchers in the arena as they will. In the cylinder "as a whole," in other words, the searching is neither unidirectional nor irreversible.[10] If the ladder carriers were free to move in whatever direction they chose, however, chaos would impend. Their movement, like that of everyday time, must be irreversible.

In general, despite the narrator's initial claim that the bodies are searching (for a *dépeupleur*), the *telos* is far less important than the continuation of motion. Conventions are established to keep the cylinder society functioning for its own sake, rather that to bring it to any end. There is, then, a basic tension within the cylinder world between two extreme conditions: stasis and chaos. Both are ultimately detrimental to the continuation of the system. Yet, while the latter is viewed as dangerous and therefore undesirable, the former is viewed more leniently.

Nevertheless, both are necessary in some form and never appear totally separated from one another.

This tension reappears in the narrator's extended discussion of the categories of bodies and their characteristics. If, by containing disorder, the "ladder laws" constitute a formal analogue of the cylinder itself, so the narrator offers another by trying to inscribe the various forms of violent agitation within a regulated hierarchy of attitudinal types. Yet, here too repressed forces flare-up unpredictably to threaten the organizational structure.

On the ladder track are found the climbers, the carriers, but also some of the sedentary. The sedentary are called semisages to distinguish them both from the true sages, or nonsearchers, and the foolish or agitated who continue to search. The semisages are, for the searchers, the object of a cult, or at least of deference, despite the fact that, impeding movement, they are somewhat bothersome. This cult of what is in fact a form of the contemplative ideal can be traced back through Plato to the Pythagoreans and beyond. In Aristotle's *Nicomachean Ethics*, it leads to the distinction between two kinds of wisdom: *phronesis*, or the practical wisdom derived from the study of changing things, and *sophia*, or the theoretical wisdom derived from the contemplation of unchanging truths. The wisdom of the sedentary is of the second, higher sort, but it remains only "partial," or impure, because they are not completely deaf to the call of the ladders and are given to fits of violence when not treated with adequate respect. Only the nonsearchers, true sages in the classical-Christian sense, are really passive and dead, as it were, to the world. They are apparently will-less, having conquered all desire, including that desire to retaliate that occasionally afflicts even the sedentaries.

Turning to the searchers and their practical wisdom, the narrator identifies three subcategories: the climbers, the carriers, the searchers in the arena. The last is further divided into those "devouring with their eyes" the climbers and "the main body of searchers" (*LO* 29). The former, tired of searching in the arena below, have turned to envious staring at those who climb.

Each of these forms of searching is associated with a conventional philosophical topos: that of the climbers and the carriers with the ladder, that of the searchers in the arena with sight. From the Bible through Wittgenstein's *Tractatus*, the ladder has referred to the search for essential knowledge and, more precisely, to the means or method of attaining it. Similarly, cognition has traditionally been represented in terms of "the desire to see." Searching with the eyes, however, is not the same as searching with the ladder, although there are affinities. Eyesight relates more to empirical observation: the mere collecting of facts in the manner of the early scientists. The still-active searchers speculate or theorize on the basis of the experience acquired in their wanderings, but do so without the rigid methodological ladders of the climbers.[11] This allows them more latitude but also less support for rising upward.

These two paths to knowledge never merge within the cylinder world (although they are never entirely cut off from one another either). The ladders are not used by either those who devour with their eyes the climbers or those who wander about the arena; the climbers and carriers do not use empirical vision to situate their ladders (*LO* 56). Only in the narrator are the two modes of acquiring knowledge combined. From a superior vantage point he observes and speculatively elaborates its system. For example: "Which suitably lit from above would give the impression at times of two narrow rings turning in opposite directions about the seeming precinct" (*LO* 29). The conditional quality of this angle of vision, however, points up the hypothetical nature of the narrator's knowledge of the system he is describing. His empirical observations have been corrected and improved by the addition of data not available through conventional sense perception.

Within the system some relation between eyesight and the quest (presumably for knowledge and in particular for knowledge of the way out of this world) is at least nascently present in every body, however undeveloped in those who climb the highest. Searching is fundamental to every body's life. Indeed, it almost begins with life itself. Babes in arms seek almost actively with the eyes: "a mite who strains away in an effort to turn its head and look behind" (*LO* 30). Toddlers explore the floor of the arena.

Only the vanquished apparently search no longer. To the "eyes of the flesh" they are indistinguishable from other bodies. They can do everything others do; they are not necessarily immobile. The essential is that they do not see and have abandoned the quest. Every body keeps his eyes lowered most of the time. The vainquished alone, convinced that the end is in vain are "in search of nothing" (*LO* 31). They see nothing; they seek nothing. Of course, "nothing" may also be an end, one that is particularly *dépeupleur* and therefore not the least vain. The quest for it has a long and familiar history in both East and West. Wherever the sense of futility prevails, to see "nothing" is to have attained the highest insight or knowledge.[12] Seated or standing against the wall, these "vanquished ones" are in any case frozen in a fixed space, and in a rigid position, "profoundly bowed" (*LO* 31). The only exception is one who is "stricken rigid in the midst of the fevering" (*LO* 31), like the madman in the Magdelena Mental Mercyseat or the celabrated *sunnyasin* of ancient India. Yet, even the vanquished are still subject to renewed fits of the "old craving" (*LO* 31): "Then the eyes suddenly start to search afresh as famished as the unthinkable first day until for no clear reason they as suddenly close again or the head falls" (*LO* 32). They thus repeat on a deeper level the experience of the climbers who have given up yet occasionally return to their ladders.

At this point the narrator touches upon features that make it difficult to fit the vanquished into his system. First, they cannot be distinguished empirically ("to the eyes of the flesh") from every body else. How, then, can he know they exist? His knowledge must derive from some intellectual complement of his sensible experience. Secondly, even if the vanquished have abandoned the search, their will to take it up again has not been totally denied; and consequently they have not withdrawn completely from cylinder life.[13]

This image of the vanquished inspires an attempt to formulate the cylinder's principle of regression. The narrator offers two versions. The first is elusive: "So true it is that when in the cylinder what little is possible is not so it is merely no longer so and in the least less the all of nothing if this notion is maintained" (LO 32). The first part of this "sentence" suggests that the absence of even the least bit is really only its disappearance. The second half can be interpreted in a number of ways. It may mean that in the smallest quantity, nothing is everything. The problem with this interpretation is that even "the least less" cannot be equated with "nothing." Even its absence would not leave absolute nothingness, but merely the absence of some thing: not an immaculate negativity, but a space that has been marked by the presence of the thing that has departed; not nothing, but to recollect the Democritean distinction which played such an important role in *Murphy*, no thing. Moreover, if that thing has only withdrawn, it might yet return. Its "re-entrance" upon the scene is facilitated by the fact that in "withdrawing" it has left traces of its passage. It would not be arising *ex nihilo*.[14] Another interpretation would read the latter half of the sentence to mean that what is missing from the least is complete nothingness. There is still something there, even in the very least bit.

Both interpretations (and there may well be others) work against the idea that the cylinder system will ever attain that state of perfect nothingness so often regarded as the desirable or inevitable *telos*. This accords with the conviction that no *dépeupleur* will ever be found and that therefore the search is vain. But it also casts doubt upon the possibility that any body can ever reach the state of perfect will-lessness that complete resignation represents. None of the vanquished will ever be a Schopenhauerian ascetic. In addition, the possibility of the cylinder ever reaching any absolute state—absolute stasis, absolute zero, absolute darkness—becomes equally questionable.[15]

To get out of this impasse, the narrator tries another formulation. "Even so a great heap of sand sheltered from the wind lessened by three grains every second year and every following increased by two if this notion is maintained" (LO 32). As in *Endgame*, however, this more quantitative or mechanistic concept of the process signals a problem underlying the narrator's entire investigation. For, of course, the grain metaphor merely returns him to the impasse when eventually there are only two grains left. The process cannot continue; the pile can never be reduced to nothing.[16]

This second formulation of the putative process of dissolution within the cylinder also has certain affinities with the Second Law of Thermodynamics, which Kenner has tried to relate to the disintegrative tendency in Beckett's work.[17] The Second Law determines the direction of thermodynamic processes. Although, according to the First Law, energy can never be lost, it may become unavailable for mechanical work. The less available energy, the less effective the functioning of the system. Its "disorder" increases and consequently its degree of entropy.

In general, any spontaneous change in the physical or chemical state obtaining at any given moment within the system, any redistribution of energy among its components, will cause disorganization and therefore will increase entropy. Heat flows from warmer to colder bodies only until the temperature of the two is equal. The system then becomes thermodynamically stable. Entropy is at its maximum. By contrast, perfect "order," or zero entropy, means maximum effective work within the system. Perfect order could only be reached, according to the Third Law, at zero degrees Kelvin, that is, at absolute zero.

There have been various attempts to apply the Second Law to systems other than those created by the controlled experiments of thermodynamics. Such attempts are not without relevance to the multiple levels of Beckett's text. For, as we have seen, the cylinder functions as a scientific phenomenon, a societal system with a history of sorts, and a hermeneutical structure. Like the Second Law itself, these textual analogues may be critically sounded in a manner that produces wider cultural resonances. In fact, the text itself suggests certain objections, either directly through the narrator or indirectly through what it reveals about the world it describes.

Doubts about the theory of entropy were first expressed in the late nineteenth century when the original mechanical proofs were shown to be untenable. A revision in terms of statistics was suggested: any closed system tends toward an equilibrium state of maximum probability. This statement had subsequently to be reformulated to accommodate entropy increases and decreases. The overwhelming tendency of the system, however, was still in the direction of thermodynamic equilibrium. In its final form—Ehrenfest's version of Boltzmann's statistical definition—the Second Law describes the situation envisioned by Beckett's heap of sand "sheltered from the wind." Its grains of sand are assumed to be monadic or indivisible units, since the findings of thermodynamics do not apply to atomic and subatomic states, where, to be sure, things become a bit more complicated.

Even in an equilibrium state, for example, the arrangement of molecules and the distribution of kinetic energy among them will change continually (cf. Brownian motion), yet thermodynamics cannot distinguish between these different microstates. A branch of macroscopic physics, it deals in averages and takes no account of such small-scale fluctuations. On the subatomic level, quantum physics affirms the unpredictability (and apparent acausality) of both particle emissions from a radioactive element and the transition of electrons from one energy level to another within the atom.

Beckett's cylinder may also be regarded as an image of the universe as a whole. Does the classic principle of increasing entropy still apply? Clausius thought it did. Helmholtz even elaborated a "theory of thermal death," which envisioned a day when all physical factors had run down to a uniform temperature and so become stabilized. All natural processes would cease, and the world be "condemned to a state of eternal rest."[18] More recent research fails to sustain this theory. There is no evidence that the universe as a whole is headed for thermodynamic equilibrium.

But what relevance does the entropy principle have for living bodies, either in the cylinder or in the world?[19] Does the Second Law of Thermodynamics help to understand the life processes? Is life merely linear, irreversible dissolution ending in death? Living bodies are not grains of sand—atoms, points, simple bodies. More complex, they are apparently less predictable. Historically, the application of the entropy principle to biology has

been connected with the conflict between biological mechanism and vitalism, a conflict that replays theological debates
over determinism and free will.

Biological mechanism, however, shares with classic thermodynamics the problem of dealing with observed entropy fluctuations. Statistical reformulations are once again somewhat
better able to manage such differences but ultimately tend to
disregard them. Like the heap of sand image, or the narrator's
cylinder model, biological mechanism works to eliminate the
unpredictable so that life can be fitted into neat causal patterns.
Mechanistic biology can accordingly be described as another
dépeupleur. To say this does not necessarily mean turning instead to a vitalism that posits uncaused causes, such as Bergson's vital impulse, Auerbach's ectropic principle, or the
narrator's hidden motor force, in order to account for the apparently spontaneous reemergence of "heated activity" in
seemingly cold bodies.

Returning to the vanquished, the narrator must admit that
they have "still some way to go" (*LO* 32). They have not quite
sunk into entropic stasis. They have stopped searching actively,
but the will to continue has not been fully quieted. They are
still ex-searchers rather than nonsearchers. Their lives are
marked by an absence of searching in which a trace of activity
(suggested by their chronic "old craving") remains. And so,
"what better name be given them than the fair name of searchers?" (*LO* 32). Accordingly, the active/contemplative opposition becomes tenuous and with it the narrator's hierarchy of
categorical distinctions.

Nevertheless, the narrator reaffirms in a slightly modified
form his initial categories of bodies: (1) those who search con-
tinuously ("the searchers"); (2) those who stop momentarily
but still search with the eyes ("the searcher-watchers, or simply
watchers"—*LO* 45); (3) "the sedentary searchers," who have
given up the search for various reasons; (4) "the vanquished."[20]
Looking at these, "an intelligence" might still be inclined to
see a progression down a "ladder" of "energy" levels leading
to relative immobility (*LO* 30)[21]. In fact, however, the overall
direction of progress is not that easy to determine. Though a

"downward" tendency seems to predominate (witness the ladder law), "upward" movement has not disappeared. A sedentary searcher can still become a searcher; a vanquished can become a sedentary searcher and, presumably even a searcher.

The narrator, seemingly unaware of the problems he has stirred up, sets out to indicate how many bodies there are in each category. His computations bring the population to 205, although his love of round numbers leads him repeatedly to prefer the figure 200. His exact count uses the number of vanquished as a basic reference. Rounding down to 200 suggests they are not counted into the final total. This raises the question of whether the vanquished exist as anything except a kind of fiction. (Even the narrator now refers to them as "the so-called vanquished"—LO 35.) Indeed, the uncertainty of categories suggests that it is ultimately impossible to fix the identity of any body in anything but a relative fashion. The difficulty of identification thus extends well beyond the domain of kinship relations where the narrator first enounters the problem (LO 36; LD 32).[22]

Given the fact that movement between categories is still possible, one may wonder what life was like at the "beginning" of the cylinder world? The "beginning," like the "end," of the cylinder world, remains "unthinkable" (LO 34). Unthinkable, in the sense that arche and telos are beyond the limits of human comprehension, or because there are no mathematical or instrumental means of ascertaining them, or because they are truly indeterminate?

The narrator does not explain; he merely offers a hypothesis, apparently extrapolating from his observations of the cylinder's present state: "All roamed without respite including the nurselings in so far as they were borne except of course those already at the foot of the ladders or frozen in the tunnels the better to listen or crouching all eyes in the niches and so roamed a vast space of time impossible to measure until a first came to a standstill followed by a second and so on" (LO 35).[23] At the beginning, then, everything was much the way it is at present, except that there were no immobilized ones, no vanquished. Bodies were already stopping in order to wait or listen but more or less complete immobilization—for it is never, or not yet, quite complete—represents a change from the "original" functioning of the cylinder.

Speculations about the origin do not, however, seem as important to the narrator as analysis of the actual system. The moment of observation is what matters: "at this moment of time and there will be no other" (*LO* 35). If he could arrive at a full explanation of the cylinder world, perhaps reducing it to a small number of fundamental principles or even to a single covering law, questions of archeology and teleology would be superfluous. The system would have already attained the functional sort of schematic perfection that so delighted Kant and the scientists, like LaPlace and Helmholtz, who followed him.

From the categories of bodies and all the problems associated with them, the narrator returns to the physical conditions of the cylinder itself, developing in greater detail aspects first mentioned in paragraph three. The models he employs, although historically and philosophically different, nonetheless all have difficulty dealing with certain factors, for example, the relation of continuity and discontinuity over time. The narrator would clearly prefer to elide such problematic aspects, but scientific honesty requires they be mentioned. Many are so important that they have contributed to the undermining of the Aristotelian/Newtonian worldview and the rise of the quantum theory. Like Einstein, the narrator often seems reluctant to accept the more radical implications of his own formulations.

First the light attracts his attention. It is of a curious sort—feeble, yellow, but with a weak sensation of red—suggesting the sulfurous half-light of Hell or the redshift of the Doppler effect. It is also unsteady, vibrating at a high but perceptible intensity varying between two and three candles. Moreover, these vibrations are not perfectly continual. When they stop, so does all activity within the cylinder. These periods of calm—called scare or respite, depending upon one's attitude—are very short, lasting only ten seconds. Then the vibrations begin again and everything returns to "order." The murmur of the cylinder also returns. The most distinctive aspect of the noise, and the only one that never varies, is that made by the light itself—"a faint stridulence as if insects" (*LO* 38)—reminiscent of the "noise" made by the thermal agitation of electrons.

The tendency for the light to shift to the red (as in the Doppler effect) suggests, moreover, that this world is moving away from its Source of Light. Thus, it resembles as well the fallen world of Platonic-Christian cosmology. In this world, there may even be no central light and therefore no ultimate reference and means of illumination. Often the narrator speaks as if there were one, but he cannot know for certain ("one or more visible or hidden sources"—(*LO* 39-40). And there is even the possibility that the narrator himself, by a Cartesian substitution, is the one who sheds light on the cylinder world.[24]

The nature of the light gives it paradoxical effects. At the same time it enlightens, it also obscures and confuses, by making it difficult for the eye to adapt. The sense of sight is impaired and eventually ruined by the oscillating murky yellow. The latter thus provides an image for the uncertainty and even treacherousness of all knowledge within the cylinder, as well as for the attendant disappointment, and even moral distress, of those who nonetheless desire to "see" things.

Their "eye-problems" allude to the ways in which the difficulty of reaching certain knowledge in this world has traditionally been explained. The fluctuating light of the cylinder suggests the distressing ambiguity of temporal existence. With no more hope of a way out, every body tries to remain satisfied with escapist myths. They do continue as well to search for the lost One, whose relation to the Way out is never specified and whose very existence has likewise become implausible. The worn but familiar methods and means of searching are retained and vary only in insignificant ways. The more they are used in the flickering light of their cylindrical cavern, the more every body's ability to "see" deteriorates. An analogous situation arises on the narrative level. The light is strong and regular enough for a detached observer to discover a certain "ladder" and to hope for the discovery of a comprehensive system. Yet, he cannot account for the light's sporadic discontinuity, its nagging irregularity. This and other inadequacies gradually undermine the narrator's confidence in his ability to see the full truth about the cylinder world.

The situation of the nonsearchers appears even worse. Unable or unwilling to endure the prospect of endless striving, they have given up. To call them vanquished, of course, implies that, too weak to struggle on, they have succumbed, in Jansenist-existential bad faith, to metaphysical despair. Yet, by also implying that they are in fact the wise, the narrator shows that he remains open to a more "positive" evaluation of their withdrawal from the search.

A truly objective observer—"the thinking being coldly intent on all these data and evidences" (LO 39)—might decide that the term *vanquished* had "the slight tint of pathos" (LO 39).[25] How would the objective scientist interpret the behavior of the nonsearchers? He might well conclude that they are simply blind. If so, it might not be objective reality that defeated the desire to see or know. Rather, the deficiency might lie with the searcher. Those blessed with better eyes might be able to "see" more adequately.[26] The narrator rejects this possibility, and keeping to the moral high ground, he insists that the problem with the nonsearchers is, not that they are less well equipped by nature, but that they have lost the will to carry on (LO 35).

Another unusual aspect of the light is its universal quality: "as though [the entire space] were uniformly luminous down to the least particle of ambient air" (LO 40). This luminous air reminds of Descartes's "subtle matter" or Newton's ether, both reworkings of the Stoic *pneuma* that pervaded all matter and interacted with opaque bodies (cf. LO 36-37). The ether concept was in fact fundamental to both the older mechanistic worldview and the plenum theories of continuous and indefinitely divisible matter. Thus, it is quite understandable that the "ladders" traditionally associated with comprehensive world systems should seem, because of the ether, to give off light rather than receive it (LO 40). The narrator's comment, however—"with this slight reserve that light is not the word"—suggests some doubt about the knowledge they bring. The luminous ether theory itself, moreover, ultimately came to grief over the problems that arose when bodies interfered with one another.

The temperature also oscillates, but more slowly than the light and between extremes that are farther apart. The slowness of the temperature shuttle vis-à-vis the light shuttle is perplexing only until analysis discovers that the difference is not in speeds but in distance covered. The two effects are therefore comparable. Indeed, the discovery of a common essence all but eliminates the difference, "and if [the space traveled] required of the temperature were reduced to the equivalent of a few candles there would be nothing to choose mutatis mutandis between the two effects" (LO 42). The two effects are accordingly reducible to one. "So all is for the best" (LO 42). One may conclude by inferring that light and heat have a single source "somewhere."

The expression *mutatis mutandis* is always a wonderful convenience in theory. Even a completely objective observer might find an actual conversion of temperature difference into candle power difficult to accomplish. More importantly, light and temperature have been shown to be qualitatively different. During the nineteenth century, science was repeatedly thwarted in its attempts to establish the qualitative identity of light and heat. Significantly, it was the theory of the indeterminable nature of light, put forth in the Copenhagen interpretation of Bohr and Heisenberg, that finally upset the traditional mechanistic cosmology.

At one point the narrator himself suggests that positivistic reductions of this sort would not serve the needs of the cylinder (LO 42). The system, it seems, requires differences—insufficiencies and excesses—in order to continue functioning. If in fact "all is for the best,"[27] it may be because the troublesome inadequacies that maintain "want," and with it the "will to live" have not been eliminated.

Thus, the complex organization and apparent certitudes of cylinder life are to a significant extent merely punctilious fictions that serve not only as a surrogate, for the unattainable way out, but also as a way of managing the painful tensions within (*LO* 38). The narrator's bogus science has analogous features. An air of strictest empiricism is spoiled by the fact that he habitually disregards the most significant of his tediously precise observations—red shift, thermal noise, heat/light incommensurability, discontinuous "ether"—because they promise to thwart his desire for a fully comprehensive, internally harmonious system. They conflict, in short, with his classical ideals.

Having established (or at least asserted) a number of quasi-positivistic certainties about conditions within the cylinder, the narrator turns again to the movements of bodies. Again he endeavors to systematize his observations, starting from an earlier rather uncertain description of the zones on the cylinder's base. He admits that the distinctness of the zones and the precision of their boundaries are purely "mental or imaginary frontiers invisible to the eye of flesh" (*LO* 43). All that follows, then, is really only a mental construct that resembles the planetary model once prevalent in atomic physics.

The narrator then elaborates the rules that govern movement between the three zones. The underlying principle is of a compromise between "order" and "license," the practical harmonization of discipline and free will in the just middle of moderation (*LO* 42). Ladder climbing, the main activity, is only possible in the area of the perimeter, known as zone one, where the ladders may be leaned agaisnt the cylinder wall. Access to the ladders (and via them to the niches) is restricted in order to keep the number of climbers constant. Climbing "freedom" is also limited. Transgressions are violently punished. In addition, there are a number of conventions by which every body abides voluntarily. Both rules and conventions serve to maintain the ladder climbing at a fixed level of intensity and regularity.

There is, however, one important condition that is not controlled by either rule or convention: that climbers will stay in zone one and that, their number being fixed, nonclimbers (watchers) will consequently never become climbers. Although this last restriction is theoretically possible, it is practically impossible, for it contravenes the principle of tolerance that enables the cylinder society to maintain itself: "the passion to search is such that no place may be left unsearched" (LO 51).

In this way the fundamental impulse behind the social life he is studying threatens to exceed the narrator's cognitive grasp and burst the bounds of his theoretical system. If climbers leave zone one, they cease to climb. If the number of climbers is to remain constant, those who wander away must be replaced. Searchers and watchers are then no longer entirely distinct, and movement between the categories is not only allowed but required by "natural justice." Even the sedentary are not wholly different; they too experience "the temptation of the ladders" (LD 46). But what of the vanquished? "The vanquished are obviously in no way concerned" (LO 52)—a statement confirming the suspicion that they have been left out of the narrator's contrived population count.[28]

By now it also becomes apparent that scientific investigation has produced not one but several "orders of ideas" each elaborated on the basis of data from somewhat (but not completely) different aspects of the cylinder world. Like the wave-and particle theories of light, these are not totally compatible. In one (based on categories of bodies according to "energy" levels), the cylinder runs down to a static state when all become vanquished. In another (based on modes of searching), the cylinder maintains itself indefinitely at a fixed level of activity.

Paragraph 12, which is in certain respects a critique of "entropy," concludes by signaling as well some problems with the notion of perpetual activity. It cannot account for those who abandon the search, nor for the possibility that the search itself might become chaotic. The narrator elides the first problem. He considers the second only much later and then with great anxiety. He does realize, however, that neither model is adequate to the functioning of the cylinder world. He is even inclined to believe that no fully adequate account will ever be produced: "All has not been told and never shall be" (LO 51).

The narrator's attempt to discover a system of laws that governs all movement within the cylinder resembles the scientist's attempt to discover those laws that govern the motion of gases in a container[29] or of particles within an atom. Just as the narrator cannot fit all his observations into neatly prescribed behavioral orders, so the scientist runs into cases that contravene the accepted laws of natural phenomena, for example, Brownian motion and quantum leaps. The narrator may attribute such unpredictable behavior to the measure of will that remains within the structural world. The analogous freedom of gas molecules and subatomic particles has been explained in terms of fundamental indeterminacy. If we cannot predict their behavior beyond a certain point, it is not simply because that point exceeds the limits of measurement. Rather, it is because the established norms and categories of interpretation—such as cause and effect, free will and determinism, stasis and dynamism, order and chaos—are not appropriate to the "between" states that are actually observed.

Viewed from another angle, the narrator's difficulties can be said to repeat the problems every body in the cylinder is having with his vision. Their failing sight is an image of his. His account of them becomes less certain, more self-doubting. Every time he returns to a detail, new ambiguities and tensions arise to frustrate his desire for precise understanding. Pilling has noted that the narrator is increasingly obliged to keep some distance if he wants to retain any understanding of cylinder life.[30] While it does give him knowledge, his position as objective observer also ensures that this knowledge will remain both less complete and less certain than he would like. His anxious dissatisfaction, so like the distressed longing he sees in every body he observes, prompts an increasing reliance upon theoretical projections and hackneyed hypotheses in an effort to fill in the gaps of a satisfying cognitive whole.

Paragraph 13 begins with the narrator about to expand the empirical approach, in the manner of Taine, to include an investigation of the effect that the cylinder climate has upon the soul. The soul, however, is a notoriously difficult thing to study. It is traditionally regarded as the scene of interaction between the material and spiritual domains, a field, as it were, upon which apparent opposites make contact and begin to converge. As the site of the passions, moreover, it has usually been considered, like Murphy's heart, too irrational a subject for logical analysis.

It is not a complete surprise, then, when the narrator quickly retreats to the body. This is the same investigator who has already evaded the problem of *pi* by burying it beneath the smooth surface of round numbers.[31] Even in the corporeal domain, however, difficulties arise when the constant mingling of opposites (by the light) frustrates the defense mechanisms (e.g., of the skin) that are supposed to maintain stability.

Just as the detrimental effects of the climate do not keep the eyes from their passion for searching, they cannot keep the bodies from their desire to copulate, which may here be regarded as an interpersonal equivalent of the desire to explore the alcoves by way of the ladders.[32] Neither actually climaxes in the longèd-for experience of ecstatic unity. A "union" of sorts, grotesque and obscene, can only be attained when the vibrations stop and everything is momentarily immobilized. At the same time an equally abominable mental or spiritual "union" is achieved when eyes made for flight "suddenly go still and fix their stare on the void or on some old abomination as for instance other eyes" (*LO* 54). This ambiguous sentence links together the void, other eyes, and eternal hatred, as if the intimate knowledge of face-to-face encounters led here not to plenitude but to vacuity, and consequently to revulsion rather than love.

These moments of fixation occur only irregularly and at such long intervals that each seems the first. They are perceived as "lulls [*coupures*]," interruptions with overtones of apocalyptic significance. Although the bodies respond with "vivacity . . . as to the end of a world," they are neither disappointed nor relieved when "the twofold storm" of light-and-temperature oscillations start up again (*LO* 54-55).

"The void or some old abomination." It has been said that nature hates a vacuum. The void has even been considered an unnatural phenomenon. This is not to say that tradition has been in complete agreement on the subject. Indeed, the controversy goes back to pre-Socratic times. Philosophers disputed its existence, and those who accepted it could seldom agree on its nature. Beckett in particular has frequently referred to the distinction Democritus made between no thing and nothing. What, then, can be said about the "void" that is supposedly experienced by every body who stares into the eyes of another during those brief lulls in which all motion apparently ceases? Murphy's encounter with Endon, like that between O and E in *Film*, suggests that this "void" may be an obscure gap or indeterminate discontinuity between bodies, more the "chaos" of spacing than perfect nothingness. If so, the "fixity" of these moments may by as elusive or illusory as the stasis of the vanquished. Recalling as well the narrator's earlier formulation—"the least less the all of nothing"—we might say that these moments are marked by a trace of the motion that has "stopped," a trace that makes renewal conceivable.

The extremely erratic moments of fixity in what otherwise seems like a system in perpetual motion have their architectural counterpart in the niches scattered across the nevertheless apparently uninterrupted upper surface of the cylinder. The latter paradox can be explained, says the narrator, by the leveling effect of omnipresent but dim light—that "conjures away the hollows [*escamote les creux*]" (*LO* 55; *LD* 48). Confronted with the former, his own "light," taking the form of an all-encompassing descriptive explanation, exhibits a similar tendency to provide more or less adequate illumination of the broad surface of things while obscuring the more troublesome irregularities. Certainly, the "perpetual motion" model has difficulty with the lulls, vanquished, and elements of stasis in general. On the other hand, his "deterioration model" cannot accommodate the various reprises that are observed, especially the desire to search and the twofold storm of temperature and light.

Since no body can see the niches, no body is aware of their formal harmony. It remains "a perfect mental image" corresponding, perhaps, less to observable reality than to the narrator's classical a priori principles. Driven by "passion," every climber's moves are made by feel [*au jugé*] (*LO* 56; *LD* 49). There is no apparent method or plan, no need for any fixed reference. The climbers have little difficulty locating the niches by instinct, trial and error. When the narrator identifies a definite directional reference, north, one may easily doubt whether it serves the needs of those climbing or his own: "She rather than some other among the vanquished because of her greater fixity" (LO 57).

That he chooses a female vanquished as the point of reference for exploration of the niches suggests a relation between the two. Both are located in the cylinder's outer zone, or circle. Some searchers enter this zone not to climb but to examine the sedentary and vanquished. Their need, or passion, drives them to investigate all hollows, whether of the cylinder or of the bodies within it. Such irregularities—extrinsic or innate (scar or birthblot [envie]—LO 59)—are in fact necessary if the search is to continue. Accordingly, "it is of course forbidden to withhold the face or other part from the searcher who demands it and may without fear of resistance remove the hand from the flesh it." Even the "eye" of the other is open to examination (LO 57-58). Everything must, however, be put back in place "as far as possible." To the extent that it is not possible to put things back exactly as they were, new irregularities may result and with them the possibility of nonidentical repetition of the same examination.[33] Perpetuation of the searching process has thus been built into the system, even though (or perhaps because) belief in a final salutory issue has been lost.

The system continues because no body may resist the impassioned problem of another (just as the sporadic lulls permit copulation with the nearest body). There are only two restrictions. The first resembles a version of the Golden Rule: "It is enjoined by a certain ethics not to do unto others what coming from them might give offence" (LO 58). This rule is followed only to the extent that it does not interfere with the quest. If every body really granted every other the respect that he wished for in turn, the interpersonal quest would no longer be possible. The latter requires firsthand empirical investigation of corporeal details. Contemplative ratiocination or mere speculation will not do.

The second restriction is more troublesome. Those waiting in a queue are immune from investigation. If somebody tries to touch one of them, the entire queue attacks. The violence generated by this transgression is the most extreme that the cylinder ever experiences. All the pent-up aggressive energy within the system is apparently released upon the "rash searcher . . . carried away by his passion" (LO 59-60). The line functions as a single corporate or societal body: "a single body" formed by "mingled flesh." The propriety of the private body may be violated, but not that of the body politic. Individual self-integrity may be sacrificed for the sake of the system, but the system protects the integrity of the group.

The cylinder world thus resembles the closed society that Bergson described, a society governed, like its cosmological analogue, by routine and mechanistic principles. Its institutions exert pressure to conform to the standard practices of the group, strictly limiting differences of conduct and stifling reflection. In the cylinder society, any exploration of irregularities in the corporate structure, any attempt to analyze the cohesion of the group—for example, by critical inquiry into its fundamental principles and established modes of thinking—is perceived as dangerous and put down by force.[34]

Totalitarian systems are constantly faced with the problem of how to deal with the aggressive drives or heated passions that are necessary in some form to the continued vitality of the community. One way is to use this violent energy to maintain order within society, for example, by incorporating it into a formal system of policing citizens and punishing transgressors. The laws of personal investigation and ladder usage do this effectively.[35]

Aggressive impulses cannot be entirely eliminated from the corporate body, however. Even a well-regulated society risks being overwhelmed by the violence it endeavors to repress, to ignore, or to employ for self-preservation. It is this possibility of pandemonium—of anarchy and chaos—that frightens the narrator and makes him appear a conservative in societal as well as scientific affairs. Even regulated and relatively restricted forms of violence ought therefore to be eliminated. His ideal is a perfectly secure and stable system. To establish it society must become perfectly harmonious.[36]

What occurs on the level of societal organization is but a replay of the important *dépeupleur* tendency of all traditional interpretative structures—scientific, historical, religious, psychological, political, and narrative. It expresses a desire for full meaning, comprehensive structures, perfect equilibrium, a final resting place. In all its often quite different historical manifestations, this desire relies upon a ritual process of purification in repeatedly displaced forms: a process by which elements that disturb, or threaten to disturb, the ideal are first contained and isolated, then ceremoniously expelled from the institutionalized "body" in question.

A second, recessive strain, to which hermetism and the carnivalesque may be said to belong, does not seek simply to reject the dominant one. Rather, it engages the latter in a critical manner. Because they remain receptive to the more indeterminate aspects of existence—for example, paradox, play, incompleteness, difference, reciprocity, passion, laughter— hermetism and the carnivalesque challenge the historically predominant ideals of harmonious self-identity and comprehensive meaning. These latter are not so much rejected as reduced to the status of questionable heuristic fictions. Pure opposites, so important to the Western tradition, are not respected. Instead, opposing forces are seen arising together, implicated in one another through a relation of similarity and difference. Pure identity, the concept upon which the notion of pure opposition rests, is never encountered. That which "is" always contains within itself the trace of what "is not." Total reconciliation or unification is perceived to be a dangerous idealization with deadening or nihilistic implications. Both scapegoating and the repression of all threatening differences are characteristically negated.

As one who seeks an ideally cohesive and fully comprehensive system encompassing all levels of cylinder life, the narrator clearly belongs to the dominant tradition. Nevertheless, his formulations allow for and perhaps indirectly encourage a carnivalesque or hermetic interpretaion of the information he himself provides with a straight face. At crucial junctures this alternative seems almost unavoidable, though it is never consciously considered, let alone accommodated within the narrator's rigid, totalizing perspective. The end of the fourteenth paragraph is only the most important of these cruxes which appear with increasing frequency as the text progresses.

In the fifteenth and last paragraph, the narrator struggles to bring his account to a satisfactory conclusion.[37] His first sentence, which begins with a series of the text's favorite filler phrases, underscores its hypothetical nature: "so on infinitely until towards the unthinkable end of this notion is maintained" (LO 60). The narrator, who has tried out a number of (not totally unrelated) explanatory models, now returns in the end to the one he always favored. What these phrases do not reveal—in fact they seem designed to obscure it—is the "space" between the last section and the penultimate. If the narrator really has been able to shoot that gap, his doubtful litany of empty phrases will provide a passage from the long and at times violent wandering of previous paragraphs into the promised land of conclusive understanding.[38]

In these ultimate moments of cylinder life ("towards the unthinkable end") there is only one searcher left, and he moves about only irregularly and intermittently, "by feeble fits and starts" (LO 60). Indeed, he looks much like the other bodies, fixed at last "in abandonment without recall." This is a state even beyond that of the vanquished who could still become somewhat agitated. It seems, in fact, that in this "final state" things have become almost the opposite of what they were heretofore. Movement is extraordinary and stasis the rule. Searchers can no longer be distinguished from vanquished. Yet, the cylinder has not reached what the narrator now considers the best of all possible worlds: total immobility. "But the persistence of the twofold vibration suggests that in this old abode all is not yet quite for the best" (LO 61).

All is not yet for the best since one last body ("this last of all if a man"—LO 61) stands up and opens his blasted eyes. Slowly, he moves toward the red-haired woman whose own immobility has long made her a suitable fixed reference. Like Murphy in his final meeting with Endon, the last one stares into her eyes until, defeated by her impenetrable gaze, he closes his own. This ultimate face-to-face encounter does not bring salvation—total knowledge, union of self and other—any more than it did for Murphy, Krapp, O, or Beckett's other characters. Neither, however, does it lead to the violent chaos that killed Murphy, or the continuation of the Unnameable's hopeless struggle, or Krapp's nostalgia, or the pain suffered by both O and the narrator of *How It Is*. Rather, here, it presages the attainment of absolute stasis "after a pause impossible to time" (*LO* 62).

The narrator regards this as the logical outcome, supposing that one by one every body will eventually cease moving: "So much roughly speaking for the last state of the cylinder and of this little people of searchers one first of whom if a man in some unthinkable past for the first time bowed his head if this notion is maintained" (*LO* 62-63). But is this in fact the case, or have the mechanism and processes of the cylinder been modified so as to make this outcome appear necessary? Does the data he has provided really generate the overview the narrator presents here? Is this conclusion in fact the most "logical"? *Can* the narrator's "notion" be maintained?[39]

His data suggested a number of explanatory models that can be grouped into two broad categories. In one, the cylinder system maintains itself in perpetual motion. In the other, it moves towards a definite *telos*. A fundamental law of the cylinder, the narrator asserts, is that balance must be maintained between license and order, between structure and free play. If perfect equilibrium existed then, according to the Second Law, the cylinder would have reached a state of maximum entropy. Barring "outside intervention" this must be permanent. While maximum entropy has traditionally been conceived in terms of stasis, it may also be seen as the zero degree of perpetual motion.[40]

In the end, then, both the narrator's broad, or basic, interpretive models predict a deadly conclusion for the cylinder world. The entropic system, in fact, is a variant of the teleological model with which the narrator began his study, and as we have seen, not unrelated to the transcendent ("trap-door") way out sought by some cylinder bodies. The perpetual-motion system transposes the static-geometric model into the realm of dynamics where it comes to resemble the immanent ("tunnel") solution proposed by others. Great though it may initially seem, the distinction between them makes little difference "towards the unthinkable end." Neither model completely explains the observed phenomena. The one cannot account for irreversible change in the form of dissolution or energy decay. The other cannot account for reversible change in the form of regeneration or renewed energy. Neither, in other words, can deal with observed discontinuities.

The cylinder itself, however, repeatedly transgresses, as it were, the laws that the narrator has established. The bodies display a propensity to unmanageable behavior. Indeterminacies and discontinuities in the cylinder functioning heighten it. The narrator becomes increasingly aware of the role that violence plays in the cylinder, but his models can account for it less and less. More than a mere machine for the recording of disinterested observations—perhaps he is a classical humanist at heart!—the narrator interprets such unruliness, and impropriety in general, seeing in it only an element of chaos that threatens to destroy the entire system as it finally destroyed poor Murphy. Rather than revise his model to allow for the possibility of genuine disorder, he maintains the classic notion of entropy.

The last scene represents the most popular view of the Second Law: a scientific end of days, a final state of maximum entropy, a stagnant equilibrium leading to thermal death. The narrator, of course, presents this state in its most reassuring, its most ideal form—complete rest. The reader, on the other hand, may well resist being reassured. In that case he may fail to close his eyes to the fact that the narrator, unable to deal with even a measure of chaos, prefers a model that culminates in total rigidity.

The conflict between narrator and reader is complicated by the former's last words—a final reiteration of the by now familiar refrain—"if this notion is maintained." By repeatedly underscoring the questionable nature of his own view of things, the narrator has all along encouraged the reader's resistance to the deadly teleology it would maintain. In the end, even his classical ending begs to be questioned.

At the same time the narrator is also raising corresponding doubts about his position as objective, "transcendent" observer and the authority of his discourse. Throughout the text, he has sought to maintain a notion of himself as the mind outside the cylinder who discovers the ultimate nature and significance of its elements by showing how they may be fit into a comprehensive system. He would restore, through the coherent unity of scientific laws and structures, what religion traditionally regards as the integral totality originally instituted by God. If he succeeded, his authoritative discourse, like the word of the Creator or the ideal functioning of the cylinder he describes, would allow "no play with the context, no gradual and flexible transitions, no spontaneously creative stylizing variants on it."[41] Should such unauthorized activity occur nonetheless, it must be regarded with doubt and suspicion, if not with outright disapproval.

Neither the narrator's discourse, however, nor the world he describes actually forms such a closed and unified system. There may be no way out of the cylinder and into some other, some higher, world. The very desire for such a Way may be part of every body's problem. But like the world that the narrator describes, his own processes of descriptive interpretation are also open to questioning, including self-questioning, and modification. The inquisitive probing into the fundamental principles of the hermeneutical, or methodological, system that the narrator's models would forcibly repress within the cylinder reappears in his own discourse to call for a reappraisal of the whole enterprise. Indeed, if this notion is maintained, there is really no more insistent subtheme in the book. In this respect it comes to resemble, almost despite itself, what Bakhtin calls an "internally persuasive" discourse.

For Bakhtin, internally persuasive discourse becomes "dialogized" when it engages and incorporates a variety of verbal and ideological points of view, approaches, directions, and values, all striving together endlessly for hegemony. From the perspective of classical information theory, based on the entropy principle, such internally "dialogized" discourse looks quite disordered and defective. For classical theory in general a plurality of structural models, which resemble one another without being harmonious, is associated with a systemic deficiency that corresponds to the amount of entropy. In other words, a range of interrelated but not totally distinguishable interpretations would be equated with loss, whether of information or of energy.

From a more Heisenbergian perspective, however, such hermeneutical pluralism à la Bakhtin, would be a manifestation of the system's fundamental indeterminism. The semantic structure of the internally persuasive or dialogized discourse is not a closed order built up out of clear and distinct bits of information. Rather, it is a structure open to the play of conflicting perspectives, none of which can ever attain determinate supremacy.

Moreover, the internally persuasive discourse elicits dialogic transmission through the "responsive understanding" of the reader.[42] The observant reader is "solicited" to carry the text's dialogue further, to continue its questioning, to develop its implications. It is this solicitous force that supplies to the transformative power of Beckett's writing. Through its deployment of carnivalized prosaic metaphors and Menippean scenarios, his work stages the consequences of the fundamental principles and beliefs of Western culture, about whose value Beckett himself appears to be quite ambivalent, to say the least.

His texts call upon the reader to respond critically and to consider thoughtfully whether these cultural notions should be maintained, and if not, how they might be modified. In general, Beckett's work asks us to consider whether the grounding notions of our heritage are not essentially nihilistic, deadening and *dépeupleur*. It asks as well whether there are not other, more positive, more realistically life-serving notions that might not replace, but would supplement them; whether it is not perhaps time for a more joyous *Science*, one that draws upon the provocative tradition to which both hermeticism and the carnivalesque belong.[43]

Literature and Its Discontents

Harboring an inevitable complicity with traditional modes and values, Beckett's work not only reproduces them but also, to some extent, contributes to their reinforcement and even legitimation. It is, in other words, symptomatic of its sociocultural context. Yet, the pathological connotations of *symptomatic* suggest that it also signals the malaise and even neuroses of our civilization. The symptomatic thus shades into the critical. Often, indeed, the two are interinvolved, and it may ultimately be impossible to decide where one ends and the other begins, or to which of the two a text essentially belongs.

In Beckett, certain things are, nonetheless, subjected to profound and sustained criticism: totalitarian thinking that requires full identity or unity within a comprehensive systematic structure, or "core," and the attendant repression of all true dissonance; the absolutism of founding oppositions and norms; and the tyranny of the fixed, central authority, or values. The workings of his critique pass, however, beyond recognized modes into the realm of the uncanny (or what Flaubert called *l'indisible*) whose effects are staged, rather than represented, in carnivalized scenarios and dialogized discourse. This raises the issue of the relation between negativity (for which Beckett was esteemed by Adorno) and a creative challenge to sociocultural norms.[1]

Stylistic conventions and innovations are not purely "formal" concerns. Mutually related to other sociocultural practices and issues, they have political significance. The invidious Sartrean distinction between the signifying and nonsignifying uses of language (what is said versus how) as well as Sartre's reservation of transformative value for the former alone, has continued to influence judgments regarding the societal "relevance" of postmodernist writers such as Beckett. From Sartre's covertly idealist perspective, an emphasis upon artistic form leads to self-referentiality and a consequent negation of "reality." Indeed, concern with style, or the way in which language is used, is implicitly to strive for the pure form of "Nothingness."[2] Similarly, Lukács condemns Beckett's excessive "literality" for destroying the rational dimension of human existence and returning it to a bestial level.

Mediating, in a sense, between these two, Stanley Cavell also perceives a "literalist" tendency in Beckett, but associates it with Logical Positivism's impossible quest for pure denotation—a linguistic analogue of the Platonic formal order. Cavell's own emphasis is on the connotative or "ordinary language" dimension of Beckett's style, which he sees as countering and contesting the denotative. Curiously, it is connotation that Sartre links with "misinformation," "non-signifying silence," and the irrational indeterminacy that he, Lukács, and Cavell himself, are ultimately worried about.[3]

As we have seen, a tendency to formalist or abstract "derealization"—a displacement of the quest for a transcendent unity—appears in both Beckett's nonfictional and his fictional writing. I would argue, however, that it is rendered problematic and challenged, though never entirely overcome, by the carnivalizing force of Beckett's style—from the overt Menippean testing characteristic of his early works to the subtle textual ironies of his later plays and fiction. These antagonistic strains constitute the complex and internally dialogized matrix of his literary production.

Fairly definite about what he rejects, Beckett is nonetheless anxious about the alternatives he finds attractive and which his texts at least implicitly put forth. This uncertainty induces the use of an exploratory, indirect, and often muted style of writing in which dialogized satire acquires distinctly carnivalesque features. Dialogic encounters in literature are perhaps the "classic" means of sounding out various strains that constitute the cultural as well as the individual self.

They enable received ideas, systems, and modes of interpretation to be openly engaged by more or less antagonistic "others"—engaged in a challenging way that may not always be possible elsewhere in society. Because it puts into play a good measure of indeterminacy, the genuinely dialogic encounter is never conclusive and may often become highly disorienting. One responds with anxiety, of course, to the extent that one is committed to the status quo ante.

Beckett writes perforce in the language(s) of our shared sociocultural heritage. The crucial issue lies in the nature of the variations he manages nonetheless to play.[4] His pluridimensional style elicits the traditional bases of understanding and judgment, frequently rendering them questionable. One discursive tendency espouses them. Others test and contest them in more or less subversive ways that facilitate and even compel their radical rethinking.

Dialogic shifts also allow variations of emotional proximity and ironic distance in the relations between author, narrator, and characters or other narrative elements. This is one function of the "echo effects" upon which Beckett so often insists (for example, in the rehearsal notes to the German production of Endgame). The texts are thus able to signal possible interpretative paths to an understanding of "reality," textual or contextual, while simultaneously indicating their shortcomings and possible dead ends.

The carnivalizing dimension of this discursive pluralism encourages the revitalization of thinking through what Heidegger calls "re-petitioning the past" or "thinking the unthought" of tradition. This involves the return and conditional privileging, with typically "uncanny" results, of what has habitually been repressed. But the repressed elements can seldom be adequately "represented," for they tend to diverge from or even to contest conventional "logical" modes. No recognizable "voice" can directly express them; they are "unsayable." Instead, they must be played out through indirect "staging" techniques, among which pluridimensional dialogism is perhaps only the best known.

Beckett critically employs the historical depth and sedimented connotative strata of ordinary language that make it both too rich and too poor a medium for the communication of logical, "sayable" information. The general "unruliness" of heteroglossia, moreover, is supplemented by its own internally complex relation to his own existential contexts. Thus, neither language nor the writer is ever fully in control, and it is their agonistic striving together that constitutes the Beckett's work of art. In this way carnivalized dialogism opens a way out of that impasse created by the shared logocentrism of those "nigger minstrels," philosophy and philology: an impasse, or dead end, from which there might at the same time seem to be no exit except into a "literature of the Unword."

The problem, as some have seen, is that in the modern world, "structures—with the categories, identities, oppositions and norms that subtend them—are too rigid, fragile, or exhausted to order life in a meaningful way that is confident enough to allow for challenges to its very meaning."[5] Significant challenge, diversity, and difference elicit fears of total chaos, or a mood of despair, frustration, and embittered resignation that cripples and perverts all forces of change.

Beckett's work calls indirectly (but not, it should be clear, in spite of itself) for the generation of structures and existential modes able to come better to terms with the challenge of internal difference and diversity, even to the extent of recognizing the necessity and creative function of radical questioning, something that continues to be applauded more often than done. The "means" it puts into practice are themselves already part of this longed for "end." Carnivalized dialogism relates negativity and affirmation, situates the quest for oneness, and makes room within its articulated structure for both relative disorder and qualified order. Beckett's textual praxis can accordingly be linked to carnivalesque contestation within the framework provided by larger processes of sociocultural transformation.

Notes

Introduction: The Accompliced Critic

1. Mikhail Bakhtin, in using the term "carnivalized dialogization" refers to the festive, free speech of the *carnivalesque* (or the more dynamic form, *carnivalization*) in dialogic form. *"Dialogization* designates the condition of subjects as speakers or users of language who are always involved in symbolic exchanges with other speakers. . . . *Heteroglossia* refers to the objective condition of language marked by a plurality of perspectives and value-laden, ideological practices that are in challenging contact with one another"—(Mikhail Bakhtin, *The Dialogic Imagination*, trans. Caryl Emerson and Michael Holquist (Austin: Univ. of Texas Press, 1980, 276). Thus, carnivalized dialogization is, for Bakhtin, a broader and more creative form of heteroglossia in which disseminating and unifying tendencies in language and culture actually engage one another. When carnivilization is absent, or when its playfully ironic contestation of official structures has broken down, the opposed forces within heteroglossia can more easily approach simple domination. See Mikhail Bakhtin, *Rabelais and His World*, trans. Hélène Iswolsky (Cambridge, Mass.: MIT Press, 1968); *Problems of Dostoyevsky's Poetics*, trans. R. W. Rotsel (Ann Arbor, Mich.: Ardis, 1973); Dominick LaCapra, *Rethinking Intellectual History: Texts, Contexts, Language* (Ithaca, N.Y.: Cornell Univ. Press, 1983), 291-325, esp. 315, and *Madame Bovary on Trial* (Ithaca, N.Y.: Cornell Univ. Press, 1982).
2. Bakhtin, *Rabelais*, 36-45.
3. This irony is often most clearly signaled *en exergue*, for example, in *Murphy*'s epigraphs and certain of the notes to the *Film* screenplay.
4. Bakhtin, *Dostoyevsky's Poetics*, 160-61, and *Dialogic Imagination*, 27-28.

5. Bakhtin, *Dialogic Imagination*, 44.

6. Bakhtin opposes dialogized parody to "polemic or autotelic parodying" (*Dialogic Imagination*, 409-10). The latter resembles the form of satire dismissed by Beckett in his essay on Jack Yates, "An Imaginative Work!" (*D* 89).

7. Bakhtin, *Dostoyevsky's Poetics*, 236n. 91.

8. Bakhtin, *Dialogic Imagination*, 272.

9. Bakhtin, *Dostoyevsky's Poetics*, 5.

10. Bakhtin, *Rabelais*, 52, 40.

11. LaCapra, *Intellectual History*, 318; Bakhtin, *Dostoyevsky's Poetics*, 185.

12. Richard Coe construes Beckett's "humor" in these essentially negative terms. See *Samuel Beckett* (New York: Grove Press, 1964). Others, such as Ruby Cohn, in *Samuel Beckett: The Comic Gamut* (New Brunswick, N.J.: Rutgers Univ. Press, 1962), explain it in terms of skepticism. Most agree with Hugh Kenner, in *Flaubert, Joyce and Beckett: The Stoic Comedians* (Boston: Beacon Press, 1962) or *Samuel Beckett: A Critical Study* (1961; reprint, Berkeley: Univ. of California Press, 1973), that irony and parody are the comic correlatives of metaphysical resignation.

13. Hugh Kenner does not regard *Murphy* as a "typical Beckett book" (*Samuel Beckett*, 52). On the other hand, Sighle Kennedy argues for *Murphy*'s crucial relation to Beckett's later work in *Murphy's Bed: A Story of Real Sources and Sur-real Associations in Samuel Beckett's First Novel* (Lewisburg, Pa.: Bucknell Univ. Press, 1971). Her discussion draws upon her own correspondence with Beckett (*D* 113), as well as upon statements Beckett made to others (e.g., "If you want to find the origin of *En Attendant Godot*, look at *Murphy*" [quoted in *En Attendant Godot: A Critical Edition*, ed. Colin Duckworth (London: Harrap, 1966), xlvi]).

1. The Poet Membered

1. The less well-known criticism now appears in *Disjecta*. When Beckett's own English version either does not exist or is substantially different from the French, I have provided my own translation.

2. *Samuel Beckett: The Critical Heritage*, ed. Lawrence Graver and Raymond Federman (London: Routledge and Kegan Paul, 1979), 215-16.

3. (*D* 43-50); James Knowlson and John Pilling, *Frescoes of the*

202 NOTES TO PAGES 14-28

Skull: The Later Prose and Drama of Samuel Beckett (London: John Calder, 1979), 3-21, 246-48).

4. Cf. Jacques Derrida's use of "dehiscence" in *Epérons: Les Styles de Nietzsche/Spurs: Nietzsche's Styles*, trans. Barbara Johnson (Chicago, Ill: Univ. of Chicago Press, 1978), 114-17.

5. Knowlson and Pilling, 246.

6. The title, "The Painting of the Van Veldes or the World and the Trousers," might therefore be said simultaneously to repeat the distinction between the two kinds of art made in the Devlin review and to signal their at least potential similarity.

7. Pilling and Knowlson, 241-56.

8. "The incoercible absence of relation, in the absence of terms or, if you like, in the presence of unavailable terms." This phrase, missing from the *Disjecta* version of "Three Dialogues," appears in the text reprinted in *Samuel Beckett: A Collection of Critical Essays*, ed. Martin Esslin (Englewood Cliffs, N.J.: Prentice-Hall, 1955), 21.

9. Beckett's own English translation reads: "the aim it sets itself" (*D* 149).

10. Lawrence Harvey, "Samuel Beckett on Life, Art, and Criticism," *Modern Language Notes* 80 (Dec. 1965): 556.

11. The published versions of Beckett's interviews which appear in Graver and Federman (Shenker interview, 146-49; Driver interview, 217-23), are generally transcribed by the interviewer from memory and so remain somewhat problematic as a record of Beckett's thought. They become especially difficult to interpret whenever Beckett, whose dislike of interviews and interviewers is known, begins in an irritated manner to favor extreme or unusually enigmatic formulations.

12. See Bakhtin's comparison of classical and carnivalesque aesthetics in *Rabelais*, 422-23.

13. See Bakhtin, *Rabelais*, passim; *Dostoyevsky's Poetics*, passim; *Dialogic Imagination*, 41-83.

14. Bakhtin, *Dialogic Imagination*, 23-24.

15. "Orpheus reflects Dionysus," writes Jane Harrison, "yet at almost every point seems to contradict him"—*Prolegomena to the Study of Greek Religion*, 3d. ed. (Cambridge: Cambridge Univ. Press, 1922), 455. This already problematic relation becomes ever more complex when Apollo is introduced into the discussion. For two differing views, see Francis Cornford, *From Religion to Philosophy: A Study into the Origins of Western Speculation* (1912; reprint New York: Harper and Row, 1957), 195-97; and Walter A. Strauss, *Descent and Return: The Orphic Theme in Modern Literature* (Cambridge, Mass.: Harvard Univ. Press, 1971), 1-19.

2. Murphy's *Caelum*

1. Deirdre Bair, *Samuel Beckett: A Biography* (1978; reprint New York: Harcourt Brace Jovanovich, Harvest/HBJ Book, 1980), 219-29; Samuel Mintz, "Beckett's *Murphy*: A 'Cartesian' Novel," *Perspective* II (Autumn, 1959): 156-65; Kenner, *Samuel Beckett*, 83-91.

2. Samuel Beckett quoted by Tom F. Driver in Graver and Federman, 219.

3. Robert Harrison in his *Samuel Beckett's Murphy: A Critical Excursion* (Athens: Univ. of Georgia Press, 1968) was perhaps the first to describe *Murphy* as a Menippean satire. His conception of the Menippea, which derives from Northrop Frye, is, however, fundamentally different from the one, borrowed from Bakhtin's work on the carnivalesque, which informs the present discussion. I am not arguing that Beckett simply imitates the ancient Menippea. Like other modern carnivalizing writers, Beckett renews both the seriocomic forms and the traditional generic patterns as he reworks them.

4. Bakhtin, *Dostoyevsky's Poetics*, 94.

5. Bakhtin, Ibid., 103, 109, 139, 148; *Dialogic Imagination*, 170.

6. Beckett, quoted by Howard Hobson, reprinted in Kenner, 100.

7. Augustine, *Confessions*, trans. R.S. Pine-Coffin (Harmondsworth, Middlesex, England: Penguin Books, 1961), 7.10.146.

8. G.S. Kirk and J.E. Raven, *The Presocratic Philosophers* (1957; reprint Cambridge: Cambridge Univ. Press, 1974), 234-35.

9. Neary's "tetrakyt" is a parodic version of the Pythagorean tetractys. Linked in a carnivalizing gesture with the belly (Scot: *kyte*), the sacred unitary figure is transformed into fourfold materialist tripe.

10. Murphy would never accept Köhler's conclusion that apes possess insight. That would muddle the clear man/animal distinction his dualism maintains. Murphy will later counter the Gestalist's argument with Descartes's example of the parrot. The man, or woman, for he has Celia in mind, who is ruled by the body has "no more insight into [the] implications [of words] than a parrot into its profanities" (*M* 38).

11. A logician might see nothing strange in trying to explain erotic attraction in syllogistic moods. Yet desire seems rather irrational, as is suggested by the more ordinary denotations of the terms *woman*, *liquor*, and *baroque* all known to cause unreasonable and unreasoning behavior in men.

12. See Plato, *Phaedrus*; Augustine, *Confessions*, 10.35.241-44.

13. (*P* 52); cf. G.W.F. Hegel, *Lectures on the History of Philosophy*, trans. E.S. Haldane (London: Kegan Paul, Trench, Trubner and Co.,

1982), 1:458. For a detailed consideration of the problem, see Martin Heidegger, *Identity and Difference*, trans. J. Stambaugh (New York: Harper and Row, Harper Torchbooks, 1969), 23-41.

14. Murphy perceives himself as a Leibnizian monad. This judgment suggests a way of interpreting his curious relation to Mr. Quigley. The latter is described as "a demented uncle who spent his time between Amsterdam [where Spinoza was born] and Scheveningen [where he died]" (*M* 53). Leibniz did in fact correspond with Spinoza. Not only did they exchange letters, but there are similarities between their philosophies. Although he rejects material existence, Murphy still "[strives] to correspond" with the Spinozan One, just as each Leibnizian microcosm, although nonphenomenal, mirrors in its own way the macrocosm. Mr. Quigley's name, moreover, simultaneously conveys in carnivalized form the contradictory meanings of *quiddity: essence, eccentricity, quibble (OED)*.

15. Cf. Beckett's comments on Proust's conception of love (39).

16. Augustine, *Confessions*, 1.19.40.

17. Emile Benveniste, *Problèmes de linguistique générale* (Paris: Gallimard, 1966), 327-35; Kurt von Fritz, *Philosophie und Sprachlicher Ausdruck bei Demokrit, Plato und Aristoteles* (1938; reprint Darmstadt, West Germany: Wissenschaftliche Buchgestellschaft, 1963), 19, 26.

18. Augustine, *Confessions*, 10.7.213-14.

19. Neary's system suffers from the same problem as the Pythagorean cosmology. Later Pythagoreans, like Philolaus, modified the Master's doctrine in response to attacks by Parmenides and the Eleatics. The starting point, which had been regarded as the embodiment of limit within the unlimited, was instead said to be the first product of the blending of the two principles. The unit, in other words, is neither limited nor unlimited; it partakes of the nature of both (Kirk and Raven, 318). Neary would like to be this original point.

20. Miss Counihan, "for an Irish girl . . . exceptionally anthropoid" (*M* 118) may be seen as a carnivalized portrayal of Cathleen Ni Hoolihan, the traditional symbol of Ireland and heroine of Yeats's play by that name. She appears also as the corporeal double of Celia's more complex (Irish) femininity. Taken together, they suggest that *Murphy*'s attitude toward Ireland may be as ambiguous as the harlot's in the last scene of Yeats's play *The Death of Cuchulain*: "I both adore and loathe"—*Eleven Plays by William Butler Yeats*, ed. A. Norman Jeffares (N.Y.: MacMillan, Collier Books, 1964), 218.

21. Kirk and Raven, 250-51, 313.

22. Reg Skene, *The Cuchulain Plays of W.B. Yeats: A Study* (New York: Columbia Univ. Press, 1974), 38-71.

23. Cf. *Des choses cachées depuis la fondation du monde*, (Paris: Bernard Grasset, 1978) 204-8, where René Girard argues that the function of Christianity is to bring all violent conflict to an end.

24. Neary's encounter with Cuchulain in the Dublin G.P.O. turns upside down the veneration of the Red Branch hero by the Irish Nationalist Movement and particularly by the insurgents of the 1916 Easter uprising. Moreover, Neary's fate carnivalizes that of the Irish artist (e.g., Beckett himself) doomed to beat his brains against the stubborn, hard-"bottomedness" of the Irish. See, for example, Beckett's "Censorship in the Saorstat," in *Disjecta*, 84-88.

25. Cf. Heinrich Heine on Kant in *Germany*, *The Works of Heinrich Heine*, trans. C.G. Leland (New York: Croscup and Sterling, n.d.). "Kant, however, lays thought before him, dissects it, analyzes it into its finest fibres, and his 'Critique of Pure Reason' is at the same time an anatomical theater of intellect. He himself always remains cold and impassive, like a true surgeon" (9:156).

26. Both *surgery* and *analysis* suggest *anatomy*, which is the term Northrop Frye uses for what Bakhtin calls Menippean satire: "The word 'anatomy' in Burton's title [*Anatomy of Melancholy*] means a dissection or analysis, and expresses very accurately the intellectualizing approach of his form. We may as well adopt it as a convenient name to replace the cumbersome and in modern times rather misleading "Menippean satire' "—*Anatomy of Criticism* (1957; reprint Princeton, N.J.: Princeton Univ. Press, 1971), 311-12. It appears that *anatomy* is far more misleading, however, for it separates into clear and simple elements what in fact belongs to a "conflict of ideas" often in an "encyclopedic farrago." Moreover, as Dominick LaCapra has pointed out, the Menippean satire "is not simply a category that allows one to identify the genre of a work but a multivalent use of language that may test the limits of genre classifications"—*Intellectual History*, 33n. 7.

27. Adrien Baillet, *La Vie de Monsieur Des-cartes* (1691; reprint Georg Olms Verlag, Hildesheim, 1972), 1:81, 84 (my translation). Frances Yates, *Giordano Bruno and the Hermetic Tradition* (reprint 1979; Chicago, Ill.: Univ. of Chicago Press, 1964), 452-53.

28. Cf. Michel Foucault's reading of Descartes in his *Folie et déraison: Histoire de la folie à l'âge classique* (Paris: Plon, 1961); with an appendix in which he responds to Derrida; Jacques Derrida, *Writing and Difference*, trans. Alan Bass (Chicago, Ill.: Univ. of Chicago Press, 1978), 31-63; LaCapra, *Intellectual History*, 259-60; Yates, 454.

29. See Jacques Derrida, *Of Grammatology*, trans. Gayatri C. Spivak (Baltimore, Md.: Johns Hopkins Univ. Press, 1976), 27-73.

30. The clocklike regularity of Kant's daily walk, for which he was mocked by Heine (136-37) is not unlike Murphy's (*M* 69). This "inhuman regularity" appears to be based upon synthetic principles that as a priori formal elements cannot be derived from sense data proper.

31. The Bildad of the Old Testament had rebuked Job for insisting upon his own innocence: "If a man suffers, it is because he has sinned before God" (Job 8:1-22, 18:1-32). Indeed, man cannot be justified: "How can he be clean that is born" (*M* 71; Job 25:4). Blake would cleanse nature of its corporeal mess by spiritualizing it into a supraindividual community. In this he follows the Socrates of the *Republic*. When Socrates deals with the problems of procreation and childrearing, he behaves like a midwife overcome with disgust at the uncleanness of the newborn child. If only he could find an answer to the question of "how he can be clean that is born," he would be able to perfect and perpetuate a truly ideal state. "The Blake League," however, "was utterly mistaken in supposing [Murphy] on the qui vive for someone wretched enough to be consoled by such maieutic saws" (*M* 71).

32. Joseph Wicksteed, *Blake's Vision of the Book of Job* (London: J.M. Dent and Sons, 1910), 36-43; Blake, *Jerusalem*, 11:27-28.

33. Murphy's harmonic problems can be related to "irregularities" in the Pythagorean musical scale. All standard musical scales, like mean time, are artificial constructs. See John Backus, *The Acoustical Foundation of Music* (New York: W.W. Norton, 1977), 123-24.

34. Leibniz, quoted in *The Dictionary of Philosophy*, ed. Dagobert D. Runes (Totowa, N.J.: Littlefield, Adam and Co., 1962), 166.

35. This possibility could perhaps have been foreseen, considering that the chit which Ticklepenny takes to the M.M.M. is also the Hindu conception of reality seen through the discovery of Brahman as *cit*, or pure consciousness. (Dr. Fist's faulty pronunciation, however, serves as an ironic and carnivalizing evaluation.)

36. Schelling, quoted in M.H. Abrams, *Natural Supernaturalism: Tradition and Revolution in Romantic Literature* (1971; reprint New York: W.W. Norton, 1971), 223.

37. Horace *Epistle* 1,1.

38. Abrams, 298.

39. Others, however, have found it already aglow with what might be called a Heraclitean fire. Heracleitus points out that not only is identity an illusion but, at the same time, that there are no clear and distinct opposites. For example: "Being and nonbeing is at the same

time the same and not the same." Aristotle, not surprisingly, accuses him of transgressing the law of contradiction. How else could one interpret the dictum: Everything forever has its opposite along with it? See Friedrich Nietzsche, *Philosophy in the Tragic Age of the Greeks*, trans. M. Cowan (Chicago: Henry Regnery, Gateway Edition, 1962), 77, 52. Such "antimony-play," as Nietzsche terms it, occurs throughout *Murphy*, but particularly when Murphy sets out on the jobpath, where he encounters such grotesques as the chandlers, Ticklepenny, Rosie Dew, and even Nelly. Heracleitus understood becoming as the eternal contention between divergent qualities striving unsuccessfully to unite. This appears transformed through contact with Hermeticism and Neoplatonism in Bruno's doctrine of identified contraries and the *coincidentia oppositorum* of the Romantics. Schelling too saw contradiction as "life's mainspring and core." But while the Romantics tended to understand opposition as absolute, Heracleitus saw the antagonists as "attached to each other and interlocked at any given moment like wrestlers of whom sometimes the one, sometimes the other is on top" (Nietzsche, *Philosophy of the Greeks*, 60). Moreover, the Heraclitean "opposites" are not part of an evolving process of oppositions, reconcilations, and renewed oppositions, moving toward a final *Aufhebung* in which all opposition would be reconciled. Instead, the contest will always endure. Thus it is that Rosie Dew will ever struggle to unite man and nature in the Cockpit of Hyde Park, or heaven and earth across a ouija board. And this appears to be because, by their very nature, she and those who resemble her, dwell within the binary opposition, resist it, disorganize it, without leading to a solution in the form of a dialectical synthesis.

40. Jaroslav Pelikan, *The Emergence of the Catholic Tradition (100-600), The Christian Tradition*, (Chicago, Ill.: Univ. of Chicago Press, 1971), 1:347.

41. Cf. Spinoza's *Ethics*, 5, prop. 35: "*Amor intellectualis quo Deus se ipsum amat* [the intellectual love with which God loves himself]."

42. Arthur Schopenhauer, *The World as Will and Representation*, trans. E.F.J. Payne (1958; reprint New York: Dover Publications, 1969), 1:15-16. Commenting upon what he, like Murphy, might have called Kant's *Critique of Pure Love*, Schopenhauer equates his concept of compassion or sympathy with "the caresses of pure love" (376). In comparison, the kind words of Vera the waitress were "not a caress" (*M* 81).

43. According to Leibniz, from whom this oxymoron is borrowed, this describes the Aristotelian entelechy, or substantial form, whose essence is paradoxically energy or activity.

44. Cf. Jacques Derrida, *Positions*, trans. Alan Bass (Chicago, Ill.: Univ. of Chicago Press, 1981), 29: "The subject and first of all the conscious and speaking subject, depends upon the system of differences and the movement of *différance*, . . . the subject is constituted only in being divided from itself, in becoming space, in temporizing, in deferral." Ross Chambers, in "Samuel Beckett and the Padded Cell," *Meanjin Quarterly* 21, no. 4 (Dec. 1962): 459, while recognizing that "as soon as [the self] asks questions about itself, it restores the where and the when: it cannot conceive itself except in space and time," finds this a reason for despairing at the absurdity of the human condition.

45. From this insight Heracleitus draws the proposition that "we are and at the same time are not" (Nietzsche, *Philosophy of the Greeks*, 77). Cf. Jacques Derrida, *Dissemination*, trans. Barbara Johnson (Chicago, Ill.: Univ. of Chicago Press, 1981), 219n. 31. See also Martin Heidegger, *Poetry, Language, Thought*, trans. Albert Hofstadter (New York: Harper and Row, Harper Colophon Books, 1971), 17-87.

46. Samuel Beckett, *First Love* (London: Calder and Boyars, 1972), 23.

47. Kennedy, 119, 123. Kennedy's is, in my opinion, the most insightful study of *Murphy* to date, and it provides many suggestions that I have developed here. She describes "Murphy's person as the 'nothing' of Mean Time." (163-64). Numerous irregularities in the movement of the sun, moon, and stars contribute to the practical difficulty of obtaining a satisfactory measure of time. Because clocks are designed to move uniformly, a fictitious "mean" sun was conceived that gave rise to mean time, which constitutes the mean solar day, the common day of civil life. In 1935, the year in which *Murphy*'s narrative takes place, mean time was given the title "universal time" by the International Astronomic Union (Kennedy, 151-54).

48. Nietzsche, *Philosophy of the Greeks*, 54.

49. Cf. Homais's profession of faith in *Madame Bovary*: "And I can't admit of an old boy of a God [*un bonhomme de bon Dieu*] who takes walks in his garden with a cane in his hand, who lodges his friends in the belly of whales, dies uttering a cry, and rises again at the end of three days"—trans. E.M. Aveline (New York: W.W. Norton, 1965), 55.

50. Cf. Bishop Butler's *Analogy of Religion, Natural and Revealed.* As John Randall, Jr., comments in his *The Making of the Modern Mind*, revised edition (1926; reprint Cambridge: Houghton Mifflin Co., 1954), "never, probably was such a double-edged sword employed to defend the Christian faith. It seems not to have occurred to the good

Bishop that if natural religion were, rationally considered, on no firmer a foundation than revelation, there might be men willing to reject them both" (299).

51. The prototype of the garret is the monadistic padded "cell" where one can live "immured in mind" (*M* 180). A windowless ("except for the shuttered judas") cube with "slightly concave sides," it is upholstered with *pneuma*, creating the illusion of being timeless and full (paradoxically of a "respirable vacuum"—*M* 181).

52. Descartes described the nervous system as an intricate network of tubes through which "animal spirits" flowed.

53. Nietzsche, *Philosophy of the Greeks*, 79-80; Martin Heidegger, *Identity and Difference*, 42-74.

54. Murphy understands unreason as absence of reason, a void, that is, from a rationalist's point of view. See Michel Foucault, *Madness and Civilization: A History of Insanity in the Age of Reason*, trans. Richard Howard (N.Y.: Random House, Vintage Books, 1973), 279-89.

55. See Nietzsche, *The Gay Science*, trans. Walter Kaufmann (N.Y.: Random House, Vintage Books, 1974), sec. 110, 111, 355, 370.

56. Jacques Derrida, *Grammatology*, 71, *Positions*, 28-29; cf. Hegel, "Who Thinks Abstractly," *Hegel: Texts and Commentary*, trans. and ed. Walter Kaufmann (Garden City, N.Y.: Doubleday and Co., Inc. Anchor Books, 1966), 114-18.

57. Derrida, *Grammatology*, 71.

58. The narcissistic relation between Murphy and Endon could be described as a burlesque double of the homosexual liaison between Bim Clinch and Ticklepenny. The name Bim (Bom, Bum) Clinch suggests, as does End-on, the circle whose end is its beginning, or more graphically the snake swallowing its own tail. And "clinching one's bim," a carnivalization of solipsism, would definitely make (at least certain forms) of union with the other difficult, if not impossible (cf. Krapp's problem). Instead of union, we find only a more chaotic form of clinch: Ticklepenny and Bim "wreathed together" (or the RMS and the Coroner "twined together"). Once again, we might say that at the beginning (or rather in the end) there is not "love" (*M* 156) but yet another ironic clinch.

59. Abrams, 185, 187.

60. Both Samuel Clarke and James Freeman Clarke did not tire of affirming the existence and superiority of God. Thus, Murphy resembles them "all but the cackle" (*M* 193). Murphy seems to affirm only his own "godlike" solipsism by the catatonic state that takes him beyond reason.

61. See Hjalmar Frisk, *Griechisches Etymologisches Wörterbuch*,

(Heidelberg: Carl Winter Universitatsverläg, 1970), 3:1072-73. Cf. the Joycean conception of purgatory, as described by Beckett in "Dante," *D* 33.

62. Neary's corporeal parody of Murphy's mental monadism is his "vague theory about his terminals being . . . connected and his life force prevented from escaping" when he crosses his icy feet on a hot-water bottle. The source of heat, however, that "tickle[s] his smattering of Greek urns" is still outside himself, as becomes apparent when the bag is replaced by "Miss Counihan's hot buttered buttocks" (*M* 207-8).

63. Cf. Pelikan, 123-32. The underlying question is whether the Mediator is already come. Murphy will later describe his position on the matter as "preterist."

64. If both players were to move only their knights, they would be able to play out about the board a "two knights mockery" that would nevertheless allow them to return to their original positions "unaltered."

65. Chess permits neither synthetic harmony (or mimesis based on the complementarity of opposites) nor simple harmony (or mimesis based on mirror images). The board by itself appears to make the former possible because the halves complement each other, a black square mating with a white square. The pieces by themselves, however, line up as mirror images, the black queen, for example, facing the white queen. Once the pieces and the board are brought into play together (as they must be for there to be a chess game) neither type of harmony is possible; the pieces can move neither mimetically nor in symmetrical patterns.

66. Cf. the ultimate word of *The World as Will and Representation*. Murphy's experience of nothingness, which "philosophy can express only negatively as denial of the will" could, from a religious point of view be understood as "ecstasy, rapture, illumination, union with God, and so on" (Schopenhauer, 409-12).

67. For a more detailed discussion of Democritus's "No-thing is more real than nothing," see my article, "The Guffaw of the Abderite: *Murphy* and the Democritian Universe," *Journal of Beckett Studies* 10 (Spring, 1985): 5-20.

68. Richard Klein, "Prolegomenon to Derrida," *Diacritics* 2, no. 4 (1972): 32; Derrida, *Positions*, 81-82, 94.

69. Murphy turns to the ultimate Being that He might remove the veil from his eye, but instead sees only his messianic double awaiting circumcision, that paradoxical mark of election that is meant to unify as it dismembers.

70. Nilsson notes that "the central point of the older chronology . . . among almost all peoples was an effort to find an agreement between the two really incommensurable periods given by the sun and moon" (quoted in Kennedy, 213).

71. Neither apparently can the scientific systems of the RMS and the coroner, for they are incapable of ascertaining precisely Murphy's "*modus morendi*" (*M* 262).

72. In Bruno's *Explusion*, the reform of the heavens begins with the Bear, which Kennedy indentifies with Cooper (86-87).

73. Was not his dream "of pins split and bunkers set at naught," of driving right to the center of the hole with total disdain for all obstacles (*M* 266)? Did he not find the passion of Robert Burns shocking? (Cf. Carlyle's commentary on Burns, quoted in Abrams, 348n. 5).

74. Kennedy, 266-67. Murphy's will and testament might also be interpreted as part of the satire of Irish nationalism that runs through the novel. In its early years, that is, in the days of Yeats and Sygne, the Abbey Theater had been the scene of experimentation and thus confrontation with established institutions. By the thirties, however, the Irish "dramatic movement," writes Richard Fallis in his *Irish Renaissance* (Syracuse, N.Y.: Syracuse Univ. Press, 1977), "had ended up being a straightjacket in which mediocrities are awfully comfortable and those who are more than mediocre are always squirming" (180).

75. Kennedy, 264-65.

76. Celia's "throwing up the kite" may be read as the burlesque double of Nelly's (that "rutting cur") throwing up Murphy's ginger cookie (*M* 100). The sublation of Kelly's kite, on the other hand, is not only a parody of the Romantic eagle and the Hegelian owl "vanishing joyfully in the dusk," but also a burlesque of Miss Dwyer as Neary's tetrakyt. Cf. Murphy's end as Absolute Rump and Rosie Dew's Panpygoptosis.

77. Abrams, 194.

78. "Neither our knowledge nor our action, in any period whatever of existence, attains that point at which all conflict ceases and all is one: the determinate line unites with the indeterminate one only in infinite approximation" (Hölderlin quoted in Abrams, 238). Cf. Beckett's formulation, "a place of impenetrable proximities" (*D* 136).

79. Abrams, 119, 121, 194.

80. Ibid., 212.

81. Plotinus quoted in Abrams, 148.

82. Beckett, quoted in Lawrence E. Harvey, "Samuel Beckett on Life, Art, and Criticism," *Modern Language Notes* 80 (Dec. 1965): 556.

83. Cf. Mintz, "Beckett's irony is a defensive gesture. . . . If Mur-

phy's system were to fall into the hands of such a philosopher as, let us say, Mr. A.J. Ayre, it would have been quickly consigned to the dustbin marked 'metaphysics.' Beckett may have used irony to protect himself against this terrible contingency" (164-65).
    84. Abrams, 186.
    85. Nietzsche, *Philosophy of the Greeks*, 68.

3. Variations on the Hermeneutic Theme

    1. Stanley Cavell, *Must We Mean What We Say?* (New York: Scribner's, 1969), 115-62. Theodor Adorno, trans. Samuel Weber in *Twentieth Century Interpretations of* Endgame, ed. Bell Chevigny (Englewood Cliffs, N.J.: Prentice-Hall, 1969), 82-114.
    2. Cavell proposes a means of escaping from "equivocation," 1-43. It derives from his conception of ordinary language, and in particular from what his discussion of *Endgame* regards as its capacity for conveying necessary implications, extralogical in nature yet "perfectly comprehensible to anyone who can speak" (123). Within the bounds of this linguistic republic, whose natives all intuitively obey the laws of their common language, true disagreement simply cannot persist. Full meaning resides, then, not in some "transcendent" realm, but in the communal experience of the shared Logos. The problem with this approach is not just that it is, after all, less innovative then Cavell believes. It also has unrealistically, unnecessarily, restrictive "implications" for the interpretation of complex literary works such as *Endgame*. If all native speakers have innate or a priori understanding of the connotations implied by any given textual moment and of the relative weight that each requires, then here can be no disagreement about the meaning(s) of any text written in that language. (Where several coexist, they are to be harmoniously arranged in a determinate order, much as medieval exegesis, governed by a similar, if somewhat more explicit, set of principles and objectives, did with holy scripture.) Conflict over interpretations could then only arise from erroneous (or perverse) uses of language.
    3. Derrida discusses this "confrontation" in terms of "two interpretations of interpretation, of structure, of sign, of play" in *Writing and Difference*, 278-93, esp. 292-93.
    4. For the difference between "closure" and "end," see Derrida, *Writing and Difference*, 250.
    5. Cf. Heidegger, *Identity and Difference*, 42-74.
    6. See, for example, Schelling's discussion of the cleavage (*Spal-*

tung) between the subjective and the objective (the ideal and the real, speculation and empiricism) that resulted from (self-) reflection and that only an idealist philosophy of nature could overcome.

7. See Dominick LaCapra, *Madame Bovary on Trial*, 19-20n. 2, for a discussion of the undecidable in the works of Derrida.

8. Cf. Nietzsche, *Philosophy of the Greeks*, 79.

9. For a discussion of Aristotle's formulation of identity, see Heidegger, *Identity and Difference*, 24-26.

10. When the English version is significantly different from the French, I have provided my own translation.

11. For a discussion of the *sorites*, or heap paradox, from the perspective of modern analytic philosophy, see Max Black, *Margins of Precision* (Ithaca, N.Y.: Cornell Univ. Press, 1970), 1-13: "To argue that the *sorites* shows that something is wrong with logic would be like maintaining that the coalescence of raindrops reveals an imperfection in simple arithmetic" (13).

12. Derrida refers to the problematic nature of the *"ça"* in *Limited Inc.*, supplement to *Glyph* (Baltimore, Md.: Johns Hopkins Univ. Press, 1977), 2:81n. 7, and in *Glas* (Paris: Galilée, 1974).

13. Cavell, 150.

14. For Heidegger's discussion of perdurance (*Austrag*), see *Identity and Difference*, 68-69. Heidegger insists that *Aus-trag* does not carry any connotation of suffering or exertion (17n. 3). Nevertheless, in Beckett's works, it can be related to what is described in *Proust* as the "suffering of being."

15. Martin Heidegger, *Being and Time*, trans. John Macquarrie and Edward Robinson (New York: Harper and Row, 1962), 435. For a detailed discussion of how Heidegger's notion of repetition relates to his conception of history, see E.M. Henning, "Destruction and Repetition: Heidegger's Philosophy of History," *Journal of European Studies*, 12, pt. 2, no. 48 (Dec. 1982): 260-82, esp. 265-66. See also LaCapra, *Intellectual History*, 188.

16. Cohn, *Samuel Beckett*, 233.

17. Cf. De Chirico's well-known painting *The Death of a Spirit* (1916), in which the "classic biscuit" figures prominently.

18. Adorno, 113.

19. Heidegger, following Nietzsche, describes how in its more extreme forms, the scientific mentality shares with philosohical idealism a fundamental mistrust and even hatred of this world. Martin Heidegger, *Basic Writings*, ed. D.F. Krell (New York: Harper and Row, 1977), 369-92.

20. Newton was profoundly interested in the apocalyptic books of

214 NOTES TO PAGES 99-126

the Bible—Daniel and Revelations—which he believed revealed the dominion of God over history as natural philosophy revealed His dominion over nature. See Richard S. Westfall, *Never a Rest: A Biography of Isaac Newton* (Cambridge: Cambridge Univ. Press, 1980), esp. 817-27.

21. Heine, 9:142-44.

22. Hippolyte Taine, quoted in René Gibaudan, *Les Idées sociales de Taine* (Paris: Editions Argo, 1928), 158 (my translation).

23. Georg Lukács, *Realism in Our Time: Literature and the Class Struggle*, trans. John and Necke Mander (New York: Harper and Row, Harper Torchbooks, 1964), 32.

24. Cavell, 130.

25. Cf. my discussion of Beckett's van Velde article, similarly entitled.

26. Cf. *How It Is* where the mud is a constant and cannot be eliminated.

27. See, for example, his recent "Catastrophe," *The New Yorker* (Spring, 1983), 26-27.

28. Cf. Heidegger's discussion in *Basic Writings*, 283-318, 369-392.

29. Cavell, 120.

30. See, for example, J.E. Dearlove, *Accommodating the Chaos: Samuel Beckett's Non-Relational Art* (Durham, N.C.: Duke Univ. Press, 1982).

31. For an extended discussion of "regulated play," see Derrida, *Writing and Difference*, 278-94.

4. Dialogues with the Double

1. Heidegger, *Identity and Difference*, 24.

2. Ibid., 45; cf. Otto Rank's more traditional, yet also clearly more problematic, idea of the double as completely different from the original, which it nonetheless resembles perfectly, in *The Double: A Psychological Study*, trans. Harry Tucker, Jr. (Chapel Hill: Univ. of North Carolina Press, 1971), 29-30; also Robert Rogers, *The Double in Literature* (Detroit, Mich.: Wayne State Univ. Press, 1970), 62.

3. Cf. Rank, *The Double*, 47; Rogers, *passim*.

4. Cf. Rank, *The Double*, 16, 73-74, 79; Rogers, 44, 58, 173.

5. Even the relation of opposition is a close relation: the opponent, as one's opposite number, is, in a sense, one's double as was the case in the ancient *agon*. Cf., "The most bitter enemy is still more of a connection than simple indifference, indifference is still more than

not knowing of one another," George Simmel, *On Individuality and Social Forms*, trans. Donald Levine (Chicago, Ill.: Univ. of Chicago Pressd, 1971), 48-49.

6. Heidegger, *Poetry, Language, Thought*, 29, 32, 53-55; and *Identity and Difference*, 64-65. Cf. Klein, 32.

7. Bakhtin, *Dostoevsky's Poetics*, 226-27.

8. Otto Rank, in his *Beyond Psychology* (New York: Dover Publications, 1941), links the double with "man's eternal conflict with himself and others, the struggle between his need for likeness and his desire for difference" (99). He also describes the artist as the hero's "spiritual double" who assures him immortality through art (97-101).

9. For repression represented as flight from double, see Rank, *The Double*, 11, 21, 28; for other examples of fear of confronting one's double, ibid., 17, 50, 73-74.

10. Ernest Fischer, "Samuel Beckett: *Play* and *Film*," *Mosaic* 2, no. 2 (1968): 113.

11. *Investment* is also the term used by Beckett to describe the mystic experience of involuntary memory in *Remembrance of Things Past* (P 22).

12. The term *appropriation* (*Ereignis* in the German) is here borrowed from Heidegger. He writes that Being and being belong to an identity whose active nature stems from the letting belong together, which is called the event of appropriation. The use of the word *Ereignis* returns us to the roots of the word: *er-eignen* (*eigen* "own," hence, *er-eignen* "to come into one's own, to come where one belongs") and eventually *er-äugnen* (*Auge* "eye," hence, *er-augen* "to catch sight of, to see with the mind's eye, to see face-to-face"). Joan Stambaugh, "Introduction" to Heidegger's *Identity and Difference*, 14.

13. Ruby Cohn, *Back to Beckett* (Princeton, N.J.: Princeton Univ. Press, 1973). 205; Martin Dodsworth, "Film and the Religion of Art," in *Beckett the Shape Changer*, ed. Martin Esslin (Englewood Cliffs, N.J.: Prentice-Hall, 1965), 21.

14. Charles C. Hampton, Jr., "Samuel Beckett's *Film*," *Modern Drama* 11, no. 3 (1968): 303-4.

15. Samuel Beckett and George Duthuit, "Three Dialogues," in Esslin, *Critical Essays*, 21.

16. Martin Esslin, "Introduction" *Critical Essays*, 4; cf. the last enigmatic exchange between D and B in "Three Dialogues," in Esslin, *Critical Essays*, 20, 22.

17. I should like to thank Professor Colin Murray Turbayne for his encouragement and assistance during the writing of the Berkeley section of this chapter.

18. Cf. Hegel's definition of *perception*: "[P]erception—the comprehension of being by throught—is the source and birthplace of a new, and in fact higher form, in a principle which while it preserves, dignifies its material. For thought is that *Universal*—that *Species* which is immortal, which preserves identity with itself." G.W.F. Hegel, *The Philosophy of History*, trans. J. Sibree (New York: Dover Publications, 1956), 77.

19. Enoch Brater, "The Thinking Eye in Beckett's *Film, Modern Language Quarterly* 36 (1975): 169-71; Raymond Federman, "*Film*," *Film Quarterly* 20, no. 2, 1966-1967: 49; Fischer, 112; Cohn, *Back to Beckett*, 207-8.

20. Federman, 49.

21. Ibid., 50-51.

22. Dominick LaCapra, *A Preface to Sartre* (Ithaca, N.Y.: Cornell Univ. Press, 1978), 126.

23. All quotations from *RTP* are my translations.

24. Cohn, *Back to Beckett*, 166-67, 169.

25. Cf. Rank's comments about the relationship between narcissism and doubles in *The Double*.

26. Bakhtin, *Rabelais*, 175-76; also Sigmund Freud, *Three Contributions to the Theory of Sex*, trans. A.A. Brill (Washington, D.C.: Nervous and Mental Disease Publishing Co., 1930), 47; cf. Jacques Derrida, *Writing and Difference*, 186-87, 181-82. This retention as means of self-unification may be linked to the return to the womb supposedly suggested in *Film*.

27. Derrida, 183; cf. Nabokov's foreword to *Despair* quoted in Rogers, 164.

28. Heidegger, *Identity and Difference*, 68-69.

29. Bakhtin, *Dostoevsky's Poetics*, 48, 213; see also Heidegger, *Identity and Difference*, 68-69.

30. Heidegger, *Poetry, Language, Thought*, 39, 49, 53-55.

31. Beckett, quoted in Federman, 47; Heidegger, *Identity and Difference*, 49.

32. Beckett, "Three Dialogues," in Esslin, *Critical Essays*, 20, 21; cf. Freud's statement about the role of failure in the creative endeavor: "A failure makes one inventive, creates a free flow of association, brings idea after idea, whereas once success is there, a certain narrow-mindedness or thick-headedness sets in, so that one keeps always coming back to what has already been established and can make no new combinations" Quoted by Ernest Jones in his *Life and Work of Sigmund Freud*, ed. Lionel Trilling and Steven Marcus (New York: Basic Books, Harper Colophon Books, 1961), 131.

33. Cf. Federman.
34. Kenner, *Stoic Comedians*, esp. 47-48, 51.

5. The Solicitation of Science

1. See Friedrich Albert Lange, *History of Materialism and Criticism of Its Present Importance*, trans. E.C. Thomas, (London: Trubner and Co., 1879), 1:53.

2. The most obvious translation is "depopulator." Beckett rejected this as the English title in favor of one that shifts the emphasis from the agent to those acted upon. Since by analogy and extension, *dépeupler* means to empty a location of its contents, whether animate or inanimate, other possible translations are "emptier," "destroyer," even "void-maker" (*videur*). This French synonym adds the meaning, "the one charged with eliminating undesirables." Because the English possibilities seemed awkward, I have chosen to use the French.

3. Ruby Cohn, *Back to Beckett*, 257. This view is based upon Cohn's belief that Beckett's title is a reference to the famous verse from Lamartine's "Loneliness [*Isolement*]": "A single being is absent, and all is depopulated [*dépeuplé*]." Another possibility, however, is Camus's *The Fall*: "One cannot wish for everyone's death nor, ultimately empty [*dépeupler*] the planet in order to enjoy a freedom that would otherwise be unimaginable" (my translation).

4. To say that the quest for abstract oneness is vain is to affirm that neither full identity nor a totalizing system is possible. While the desire for such an end is inherently life-denying, the affirmation of its impossibility need not imply simple despair. It may even open the way for a less woeful or jaundiced view of actual existence. Like Hamm's "no to nothingness," it is a denial that may lead in positive directions.

5. It is often forgotten that Belacqua is a comic figure in the *Divine Comedy*. His indolence is contrasted with Dante's eagerness to know all that can be known and to climb out of the inferno/purgatory of earthly life into the transcendence of paradise. The general feeling among critics is that Beckett advocates the Belacquan pose. Yet, both his fictional and his nonfictional work suggest that his attitude is by no means so unambivalent.

6. It is curious to note that although a cylinder is formed by rotating a rectangle around its axis, the same rectangle leaned against the sides of the cylinder is incommensurable with it.

7. Cf. Nietzsche, *The Gay Science*, sec. 110, 111.

8. Knowlson and Pilling, 159-160.

9. Ibid.

10. Cf. Loschmidt's "reversibility objection" to the Second Law of Thermodynamics. See Max Jammer, "Entropy," *Dictionary of the History of Ideas* (N.Y.: Scribner's, 1973), 2:117.

11. *Speculate* from the Latin *specere* "to look at"; and *theorize* from the Greek *theorein* "to look at, to view."

12. This perspective, which recalls the Schopenhauerian pessimism that cast a pall over much late-nineteenth-century thinking as well as the gloomy absurdism of the post-World War II era, has often been attributed to Beckett himself. *Le Dépeupleur*, however, treats the vanquished, if not always critically, at least not without reservations.

13. Initially, the narrator had supposed that perpetual defeat would lead the entire cylinder society to collapse in despair. To explain the fact that this has not already happened, he postulated the resurrectability of the exhausted desire to search. Now it seems that the more information he acquires (or the more details he adds), the less likely his original prediction becomes. The system does not seem ever to have been heading toward the end he envisioned.

14. Cf.: "On this earth that is Purgatory, Vice and Virtue—which you may take to mean any pair of large contrary human factors—must in turn be purged down to spirits of rebelliousness. Then the dominant crust of the Vicious and Virtuous sets, resistance is provided, the explosion duly takes place and the machine proceeds. And no more than this; neither prize nor penalty; simply a series of stimulants to enable the kitten to catch its tail. And the purgatorial agent? The partially purged" (*D* 33).

15. This interpretation is consistent with the narrator's first attempt to comprehend the cylinder in terms of a fundamental law: "all should die but with so fluctuant a death as to excape the notice even of a visitor (*LO* 18).

16. Cf. that aspect of quantum field theory that describes continuous short-term creations and annihilations of particle-pairs ("active vacuum field"). The result is a continual fluctuation of the number of particles, and even of the total energy, so long as the energy fluctuations do not exceed the limits of detectability consistent with the quantum uncertainty principle. Mary B. Hesse, "Models in Physics," *British Journal for the Philosophy of Science* 4: (1958): 198-214.

17. Kenner, *Samuel Beckett*, 151-52.

18. Hermann von Helmholtz, "On the Interreaction of Natural Forces," in *Popular Scientific Lectures* (1881; reprint New York: Dover Publications, 1962), 74.

19. Social theorists such as Herbert Spencer and Georges Sorel used the entropy principle to explain processes of societal decline and transformation, while Henry Adams applied it to the course of human history as a whole. Helmholtz thought that cytological processes might be associated with entropy decrease. In the 1940s, Claude Shannon proposed an information theory in which entropy figured prominently.

20. Although there are four categories of bodies, there are only three zones in the cylinder. These two ways of distinguishing are therefore only imperfectly commensurable.

21. Cf. "the rational being [intelligence]," who might have been tempted to provide a rational explanation for the situation of Hamm and Clov (E, 33).

22. Cf. the opening sentence of "Dante". "The danger is in the neatness of identification" (D 19).

23. Helmholtz's "heat death" theory implied the existence of an initial state of minimum entropy. The universe had a definite beginning, "which must have been produced by other than now acting causes."

24. See Heidegger, Basic Writings, 243-82.

25. Lange, in his History of Materialism, points out how all forms of idealism, even those according an important place to the study of nature, such as Aristotelianism or Hegelian dialectics, place great emphasis on the ethical and therefore anthropic domain to the ultimate detriment of the material and natural. In particular, Lange discusses the moral character of teleology (53).

26. Cf. Einstein's first "thought experiment" in his 1920 controversy with Bohr. See Max Jammer, The Philosophy of Quantum Mechanics (N.Y.: John Wiley, 1966), 115-16.

27. Near the conclusion of the text (LO 53), this same Panglossian expression is used to suggest that le mieux would be a static condition in which the double vibrations not only become completely commensurable but stop altogether. This is an example of how the last paragraph contradicts the normal functioning of the cylinder in order to force the end. The Leibnizian optimism that Voltaire was parodying did include the assertion that this world is progressing and developing toward perfection. But for Leibniz himself, the world is neither perfect already nor likely to become so. Static perfection, moreover, even if it were possible, would be a stupid bore and therefore undesirable. See his comments on the beatific vision in The Principles of Nature and Grace, The Philosophical Works of Leibniz, ed. George Martin Duncan (New Haven: Tuttle, Morehouse and Taylor, 1890), 217.

28. The French version reads: "In all evidence the vanquished are not to be taken into account" (*LD* 46).

29. These gas laws might, following Murphy's etymology, be called the laws of chaos.

30. Knowlson and Pilling, 163-64.

31. A similar gesture relegates the "soulscape" of *Watt* to the addenda.

32. Cf. Sigmund Freud on the sexual symbolism of ladders, *Interpretation of Dreams*, trans. James Strachey (New York: Hearst Corp., Avon Books, 1965), 390.

33. Cf. the definition of indeterminacy as an essential limitation or imprecision of measurement for reasons of "subject-object" interference.

34. Cf. Edmund Burke's idea of the good society. Burke insisted that basic principles and beliefs should never be subjected to conscious examination that destabilizes the social order and leads to radical change or discontinuity, as he felt it did in the French Revolution. The good society evolves organically in simple continuity with historical tradition.

35. Joseph de Maistre, the most cogent defender of such institutionalized violence, recognized, in particular, the social importance of sacrificial scapegoating. Recently, certain aspects of de Maistre's view have been developed by René Girard in *Violence and the Sacred*, trans. Patrick Gregory (1977; reprint Baltimore, Md.: Johns Hopkins Univ. Press, 1979). Orwell's *Animal Farm* and *1984* both dealt with the important cathartic functions that continued forms of other-directed animosity may have in a repressive society in a much more limited way.

36. This is the function Girard attributed to Christianity in *Des choses cachées depuis la fondation du monde* 204-8. Here the narrator chooses the Schoperhauerian/Eastern variant that has strong affinities with the thermal-death theory deriving from the principle of entropy.

37. In the mid-sixties, Beckett himself abandoned the text after the fourteenth section because, Pilling believes, "he could not see how to bring to an end a world that was going about its business almost without reference to him, and which grew more elaborate and complicated with each attempt he made to describe it." In 1970, he added a final paragraph "divorced in time from the events that occupy the main body of the text." Still, "it is difficult to feel . . . that this was an entirely satisfactory strategy, however important it may have been to Beckett (usually . . . content to abandon works that are slipping out of control)" (Knowlson and Pilling, 157).

38. There is a sense in which this last paragraph is actually, or could have been, the sixteenth, or foursquare section that completes the whole in classical fashion. Clearly, that is what the narrator's approach to problems would lead him to prefer. What is lacking is a fifteenth paragraph that would bridge the gap in a convincing manner. As it is we have only the miraculous "transition" effected by the narrator's incantatory "so on indefinitely" (*LO* 60). Such mumbo jumbo, following hard upon his observation of the searchers interest in discovering any body's concealed *envie* ("desire," "lack," but also "mark" or "blemish" that signals a secret desire), merely calls attention to the fact that, in the end, neither reality nor the narrator's account of it is going to fulfill his classical expectations. (Cf. the naevus on Murphy's end by which he is identified and which marks the excessiveness of his nature.)

39. One fairly obvious sign that his conclusion may be forced: the reversal of an earlier causal relation. The movement of bodies now determines light, temperature, and noise, rather than vice versa.

40. Maximum entropy is understood as the equalization of heat transfer. Apparently, this model does not allow for any excess of disorder. Zero entropy, or perfect "order," means the continued maintenance of heat transfer at its highest possible level. This can only be attained at zero degrees Kelvin, or absolute zero, a theoretical construct. Zero perpetual motion, on the other hand, is stasis, while maximum perpetual motion means endless repetition of the same routine, an impossible dream.

41. Bakhtin, *Dialogic Imagination*, 343. See also LaCapra, *Intellectual History*, 291-324.

42. Bakhtin, *Dialogic Imagination*, 345-46.

43. Supplementarity is not a matter of substituting the latter for the former. That is not only impossible, it means missing the point of the carnivalesque mentality that informs Beckett's work. Supplementarity poses the question how we are to go on, whether established notions are to be maintained as they are or modified through contact with notions that contest their authority in significant ways.

Conclusion: Literature and Its Discontents

1. For an extended discussion of the relations among the symptomatic, the critical, and the transformative in the work of Flaubert, see LaCapra, *Madame Bovary on Trial*.

2. Examples of Beckett criticism that share aspects of this per-

spective are Coe's *Samuel Beckett* and Dearlove's *Accommodating the Chaos*. I call Sartre's position idealistic because his defense of "content" and "reality" against the mortal danger of "empty" formalism is nonetheless predicated upon a belief that form constitutes the "material" aspect of the Word. For an analysis of the continuities and discontinuities in Sartre's aesthetics, see LaCapra, *A Preface to Sartre*, esp. 47-91.

3. Sartre addresses the problem of relating "signifying" and "nonsignifying" dimensions of language in *Between Existentialism and Marxism* (NY: William Morrow and Co., 1976), 228-85. Certain aspects of his investigation are developed in a more sustained and radical way by Heidegger, for example, *Basic Writings*, 143-88, 283-318, 369-92.

4. Cf. "By structure . . . I mean the endless substantial variations of these three beats, and interior intertwining of these three themes into a decoration of arabesques—decoration and more than decoration" (*D* 22).

5. LaCapra, *Madame Bovary on Trial*, 212.

Index